The Trade Impact of European Union Preferential Policies

Luca De Benedictis · Luca Salvatici
Editors

The Trade Impact of European Union Preferential Policies

An Analysis Through Gravity Models

Springer

Editors
Prof. Luca De Benedictis
University of Macerata
Department of Economics and Financial Institutions
Via Crescimbeni 20
62100 Macerata
Italy
debene@unimc.it

Prof. Luca Salvatici
University Roma Tre
Department of Economics
Via Silvio D'Amico 77
00145 Roma
Italy
lsalvatici@uniroma3.it

Financial support for the publication of this book received from the Italian Ministry of Education, University and Research (Scientific Research Program of National Relevance 2007 on "European Union policies, economic and trade integration processes and WTO negotiations") is gratefully acknowledged. We are extremely grateful to Filomena Pietrovito for superbe assistance in the preparation of individual chapters and the editing of manuscripts.

Additional material to this book can be downloaded from http://extra.springer.com

ISBN 978-3-642-16563-4 e-ISBN 978-3-642-16564-1
DOI 10.1007/978-3-642-16564-1
Springer Heidelberg Dordrecht London New York

Library of Congress Control Number: 2011930926

Cover design: eStudio Calamar S.L.

Printed on acid-free paper

Springer is part of Springer Science+Business Media (www.springer.com)

To our teachers and students, and to our families

Foreword

Trade preferences are an important structural component of the relations between the European Union (EU) and the developing world, although their effectiveness in promoting developing country exports has sometimes been questioned. However, developing countries have been consistently asking developed countries for deeper and wider preferential trade concessions, preference erosion has always been and continues to be a contentious issue in multilateral negotiations, and firms in developed countries complain about the increased competition they have to face as a result of trade preferences.

EU trade preference schemes form a diverse and complicated set of tangled trade concessions (a "spaghetti bowl", as Bhagwati put it), with preferences of different degrees – in terms of both the depth of preferential margins and the width of product coverage – granted either on a unilateral or reciprocal basis.

As the editors explain in their introduction to this volume, its goal is twofold: to provide new evidence on the impact on trade of EU preferential trade regimes, and to contribute, on methodological grounds, to the literature assessing the impact of trade policies using the gravity model.

The book is the result of the synergic activities performed within two broader research projects: *AgFoodTrade* ("New Issues in Agricultural, Food and Bio-energy Trade"), financed by the European Commission through the 7th Research Framework program (Grant Agreement no. 212036), and *PUE&PIEC* ("European Union Policies, Economic and Trade Integration Processes and WTO Negotiations"), financed by the Italian Ministry of Education, University and Research (Scientific Research Program of National Relevance 2007).[1] We believe the decision to join forces to analyze the effectiveness of EU preferential trade schemes has been successful and generated significant benefits in terms of additional activities and results achieved for each of the two publicly financed research projects.

[1]More information on the two research projects and their outputs can be found at http://www.ecostat.unical.it/Anania/PUE&PIEC.htm and http://www.agfoodtrade.eu/.

We have strongly supported the decision to produce a volume, rather than publish the results of the research activities in scientific journals only. As a result, the new evidence generated on the effectiveness of EU trade preferential schemes and the advances proposed in the use of the gravity model to assess the implications of trade preferential schemes are now more easily available well beyond the boundaries of the scientific community. The intended primary target of the book are relevant actors involved in trade policy design and implementation in the public sector and policy makers. We believe that scientific research funded through public resources has the responsibility to maximize its societal impact by making a significant effort (which implies investing human and financial resources) to reach stakeholders potentially interested in its results. Even more so when, as in this case, the focus of the research is the effectiveness of important policies and the factors which may reduce or enhance it.

Nevertheless, the target readership of the volume is even broader, as it aims to provide a valuable tool in graduate teaching and for students with an interest in preferential trade policies and in the gravity model. This is one of the reasons why data sets and listings of programs used to generate the results are made available in the publisher's web page for the book, allowing for replications of results as well as analyses of the data different from those performed by the authors.

We hope readers will share our view that the efforts by the editors and the authors have produced a very useful tool for both, trade policy makers and analysts as well as policy analysts to be.

Arcavacata di Rende, Italy
Paris, France

Giovanni Anania
PUE&PIEC, coordinator

Jean-Christophe Bureau
AgFoodTrade, coordinator

Contents

Abbreviations

AVE	Ad Valorem Equivalents
ACP	African, Caribbean and Pacific
ASEAN	Association of Southeast Asian Nations
ATM	Autonomous Trade Measures
AC	Average Cost
CARIFORUM	Caribbean Forum of African, Caribbean and Pacific States
CEEC	Central and Eastern European Countries
CEPII	Centre d'Etudes Prospectives et d'Informations Internationales
CN	Combined Nomenclature
CIS	Commonwealth of Independent States
CGE	Computable General Equilibrium
CES	Constant Elasticity of Substitution
CIF	Cost of Insurance and Freight
CU	Custom Unions
DM	Davidson-Mackinnon
DC	Developing Countries
DOTS	Direction of Trade Statistics
EAC	East African Community
ESA	Eastern and Southern Africa
EPA	Economic Partnership Agreements
Euro-Med	Euro-Mediterranean
Euro-Med	Euro-Mediterranean Partnership
EC	European Community
EU	European Union
EBA	Everything But Arms
FC	Fixed Costs
FDI	Foreign Direct Investment
FOB	Free On Board
FTA	Free Trade Agreements
F&V	Fruit and Vegetable

FAT	Funnel Asymmetry Test
GATT	General Agreement on Tariffs and Trade
GSP	Generalized System of Preferences
GMM	Generalized Method of Moment
GSP	Generalized System of Preferences
GTAP	Global Trade Analysis Project
GDP	Gross Domestic Product
GCC	Gulf Cooperation Council
HS	Harmonized System
IV	Instrumental Variable
IMF	International Monetary Fund
LDC	Least Developed Countries
LSDV	Least Square estimator with Dummy Variable
MTPI	Mercantilistic Trade Preference Index
MTPI	Mercantilistic Trade Preference Index
MA	Meta-Analysis
MRA	Meta-Regression Analysis
MFN	Most Favored Nation
MTR	Multilateral Trade Resistance
NEGB	Negative Binomial
NBPML	Negative Binomial Regression Model
NGO	Non-Governmental Organizations
NRPTA	Non-Reciprocal Preferential Trade Agreements
OLS	Ordinary Least Squares
OCT	Overseas Countries and Territories
POISS	Poisson
PPML	Poisson Pseudo Maximum-Likelihood
PM	Preferential Margins
PTA	Preferential Trade Agreements
RTA	Regional Trade Agreements
RoO	Rules of Origin
SAD	Single Administrative Documents
SADC	Southern African Development Community
SAA	Stabilization and Association Agreements
TDC	Tarif Douanier Commun
TRQ	Tariff Rate Quotas
UN	United Nations
UNCTAD	United Nations Conference on Trade and Development
WLS	Weighted Least Squares
WDI	World Development Indicators
WTO	World Trade Organization
ZINBPML	Zero-Inflated Negative Binominal Model
ZIP	Zero-Inflated Poisson
ZIPPML	Zero-Inflated Poisson Model

Contributors

Mariarosaria Agostino Department of Economics and Statistics, University of Calabria, Via Pietro Bucci – Cubo 1C, 87036 Rende (CS), Italy, m.agostino@unical.it

Francesco Aiello Department of Economics and Statistics, University of Calabria, Via Pietro Bucci – Cubo 1C, 87036 Rende (CS), Italy, f.aiello@unical.it

Giovanni Anania Department of Economics and Statistics, University of Calabria, Via Pietro Bucci – Cubo 1C, 87036 Rende (CS), Italy, ganania@unical.it

Jean-Christophe Bureau AgroParisTech–Paris, UMR Économie publique, 16, rue Claude Bernard, 75231 Paris, Cedex 05, France, bureau@grignon.inra.fr

Paola Cardamone Department of Economics and Statistics, University of Calabria, Via Pietro Bucci – Cubo 1C, 87036 Rende (CS), Italy, p.cardamone@unical.it

Maria Cipollina Department of Economics, Management and Social Sciences, University of Molise, Via Francesco de Sanctis, 86100 Campobasso, Italy, cipollina@unimol.it

Luca De Benedictis Department of Economic and Financial Institutions, University of Macerata, Via Crescimbeni 20, 62100 Macerata, Italy, debene@unimc.it

Federica Demaria Department of Economics and Statistics, University of Calabria, Via Pietro Bucci – Cubo 1C, 87036 Rende (CS), Italy, demariaf@unical.it

Lars Nilsson European Commission, DG Trade, Rue de la Loi/Wetstraat 170, 1040 Bruxelles/Brussel, Belgique/België, Belgium, lars.nilsson@ec.europa.eu

Alessandro Olper Department of Agricultural and Environmental Economics and Politics, University of Milano, Via Celoria 2, 20133 Milano, Italy, alessandro.olper@unimi.it

Filomena Pietrovito Department of Economics, Management and Social Sciences, University of Molise, Via Francesco de Sanctis, 86100 Campobasso, Italy, filomena.pietrovito@unimol.it

Valentina Raimondi Department of Agricultural and Environmental Economics and Politics, University of Milano, Via Celoria 2, 20133 Milano, Italy, valentina.raimondi@unimi.it

Luca Salvatici Department of Economics, University Roma Tre, Via Silvio D'Amico, 77-00145 Roma, Italy, lsalvatici@uniroma3.it

Margherita Scoppola Department of Economic Development, University of Macerata, Piazza Oberdan 3, 62100 Macerata, Italy, scoppola@unimc.it

Daria Taglioni World Bank, Washington, USA and Centre for Economic and Trade Integration at The Graduate Institute of International and Development Studies, Rue de Lausanne 132, 1211 Geneva, Switzerland, dtaglioni@worldbank.org

Francesco Trivieri Department of Economics and Statistics, University of Calabria, Via Pietro Bucci – Cubo 1C, 87036 Rende (CS), Italy, francesco.trivieri@unical.it

List of Figures

List of Tables

Chapter 1
Introduction

Luca De Benedictis and Luca Salvatici

Abstract The volume introduced by these notes focuses on the impact of European Union (EU) preferential policies on the trade volume with preferential partners. The first part of the book includes four chapters on the evolution of EU preferential policies, the methodology used to calculate trade preferences, an overview of the gravity model, and a meta-analysis of the literature on ex post Preferential Trade Agreements (PTA) evaluation. The second part includes five empirical analyses of the trade effect of different EU preferential regimes. The evaluation is carried out under the common framework of the gravity model of international trade. This introductory chapter makes the case for sound trade policy evaluation, and describes it as a good mixture of meticulous account of policy instruments, disaggregated trade and tariff data, specific information at the sectoral and (possibly) preferential regime of entry into the EU market, and finally of replicable econometric analysis.

1.1 Trade Preferences: A Controversial Issue

The analysis of preferential trade regimes is a classical research topic in international trade theory (Viner 1950). It has recently gained momentum also from an empirical stand point with the diffusion of ex ante analysis through computable general equilibrium modelling and ex post impact evaluation through modern econometric techniques. The issue has also moved more centre-stage in the political discussion since the beginning of this decade, in part due to the success of development Non-Governmental Organisations (NGO) in using the Millennium

L. De Benedictis
Department of Economic and Financial Institutions, University of Macerata, Via Crescimbeni 20, 62100 Macerata, Italy
e-mail: debene@unimc.it

L. Salvatici
Department of Economics, University Roma Tre, Via Silvio D'Amico, 77, 00145 Roma, Italy
e-mail: lsalvatici@uniroma3.it

L. De Benedictis and L. Salvatici (eds.), *The Trade Impact of European Union Preferential Policies*, DOI 10.1007/978-3-642-16564-1_1,

Development Goals to gain commitments from the G8 governments to increase development aid, and in part due to the difficulty in the Doha Development Round trade negotiations. Too often, however, public debate on these issues revolves around received wisdom and oft-stated positions grounded in specific anecdotes or particular circumstances. The shared goal of the essays included in this book is to bear the rigour and techniques of modern applied economic analysis in providing an evidence-based evaluation of some of the controversial issues related to the trade enhancing role of Preferential Trade Agreements (PTA) involving the European Union (EU) and its international trade partners.

The EU is the first target market for Developing Countries' (DC) and Least Developed Countries' (LDC) exports. The EU is an important target market for developing countries' and LDC exports in general, and is especially important for most former colonies of EU member states. Trade preferences for developing countries have been used by the EU since the early 1960s, and are an important opportunity to increase access to the EU's market and to overcome some structural difficulties of DC and LDC. PTA, either reciprocal or not, are expected to play a central role in inducing trade opportunities for numerous developing countries, remarkably for the poorest ones. In this respect, the EU's trade policy is fairly complex, and various preferential agreements are granted to EU's trade partners.

There is little doubt that the original intentions of the EU, as well as those of other developed countries, in introducing preferential policies are (at least in theory) for the good. The aim of the non-reciprocal trade preferences regime is to give a direct incentive in terms of tariff reduction that would foster exports to the EU market, in order to support development and reduce poverty in former European colonies, in particular, and in poorest countries, in general. The empirical literature on the trade effect of EU trade preferences by and large confirms expectations of a robust and positive impact of PTA on trade, but results are heterogeneous for different countries and sectors. On the other hand, some critics claim that non-reciprocal preferences have perverse side effects, since they result in trade diversion and ossify market structures under sheltered market niches (Borchert 2009). Some critics have highlighted the tension between multilateralism and regionalism and have pointed to the potential welfare cost of the latter.

Hudec (1987) makes a political economy argument about the perverse effects of non-reciprocal trade preferences on beneficiary countries' trade policy. He shows how tariff preferences can have an adverse impact on the beneficiary country. Preferential schemes reduce the willingness of the beneficiary country's export sector to oppose its own government's protectionist policies. When a country has achieved free access to its major trading partner markets, its incentive to liberalise its own market as an instrument to foster the partner's trade openness disappears. In addition, when preferences eligibility is withdrawn, access to export markets becomes conditional on trade policy on the basis of reciprocity, which requires a country to reduce its own protectionist policies and reap associated gains in efficiency and competitiveness. This view is shared by Panagariya (2002) and Özden and Reinhardt (2005). The latter estimate the effect that Generalized System of Preferences (GSP) removal has had on former beneficiaries of trade policies. They find that countries excluded from a GSP scheme subsequently adopt lower trade barriers than countries that remain eligible. Thus, participating in non-reciprocal preferences through institutional frameworks such as the GSP, discourages developing countries from liberalisation.

More relevant for our analysis is the opposite claim that criticizes preferential trade policies as being ineffective. In point of fact there would be, as often, a gap between the rhetoric of preferences and reality: preferential margins simply cannot fully compensate for the lack of basic competitiveness in developing economies. Starting from the very little ex post evidence on the effects of preferential schemes on the export performance of the beneficiaries, the empirical literature on preference schemes highlights several difficulties limiting the benefits available for the recipient countries.

It has been suggested that preferences are not effective due to their limited scope and because they exclude goods that are important for DC economies. This idea is propounded because many unilateral agreements are temporary and introduce an element of uncertainty which is unfavourable to investment and the creation of long-term trade flows; that the administrative costs of proving eligibility for preference negate some of the margins, while rules of origin limit the benefits (Panagariya 2002). This strand of literature focuses on the deficiencies and limitations of preferential programs, underlining the shallowness of the preferences granted to developing countries.

These claims are supported by the fact that preferential tariffs have not generated significant trade flows (Ongluglo 1999), and some authors even claim that countries which do not benefit from preferences can end up exporting more, and become better off eventually (Özden and Reinhardt 2005). For Brenton and Ikezuki (2005) evidence suggests that trade preferences have not enabled beneficiaries as a group to increase their market shares in the main preference-granting markets. Accordingly, preferential tariffs can theoretically promote trade and development but the significance of tariff preference effects is questionable. First, there are many exclusions and limitations. Second, costs of compliance diminish in practice the utilisation and the benefits of preferences. Evidence suggests that many goods imported from developing countries are eligible for preferences but only some of them are used.

To summarize, while the use of PTA has been blamed for its ineffectiveness or for its side effects, the empirical analysis of the trade enhancing effect of preferential agreements does not offer a uniformly strong conclusive evidence. The prominent impression that is received in scrutinising this literature is the very high variability of existing results, depending on the empirical technique being applied, the method in the quantification of the preferences, and the characteristics of data used. But when this variability of results is examined in a meta-analysis this impression changes. In their comparative empirical study of the literature on EU's PTA, Maria Cipollina and Filomena Pietrovito (Chap. 5) in this volume, offer the following robust meta evaluation: the effect of PTAs on trade is positive, statistically significant and economically relevant. This is by no means the strong conclusive evidence we are looking for, as it just emphasises the conditional average PTA trade effect revealed by the literature. Moreover, the lack of precision in the different estimates of the trade effect of PTA calls for more empirical evidence, sound and consensual econometric techniques and higher quality data in terms of sectoral disaggregation, and also in the ability to track the different preferential regime of entry into the EU for any given product and exporter country.

This is an appropriate moment for the evaluation of the impact of EU's PTA on partner countries' exports. The European Commission has just launched a phase of revision of the EU trade policy and appraisals of this impact (see Gasiorek et al. (2010) for a comprehensive evaluation of the EU's GSP) are the needed quantitative evidence upon which the new EU trade policy should be based on. This book offers further evidence.

1.2 Trade Policy and Trade Policy Analysis

In planning the collection of essays included in this volume we did not consider trade policymakers as the exclusive final consumer of the book. Trade policy analysis has gone a long way from the partial equilibrium diagrams that monopolised the trade policy literature only a couple of decades ago. The literature has evolved along three main directions. (1) The first has to do with the economic analysis of the GATT\WTO multilateral trade system (Bagwell and Staiger 2002), that overcomes the unilateral economic argument for free trade in favour of a theory of mutual concessions driven by exporter interests, where the Gatt/Wto principles cast their logic into governments' need to escape from the resulting terms-of-trade-driven Prisoner's Dilemma. (2) The second has covered trade policy instruments in high details moving away from the classical dichotomy between tariffs and non-tariffs barriers. Meticulous descriptions of the normative structure of the variegated countries' trade policy palette and comprehensive legal studies have enriched trade economists' knowledge (Choi and Hartigan 2004; Kerr and Gaisford 2008). (3) The third one has been devoted to the articulation of ex ante analysis of trade policy through Computable General Equilibrium (CGE) modelling (Francois and Reinert 1998). In these main streams of the literature, the investigation of the effects of trade policy is carried out through comparative static analysis or simulation techniques, and little role has been played by ex post observational studies and by econometrics. But in recent years things have been developing also in a different direction. This volume specifically focuses on this latter change, offering both an overview of the main ingredients of this field of research, including data characteristics, preferential margins, functional forms of the regression and estimation techniques, and a collection of original studies evaluating the impact of different EU's preferential regimes under the common framework of the gravity model of international trade.

We believe that PhD students in international trade, researchers in empirical international relations and scholars in development economics and international trade would benefit from the material included in the book and would take advantage of the "learning-by-doing" approach that guided us in making all the empirical analysis included in each chapter fully and easily replicable, using the Stata do-files and the datasets included in the Springer webpage of the volume.

1.3 Methodology

From Tinbergen (1962) to Helpman et al. (2008), the gravity model has been used to estimate the volume of bilateral trade as a function of two main components, the economic size of the two countries and the distance between them. There is also a third component that encompass the role played by heterogeneity in that relationship, and which has been used to estimate the effect of trade preferences on trade flows. Therefore, the econometric analysis of the trade impact of preferential trade policy is based on ex post observational studies.

As recently summarized by Imbens and Wooldridge (2009), program evaluation through econometric techniques applied to observational data, rather than on controlled randomised experiments, is always plagued by serious obstacles to the estimation of causal effects. One notable exception is when the identification and estimation of the policy effect can rely on robust evidence of what has been variously named as unconfoundedness, ignorability, exogeneity, or selection on observables. All these expressions refer to the assumption that when some units (i.e. countries or sectors of a country in our case) are exposed to a preferential fiscal treatment at the border (i.e. a PTA), while others are excluded from such treatment. The adjustment for differences in observed covariates or pre-treatment characteristics, removes all biases in the comparison between treated and control units, such that the difference in the outcome (increase in trade flows in our case) can only be due to the effect of the treatment.

Also when evaluating the impact on DC trade flows of the EU's preferential trade policies the fundamental issue is essentially a problem of missing data. In observational data we can only observe trade flows of treated units and untreated units, but not the counterfactual trade flows of treated units had they not been treated. This information, that would permit to correctly estimate the average treatment effect, is missing. Without any natural counterfactual the second best alternative is to chose a comparison group similar to the group of countries that received preferential treatment, so that the only possible differences between the two groups is in the treatment.

Formally,

$$X_{ij} = \alpha + \beta T_{ij} + Y_{ij}\gamma + \varepsilon_{ij} \tag{1.1}$$

where X_{ij} is the volume of imports of country i from country j, and Y_{ij} is a matrix of covariates, which in the gravity equation includes countries' GDP, distance and the multilateral resistance term. In some cases, country i grants preferences

T_{ij} to country j, so that the treatment dummy equals to 1 if country i is granting a preference to country j, and 0 otherwise. In other terms,

$$X_{ij} \equiv [X_{ij}(1)T_{ij}] + [X_{ij}(0)(1 - T_{ij})] \tag{1.2}$$

Following Ravallion (2008) and denoting X_{ij} (1) as $X^{T}{}_{ij}$ and X_{ij} (0) as $X^{C}{}_{ij}$, (1.1) can be applied to a subsample of countries in a PTA and others which are excluded from it.

The following system:

$$X_{ij}^{T} = \alpha^{T} + Y_{ij}\gamma^{T} + \eta_{ij}^{T} \quad \text{if } T_{ij} = 1 \tag{1.3}$$

$$X_{ij}^{C} = \alpha^{C} + Y_{ij}\gamma^{C} + \eta_{ij}^{C} \quad \text{if } T_{ij} = 0 \tag{1.4}$$

is usually estimated as a single regression, multiplying (1.3) by T_{ij} and (1.4) by $(1 - T_{ij})$ and using the identity (1.2) we get

$$X_{ij} = \alpha^{C} + (\alpha^{T} - \alpha^{C})\ T_{ij} + Y_{ij}\gamma^{C} + Y_{ij}(\gamma^{T} - \gamma^{C})\ T_{ij} + \varepsilon_{ij} \tag{1.5}$$

where $\varepsilon_{ij} = \left(\eta_{ij}^{T} - \eta_{ij}^{C}\right)T_{ij} + \eta_{ij}^{C}$. The average treatment effect of the PTA, $(\alpha^{T} - \alpha^{C})$ would be consistently estimated only if $(\gamma^{T} - \gamma^{C})$ is null, and if the participation to the PTA is uncorrelated with the error term.

Since the agreement on a trade preferential treatment is certainly not random, the researcher is forced to pursue second best empirical strategies. On the one hand, the theoretical derivation of the gravity equation offers precious guidance. On the other hand, the inclusion of countries' economic size, distance and multilateral resistance as main covariates to control for the effect of variables that are strongly related to PTA participation; controlling for country heterogeneity through the appropriate use of country and country-pair dummies, and the proper handling of errors' structure, allow the unconfoundedness condition to hold. In some recent cases reweighting of the gravity equation through propensity score or instrumental variables has been performed (Millimet and Tchernis 2009; Baier and Bergstrand 2007), but more generally, if the selection bias from unobserved characteristics is likely to be negligible, then the evaluation of the impact of PTA on trade flows through the gravity model may provide a good comparison with unfeasible randomised estimates.

1.4 The Novelties of This Book

We believe that the present volume, in spite of the quality of each single chapter, has the value of being better than the sum of its parts. This quality is at least associated to six main distinguished features that make it different from other analyses of EU's PTA.

The first feature is the homogeneity in the empirical technique used. All the evaluations of EU's PTA have been undertaken under a common framework. All the empirical analyses use the gravity model as an interpretative tool. Each author with her or his own peculiarity always makes reference to a common background literature and to a common referential model. This makes the interpretation of the impact evaluation easier, and encourages the reader to follow different variants of the same model in eventually planning her own empirical analysis.

The book offers four survey-like chapters that set the scene for the subsequent empirical analyses; the description of the evolution of EU preferential policies, the overview of the methodology used to calculate trade preferences, the review of the theoretical background, and the empirical strategy that makes the gravity model a useful tool for ex post PTA evaluation, and finally a meta-analysis of the literature, all together make an updated overview of the most recent methodological advances on the topic.

All empirical chapters use highly disaggregated data at the sectoral level. Commonly, the gravity model is applied to aggregate data and it is used for the whole economy. The very disaggregated level of commodity observation pursued in each chapter permits to take into account the heterogeneity among products, heterogeneity which appears at two levels: first, the nature and the intensity of EU protection, and second the degree of export variety.

More precise information on preferential margins was used in this book than in previous studies. In a gravity model setting, using an explicit measure of the preference margins provides a more refined measure of trade preferences compared to the binary variables commonly used in the literature. Thus, contrary to the majority of empirical literature using gravity equation, in this book, preferences vary with the exporter as well as according to products.

Our framework incorporates recent advances in the modelling of gravity equations. In particular, one of the most debated issues in the recent literature on the gravity model is the inclusion of zero-trade flows in the analysis (Santos-Silva and Tenreyro 2006). In all chapters, this issue is discussed in the context of the data used, and generally nonlinear estimators or Heckman two-step procedures have been used to include zeros in the estimate and to account for selection.

Finally, we believe that an empirical analysis increases its individual and social value if it is made fully replicable (King 2003; Hamermesh 2007). Therefore, we allow the reader and the practitioner to have access not only to the data used in the empirical analysis but also to the code that makes it possible to completely replicate the analysis from the (publicly available) raw data to the tables of results and the figures included in each essay. Whenever one author is still working on a different research project using the same dataset, a subsample of the original data is made available. The complete dataset can always be directly requested to the authors of a specific chapter.

All datasets and code files are compilable in STATA 9.0. STATA is the data analysis and statistical software more often used by the authors of this volume and by applied trade economists in general. Some particular analysis on preferential margins has been performed using GAMS. In the Springer webpage of the volume, the interested reader will find for each chapter a text file containing the instructions about the analysis to be performed.

1.5 Outline of the Book

We take as a starting point that, in spite of the fact that one of the main objectives of trade preferences is to create the necessary stimulus to promote trade from developing countries, the effectiveness of trade preferences has largely been disputed. Our goal is to provide further evidence about the trade impact, highlighting in which sectors more generous preferences may boost trade, and where preference erosion may have the largest impact.

A quick summary of the chapters will give a flavour of the issues covered in this book. Chapter 2 by Lars Nilsson provides an overview of EU preferential trading arrangements towards developing countries. It presents the main features of the various arrangements and how they have evolved over time. This is a necessary background information for the following chapters, but the chapter also describes the relative importance of preferences in EU imports from developing countries and the extent to which the preferences are used. More importantly, the author points out that one issue largely overlooked in the literature is the importance of the value of the import flows. A significant number of preference eligible goods are imported into the EU from developing countries at relatively low values: while the overall use of EU trade preferences is high, preference utilisation rates of these imports are markedly lower compared to the overall high use of EU trade preferences.

There is more to imports and tariffs than first meets the eye, and Chapter 3 by Maria Cipollina and Luca Salvatici provides an introduction to the complexities of the EU import tariff regimes. Several definitions are feasible and have been used in the literature. Tariff margins can be expressed in absolute or relative terms; both provide different information about trade policy. However, regardless of the definition used and the way that it is expressed, in the context of trade policy, there remains the problem of how tariff margins should be aggregated which, in fact, is almost a separate strand of literature (Cipollina and Salvatici 2008). The authors review some of the available absolute and relative tariff margin definitions and compute them in the case of the European Union (EU) policies. Then they focus on the aggregation problem and define an aggregate preference index – Mercantilistic Trade Preference Index (MTPI) – in the spirit of the theoretically consistent protection indexes introduced by Anderson and Neary (2003). MTPI for the preferences granted by the EU to various sectors are computed using a partial equilibrium model based on Bureau and Salvatici (2004, 2005). The main message coming out from this chapter is that any donor country's preference schemes should be seen in light of the donor's overall trade openness taking into account trade preferences offered to competitor countries.

In Chapter 4, Luca De Benedictis and Daria Taglioni present a selective overview of the gravity equation that is going to be used in the subsequent chapters. Gravity has long been one of the most successful "empirical fact" in economics. Over the years there has been dramatic progress both in understanding the theoretical basis for the equation and in improving its empirical estimation. The authors review these developments, starting from Tinbergen's (1962) original analysis, derive the theoretical foundation of the modern version of the model (Anderson and van Wincoop 2003; Helpman et al. 2008) and discuss the empirical strategies to correctly estimate it. They examine some well-known issues, such as the use of country fixed effects to control for Multilateral Resistance and the ways to include the information embedded in the zero-trade flows in the estimatimation of the volume of trade. They also focus on less discussed matters such as the role of dynamics and interdependence. The authors argue that awareness of old and new problems in the estimation of the gravity equation will lead to a more accurate estimation and interpretation of the policy impact on trade flows.

The value and use of EU preferential trading arrangements have been debated off and on for a number of years in a number of various contexts. Several studies have analysed the impact of EU trade preferences on imports from developing countries. Existing studies report very different estimates: Chapter 5 by Maria Cipollina and Filomena Pietrovito combines, explains, and summarizes the results obtained by this literature using a Meta-Analysis (MA) approach. The authors test the estimation results for sensitivity to alternative specifications and different control variables. After filtering out potential biases, the MA confirms expectations of a robust and positive effect of preferential trade agreements. The results from the studies that use dummies tend to be higher in absolute terms than the results from studies using a measure of margin: the former indicates a positive impact of preferences on trade of around 70% while the latter suggest that an increase in preferences of 10% increases trade by about 4%.

This sets the scene for the other five chapters, which employ a gravity model framework to verify whether EU preferences for developing countries have helped to increase their market shares. All applications share some crucial methodological choices, such as the usage of explicit measures for the preferential margins as well as controlling for heterogeneity, endogeneity and zero-trade flows. They use disaggregated flows at the product level, comparing flows to the EU and not to other export markets. This means that they will not be able to pick up whether a developing country is exporting more to the EU as a result of preferences in a given sector than it is exporting to other developed countries. They can, however, pick whether a country is exporting to the EU more than a country which does not have preferences, and capture the importance of preferential flows of one product compared to flows of the same product from the same country when the preference is not requested and receives Most Favoured Nation (MFN) treatment.

In Chapter 6, Maria Cipollina and Luca Salvatici assess the impact of trade policies both on the number of bilateral trade flows (*extensive margin*) and on volumes traded (*intensive margin*). Using a theoretically grounded gravity equation they estimate a cross-sectional sample selection models for 4,941 commodities (6-digit HS level) from 169 DC to 25 EU member countries, allowing for heterogeneous trade costs and substitution elasticities across industries. Preference margins are measured in relative terms and definition focuses on actual preferences with respect to possible competitors, rather than theoretical margins with respect to bound MFN tariffs. Moreover, the information on actual preferential trade flows allows providing improved estimates of the impact of trade preferences by accounting for the share of preferential flows on total imports. By and large, EU preferences discourage export diversification of industrial goods, but promote it in the case of agriculture. As far as the intensive margin is concerned, large impacts are associated to sections with low duties and large margins are less effective in the presence of high bilateral duties, as in the case of agricultural products and textiles.

Francesco Aiello and Paola Cardamone (Chapter 7) evaluate whether Everything But Arms (EBA) was effective in increasing exports from LDC to the EU, over the period 1995–2006. The analysis is carried out by considering five products (cloves, coffee, crustaceans, molluscs and vanilla beans) which meet three criteria relating to the export intensity of LDC, the actual preferences of EBA and the intra-year distribution of EU tariffs. By using very disaggregated data (8 digit level) the estimates of the negative binomial model contrast with those obtained in previous works since the authors show that the EBA initiative exerts for some products a positive role in enhancing LDC exports to the EU: in particular, the exports of crustaceans and vanilla were positively affected by the preferential treatment.

Paola Cardamone (Chapter 8) deals with the fruit and vegetable market which is among the most important agricultural ones for the EU in terms of both production and trade. More specifically, the chapter focuses on European imports of fresh grapes, pears, apples, oranges and mandarins over the period 2001–2004 addressing the need to assess the impact of EU preferences using higher frequency trade data than annual flows. As a matter of fact, the distinguishing feature of this chapter is that monthly rather than yearly data are used in order to take into account that both imports and protection vary seasonally. Furthermore, the author determines a measure of preferential margins by considering quotas and the entry price system as well. Following the seminal work by Santos-Silva and Tenreyro (2006), she estimates a Poisson model controlling for the heterogeneity bias and the heteroskedasticity of the error term of the multiplicative gravity specification. As in the previous chapter, limiting the analysis to a small set of products allows to work at a very detailed level (8 digit). Overall, the results show that the GSP scheme is successful in enhancing EU imports of apples and fresh grapes while regional trade agreements seem to achieve the goal of increasing EU imports of fresh grapes, pears and mandarins.

Alessandro Olper, Valentina Raimondi and Margherita Scoppola (Chapter 9) focus on the 2003 reform of the Common Agricultural Policy in the rice sector. Because the EU grants trade preferences to a considerable number of developing countries, the reform of the domestic policy also entailed erosion of preferences. Moreover, because EU preferences to rice imports are granted by means of Tariff Rate Quotas (TRQ), to compute the preferential margin one needs to evaluate the tariff equivalent of the TRQ. The literature to date has assessed this tariff equivalent by assuming perfect competition in international agricultural trade. This chapter proposes a new empirical approach to calculate the tariff equivalent of the tariff rate quota, which is shown to be consistent with the assumption of economies of scale and imperfect competition in international trade. The results show that the way in which preferential margins are calculated matters significantly when assessing the existence and extent of preference erosion and estimating the values of trade elasticities. Under the standard method for computing the tariff rate quota equivalent, no clear-cut evidence of preference erosion emerges, while the opposite is true when the tariff equivalent proposed in this chapter is used. The method to calculate the margin also significantly affects the estimated values of the trade elasticities; more specifically, the results show that, by using the preferential margins based on the standard tariff equivalent of tariff rate quotas, the impact of trade preferences is lower than when one assumes economies of scale and imperfect competition. Finally, estimations highlight that the trade impact of preferences is currently still very high for almost all preferred countries.

Finally, Mariarosaria Agostino, Federica De Maria and Francesco Trivieri (Chap. 10) use a gravity model to investigate the effects of the costs of compliance arising from factors related to the scheme requirements, such as rules of origin, technical, sanitary and traceability requirements. As mentioned above, this is a crucial issue: if costs of compliance outweigh the benefits of a trade preference, then a larger preference margin would not necessarily provide a greater incentive to export. The authors focus on the agricultural sector as developed countries have always shown a certain reluctance in granting deep and effective tariff reductions to agricultural imports, and many MFN duties on agricultural commodities are still very high, which makes the benefit from any preferential agreement potentially relevant. A cross section non linear model is estimated for 669 agricultural exports from 136 DC and results confirm that the costs of compliance do play a role in making the schemes work: the higher the compliance costs, the lower the impact of the preferential margins. Furthermore, the marginal effect of the preferential margins differ across regimes, and the influence of costs on the preferential margin impact is proportionally higher for the Cotonou and GSP-Drugs schemes.

1.6 Conclusions

The general result of the essays included in the volume indicates that by and large EU's preferences support exports of developing countries to the EU market, though the impact on trade differs with the degree of preference. That is, trade preferences have helped to increase exports from developing countries, but the deeper the preferences, the greater the effect. These results reinforce the choice to work at the disaggregated level, in order to catch this product specificity that is rarely taken into account in international trade models. Using trade at a very high level of data and temporal disaggregation, the volume's essays show that the EBA initiative, the GSP scheme as well as regional trade agreements all exert (at least) for some products a positive role in enhancing developing countries' exports to the EU.

The increase in the value of trade flows ranges from 0.1 to 3% of total trade flows. These are rather small percentages, but these increases should be seen against the fact that about 60% of EU imports enter the EU market at MFN-0 rates. These 60% of imports should not be affected (at least not directly) by any preferential trading measures. Hence, the figures of 0.1–3% can only affect the other 40%, that is to the dutiable imports. The impact of EU trade preferences then increases to between 0.25 and 7.5%, where the latter figure is certainly far from trivial. Moreover, with low MFN tariffs, relatively few tariff peaks, and the composition of exports, the extent to which bilateral preference regimes can help developing countries is, in principle, structurally limited. In other words, the preference margins are typically low because the underlying MFN tariffs are low, and this inevitably means the scope for offering preferential access via tariff reductions is constrained, and is a structural feature arising from the EU‘s (but for agriculture) low level of MFN tariffs.

Moreover, market access is not just about the level of the tariffs being imposed by the importing country – there are various well-known other reasons why access to markets may be impeded ranging from internal domestic infrastructure issues, to issues of trade facilitation, as well as technical measures and standards. However, the role of tariff barriers shouldn't be easily dismissed, since there is evidence that notwithstanding the trade preferences rhetoric, developing countries still appear to be substantially restricted in their trade with the EU due to the interaction between the EU's MFN tariff profile and the structure of developing countries' exports (Antimiani et al. 2008). In this respect, developing countries rightly claim that their market shares in developed markets remain limited, in spite of complex and sometimes extensive preferential access granted by rich countries to them.

Using disaggregated data allows gauging another alleged disadvantage of the trade preferences; namely that countries could become dependent on the preferences and focus their economy around one product rather than allocating resources throughout the economy. Even if there is some evidence that the EU's preference regimes have led to a reduction in the number of exported products, especially in the industrial sector, it is worth emphasizing that overall EU preferences have led to a diversification of exports into new products.

There are a number of important caveats when considering the policy implications arising from these results. Even if essays included in the volume analyse the impact of compliance costs, we don't examine all possible determining factors influencing the degree of preference utilization rate. In the same vein, even if the essays deal with preference rents, they do not to assess the extent to which the exporters in the beneficiary countries are able to appropriate them. More generally, this book does not consider the extent to which EU's trade policy accomplishes the needs of developing countries and does not aim to put forward recommendations for possible improvements in this respect.

Although our main goal is to challenge current thinking about what is the impact of current trade policies, some normative conclusions can be attempted. The international architecture of trade policies is not a product of "intelligent design" but is instead evolutionary. The EU's preferential policies are at a turning point and the mid-term assessment of the impact of EU's GSP revision offers a valuable occasion for analysis and planning. In the years ahead, the EU has an opportunity to redefine the rules and tools that govern its trade policies.

Preferential schemes are likely to remain a feature of the international architecture in a multi-polar world, even though they are likely to be a declining share of total trade flows. The role of preferences has eroded under the impact of two phenomena. Firstly, the EU is going (sooner or later) to progressively lower its trade barriers either in favour of all WTO members and/or in favour of regional partners. Secondly, the types of preferences granted are becoming 'outdated' since tariff and quantitative restrictions are no longer the only instruments of protection. Other obstacles, such as veterinary and quality standards, play an increasing role, against which tariff preferences are useless.

Preferences are also bound to remain fragmented, creating a complex web of networks to achieve various objectives. Accordingly, the rules of the game and the tools of preferential policies need to evolve to focus on transparency and results, in order to rise to the challenge of the new development agenda. For such a large and fragmented policy, there is a need for much greater information, freely available, to allow participants to coordinate, plan and use more effectively.

Detailed and timely data are needed, as they enable new models for policy analysis. Disaggregated gravity models have to move from being interesting innovations, to become a much bigger share of research activity. These analytical efforts are essential to benchmark different schemes which can then drive improvements in performance.

Acknowledgments We acknowledge financial support from the "New Issues in Agricultural, Food and Bio-energy Trade (AGFOODTRADE)" (Small and Medium-scale Focused Research Project, Grant Agreement no. 212036) research project funded by the European Commission, and the "European Union policies, economic and trade integration processes and WTO negotiations" research project funded by the Italian Ministry of Education, University and Research (Scientific Research Programs of National Relevance 2007). We are grateful to Giovanni Anania, Mariarosaria Agostino, Federica De Maria, Lars Nilsson and Francesco Trivieri for the comments.

Chapter 2
European Union Preferential Trading Arrangements: Evolution, Content and Use

Lars Nilsson

Abstract This chapter provides an overview of European Union (EU) preferential trading arrangements towards developing countries. It presents the main features of the various arrangements and how they have evolved over time. It is noted that EU trade relations *vis-à-vis* developing countries are in general moving away from unilateral preferences towards reciprocal agreements. The chapter also describes the relative importance of preferences in EU imports from developing countries and the extent to which the preferences are used. It highlights that a significant number of preference eligible goods are imported into the EU from developing countries at relatively low values and that the preference utilisation rates of these imports are markedly lower compared to the overall high use of EU trade preferences.

2.1 Introduction

Preferential trading schemes originated in developing countries' mistrust of the international trading systems and the General Agreement on Tariffs and Trade (GATT). Until the early 1960s, lowering of tariffs through GATT negotiations had mainly been accomplished on industrialized goods which the developed countries rather than the developing countries traded with each other. Partly as a consequence of the developing countries' dissatisfaction with the GATT, the United Nations Conference on Trade and Development (UNCTAD) was founded. The first conference was held in 1964 and resulted in demands from the developing countries for promotion of an increase of their export earnings and for a continuation of industrialization of their countries.

The opinions expressed in this chapter are the author's own and do not necessarily reflect any views of the European Commission.

L. Nilsson
European Commission, DG Trade, Rue de la Loi/Wetstraat 170, 1040 Bruxelles/Brussel, Belgique/België, Belgium
e-mail: lars.nilsson@ec.europa.eu

L. De Benedictis and L. Salvatici (eds.), *The Trade Impact of European Union Preferential Policies*, DOI 10.1007/978-3-642-16564-1_2,

To achieve these objectives, the developing countries demanded non-reciprocal preferential tariff treatment. The preferences would give the developing countries better access to the developed countries' markets and an advantage over suppliers from industrialized countries. The European Union (EU) introduced its first Generalised System of Preferences (GSP) in 1971 and was followed by many other industrialised economies. However, it was not until the end of the 1970s that such unilateral non-reciprocal preferences for developing countries were legalised through the GATT when the so called "enabling clause" (GATT 1979) was adopted under the Tokyo Round.[1]

EU trade preferences have taken and still take different shape depending on which the beneficiary countries are. All developing countries are eligible for the EU's GSP scheme, while only the African, Caribbean and Pacific (ACP) countries *were* eligible for the more far-reaching non-reciprocal preferences under the Lomé Conventions and the Cotonou Agreement, and *are* so for the on-going negotiations of reciprocal preferences under the latter's successor, the Economic Partnership Agreements (EPA). In addition, non-reciprocal preferences have been introduced for countries in the EU's neighbourhood. The EU has also concluded free trade agreements with the Mediterranean countries as well as with Chile, Mexico and South Africa and negotiations with other countries and/or regions are on-going.

This chapter describes the evolution, content and use of EU trade preferences. Section 2.2 presents the scope, coverage and change over time of the EU GSP and preferential arrangements for non-ACP countries. A summary of on-going EU Free Trade Agreement (FTA) negotiations with developing/neighbourhood countries is also provided. Section 2.3 provides the same description of the preferential schemes applicable to the ACP. Section 2.4 presents the relative importance of preferences in EU imports from developing countries and the extent to which the preferences are used, with a particular emphasis on the preference utilisation rate of small import flows. Finally, Section 2.5 concludes.

[1]Article 1 of the GATT stipulates that no GATT contracting party must be treated worse than any other contracting party (also known as the Most Favored Nation (MFN) principle). The "enabling clause" permits developed countries to discriminate between developed, developing and Least Developed Countries (LDC) which would otherwise violate Article I of the GATT. Note that there are no World Trade Organization (WTO) definitions of "developed" and "developing" countries. WTO members announce for themselves whether they are "developed" or "developing" countries. However, other members can challenge the decision of a member to make use of provisions available to developing countries, see http://www.wto.org/english/tratop_e/devel_e/d1who_e.htm. Least developed countries are defined by the United Nations, see http://www.unohrlls.org/en/ldc/related/62/.

2.2 The European Union Preferential Arrangements for Non-African, Caribbean and Pacific Countries

2.2.1 The European Union Generalized System of Preferences

In 1971, the European Community (EC) introduced its first GSP scheme. It has been modified and improved on several occasions since, most often in terms of product coverage and preferential margins. GSP preferences, which are available to all developing countries, were offered in the form of duty free quotas and ceilings until the mid-1990s when all quantitative restrictions were removed and preferences instead were given in the form of reductions of the applied MFN tariff, the size of which depended on the *sensitivity* of the product.

Special incentive schemes under the GSP have been in place for close to 20 years. For example, countries combating drug production and trafficking received additional preferences already in 1991. Similarly, LDC have received preferences superior to those under the general arrangement since 1977.

In 2002, the EU broadened the number of sub-schemes under its GSP to five (a general arrangement; special incentive arrangements for the protection of labour rights; special incentive arrangements for the protection of the environment; special arrangements for least-developed countries; and special arrangements to combat drug production and trafficking, "GSP drugs," (Council Regulation (EC) 2001). The arrangements to combat drug production and trafficking provided for duty-free access for all industrial products (and some agricultural products) included in the general arrangement and as well as for certain agricultural products which were not covered by the general arrangement.

The same year, India challenged the EU's "GSP drugs" regime claiming that it was inconsistent with Article I of the GATT, the MFN principle, and not justified under the enabling clause. Two years later, in 2004, the WTO's Appellate Body found that the EU had not been able to demonstrate that its 'drug' regime is based on objective and transparent criteria that would allow all developing countries similarly situated to qualify for these preferences. As a result, when the EU adopted its next scheme, which ran from 2006 until the end of 2008, it included a newly revised "GSP-Plus" scheme for vulnerable countries with special development needs. However, the special incentive arrangement for sustainable development and good governance entered into force already on 1 July 2005 and repealed the special arrangements to combat drug production and trafficking (Council Regulation (EC) 2005).

In July 2008, the EU adopted the latest revision of its GSP scheme which runs from 1 January 2009 until the end of 2011. However, in May 2010 the Commission proposed that the current regulation should be extended to 31 December 2013 because of the time frame needed for an agreement on a successor regulation through the ordinary legislative procedure (EC 2010). The current GSP contains three different sub-arrangements, the general or standard scheme, GSP-Plus and the Everything But Arms (EBA) initiative, which was introduced for the first time in 2001.

The standard scheme covers 176 developing countries and about 6,200 products. Non-sensitive products (slightly less than half of the products covered) enjoy duty-free access, while sensitive products (mainly agricultural products, but also textile, clothing and apparel, carpets and footwear) benefit from a tariff reduction of 3.5% points of *ad valorem* duties compared to the applied MFN tariff and a 30% reduction of specific duties (with a few exceptions).[2] For textiles and clothing, the reduction is 20% of the *ad valorem* MFN duty rate.[3]

The GSP-Plus scheme is designed for vulnerable countries with specific development needs. The scheme covers 15 countries and allows for duty-free entry to the EU market of the goods covered by the general GSP scheme and for some additional products. To be eligible, beneficiaries must meet a number of criteria including ratification and effective implementation of key international conventions on human and labour rights, sustainable development and good governance, and demonstrate that their economies are dependent and vulnerable. Poor diversification and dependence are defined as meaning that the five largest sections of a beneficiary's GSP-covered exports to the Community must represent more than 75% of its total GSP-covered exports. GSP-covered exports from that country must also represent less than 1% of total EU imports under GSP.

Finally, the LDC are eligible for duty free access to the EU market without any restrictions for all products except Arms under the EBA initiative, which also forms part of the EU GSP scheme.

Beneficiaries of the GSP are subject to "graduation" which is triggered when a country becomes sufficiently competitive in one or more product groups and therefore no longer considered to be in need of preferential access to the EU market. The graduation mechanism consists of a single criterion; the share of the Community market expressed as a share of preferential imports. The share is 15% in general, but 12.5% for textiles and clothing, split into two sections, thereby, in practice, restricting access to the GSP scheme for Brazil, China, India, Indonesia, Malaysia, Vietnam and Thailand (Council Regulation 2008, Annex I, Column C). Close to 98% of China's exports have graduated from the EU's GSP scheme in 2009.

Any GSP arrangement may be temporarily withdrawn for serious and systematic violations of core human and labour rights conventions and on other potential grounds related to e.g., customs control identified in the Regulation. This is currently the case for Belarus (preferences withdrawn in 2007) and Myanmar (preferences withdrawn in 1997). Similarly, GSP-Plus benefits may be temporarily withdrawn if national legislation no longer incorporates the relevant conventions

[2]Tariffs are suspended if preferential treatment results in (*ad valorem*) duties of 1 percent or less, or in specific duties of 2 Euros or less.

[3]This concerns mainly products in chapters 50–63 of the Harmonized System (HS).

or if that legislation is not effectively implemented. To this end, benefits under the GSP-Plus were withdrawn for Sri Lanka in August 2010.[4]

The safeguard clause entails restoring the Common Customs Tariff duties and is generally implemented when imports of a product cause serious difficulties to a Community producer of like or directly competing products. Serious difficulties are assessed using criteria measuring Community producers' market share, production, stocks, production capacity, bankruptcies, profitability, capacity utilisation, employment, imports and prices. Investigations are opened at the request of a Member State or on the Community's own initiative, and must in principle be completed within six months, unless an extension decision is granted.

The rules of origin in the GSP are used to determine where goods originate, i.e., where they are deemed to have been produced or manufactured in order to grant preference to the right beneficiary (for more information, see EC 2008). However, the rules of origin are not part of the GSP regulation(s). Instead they are governed by separate regulation(s) (Commission Regulation (EEC) 2454/93 as subsequently amended (most recently by Commission Regulation (EC) 214/2007)). A reform of the rules of origin under the GSP has been on its way since 2005 when the Commission adopted a Communication on the future of rules of origin in preferential trade arrangements (EC 2005). The new GSP rules of origin apply as of 1 January 2011 (as regards the rules for determining origin) and on 1 January 2017 with a transitional period until 1 January 2020 as regards procedures (Commission Regulation (EU) No 1063/2010).[5]

The Commission is currently reflecting on the EU's trade policy towards developing countries. At a conference organised by the Commission in March 2010, discussions were held on how EU trade policy could take better account of, or be tailored towards, developing countries' needs with a particular attention paid to the fact that larger emerging economies have different development needs than poor and vulnerable countries. The objective of the process is to help shape the policy line in this area for the coming Commission mandate and beyond.

One discussion topic at the conference was the EU GSP Scheme and how it can maintain its effectiveness as a development tool. The basis for discussion of this issue was the comprehensive external evaluation of the EU's GSP scheme that has been carried out by University of Sussex (Gasiorek et al. 2010). The conference also marked the launch of a public consultation on the review of the EU's GSP scheme. The results of this consultation will feed into the Commission's future proposal to the European Parliament and Council on an updated GSP regulation, which is expected to be adopted by the Commission in May 2011.

---

[4]The withdrawal of preferences normally enters into force 6 months after the decision is announced, giving the country concerned time to address the situation.

[5]For more information, see the homepage of Directorate General Taxation and Customs Union (TAXUD) at http://ec.europa.eu/taxation_customs/customs/customs_duties/rules_origin/preferential/article_781_en.htm.

2.2.2 *Preferential Arrangements for Non-African, Caribbean and Pacific Countries*

The World Bank classified the former candidate countries in Central and Eastern Europe (CEEC), with the exception of Slovenia, as developing countries.[6] Before EU membership their trade relations with the EU were governed by the so-called Europe Agreements, which aimed to progressively establish an FTA between the EU and the respective country. Asymmetric liberalisation was applied so that EU markets were opened more quickly for goods from the CEEC than vice-versa. EU trade relations with another candidate country, Turkey, are governed by a customs union for industrial products, including processed agricultural products.

The trade provisions of the Europe Agreements entered into force in 1992 for the Czech Republic, Hungary, Poland and Slovakia, in 1993 for Romania and Bulgaria, in 1995 for Estonia, Latvia and Lithuania and in 1997 for Slovenia.[7] The customs union with Turkey entered into force in 1995.

In addition, the EU has a number of bilateral or regional FTAs with other developing countries. The EU has concluded and currently implements Association Agreements with Southern Mediterranean countries (with the exception of Syria[8] and Libya), which provide for asymmetric (in favour of the Mediterranean countries) preferences on manufactured goods and on certain agriculture, processed agriculture and fisheries products. These agreements entered into force in the late 1990s for the Occupied Palestinian Territory (1997) and Tunisia (1998) and during the first 5 years of the 2000s for the other countries [Algeria (2005), Egypt (2004), Israel (2000), Jordan (2002), Lebanon (2003) and Morocco (2000)].[9] Liberalisation of trade in services and investment, also form part of the Association Agreements' key objectives. To this end bilateral negotiations were launched in 2008 with some Southern Mediterranean partners.

Bilateral FTAs have also been established with Chile, Mexico and South Africa. The EU's FTA with Chile was concluded in 2000 and entered into force in February 2003. The agreement creates a free trade area in goods, services and government procurement, liberalises investment and capital flows and strengthens the protection of intellectual property rights and goes beyond WTO commitments.

---

[6]These countries are all new member states of the EU as of 1 May 2004, except for Bulgaria and Romania, which became members of the EU on 1 January 2007.

[7]In the case of Slovenia, EU imports were governed by annually renewable autonomous trade preferences in the 1990s before the entering into force of the Europe Agreement. In case of the three Baltic States, the dates refer to trade provisions of agreements prior to the Europe Agreements. See http://ec.europa.eu/enlargement/press_corner/key-documents/index_archive_en.htm for more information.

[8]The EU's Cooperation Agreement with Syria should be replaced by a Euro-Mediterranean Agreement similar to those concluded by the European Community with its other Mediterranean partners. The agreement was signed in 2004 but is pending Syrian ratification.

[9]The years refer to the entry into force of the trade in goods part of the agreements. See the WTO's database on regional trade agreements, http://rtais.wto.org/UI/PublicMaintainRTAHome.aspx.

The EU-Mexico FTA entered into force in October 2000. It covers trade in goods and services and has specific chapters on access to public procurement markets, competition, intellectual property rights and investment. The FTA with South Africa was signed in 1999 (and entered into force in 2004) and aims, among other things, to establish a free trade area over a 12 year period covering 90% of bilateral trade.

The EU introduced Autonomous Trade Measures (ATM) for the Western Balkans (Albania, Bosnia and Herzegovina, Croatia, the former Yugoslav Republic of Macedonia, Montenegro, Serbia and Kosovo) in 2000.[10] The ATM are similar to the EBA in that they provide for duty- and quota-free access for almost all products from the beneficiary countries. Only wine, sugar, baby beef and certain fisheries products enter the EU under preferential tariff quotas. These preferences were renewed in 2005 and currently last until 2010. As of 2008, Moldova benefits from a similar arrangement.

However, the ATM have been superseded by reciprocal Stabilisation and Association Agreements (SAA) with most of the Western Balkan.[11] The trade part of the SAA came into force through Interim Agreements with the former Yugoslav Republic of Macedonia in 2001, Croatia in 2002, Albania in 2006, Bosnia and Herzegovina and Montenegro in 2008 and with Serbia in 2010.[12]

Croatia and the former Yugoslav Republic of Macedonia further have the status as candidate countries for EU membership and Croatia are currently negotiating the terms for its accession. Albania, Montenegro and Serbia have also applied for membership. As a result of these countries' political status in relation to the EU, in addition to the fact that they are not included among the list of GSP beneficiaries, it has been decided not to analyse their trade with the EU further in this chapter.

2.2.3 *On-Going Free Trade Agreements Negotiations with Developing/Neighbourhood Countries*

Negotiations with six Central American countries (Costa Rica, Guatemala, Honduras, Nicaragua, Panama and El Salvador) were concluded in May 2010. With Mercosur, negotiations have officially been on hold since 2004 but the Commission proposed to Mercosur to re-launch the negotiations in May 2010. In the case of the Andean Pact, negotiations with Colombia and Peru were concluded in the first

[10]The ATM are sanctioned by a WTO waiver.

[11]SAAs are in force with the former Yugoslav Republic of Macedonia (2004), Croatia (2005), Albania (2009) and Montenegro (2010) and have been signed with Bosnia and Herzegovina and Serbia.

[12]See the WTO's database on regional trade agreements, http://rtais.wto.org/UI/PublicMaintainRTAHome.aspx.

half of 2010, while negotiations with Ecuador are still pending and uncertain in the case of Bolivia.[13]

Negotiations with the Gulf Cooperation Council (GCC) have reached an advanced stage but the negotiations have been suspended. The main outstanding issue is the treatment of export duties under the FTA. As of April 2011, sixteen rounds of negotiations (launched in 2008) with the Ukraine have taken place and negotiating directives were adopted for Armenia and Georgia in June 2010. When these two countries have made sufficient progress in implementing some key recommendations, the Commission will propose launching negotiations. A preparatory process, before negotiating directives are adopted, is ongoing with Moldova.

In March 2010, it was agreed to take a "pause" in the negotiations with a regional grouping of 7 Association of Southeast Asian Nations (ASEAN) countries. The Commission will pursue FTA negotiations in a bilateral format with countries of the ASEAN which are willing to do so. Vietnam has given a political signal that it is ready to engage along this path and negotiations with Malaysia and Singapore are on-going. Negotiations with India were launched in 2007; nine rounds have been held as of April 2010.

2.3 Preferential Arrangements for African, Caribbean and Pacific Countries

The first EU non-reciprocal trade agreements with a set of ACP countries basically originated in the reciprocal preferential schemes that some founding EU countries had with their former colonies in, mainly, francophone Sub Saharan Africa through the two Yaoundé agreements of 1963 and 1969. Similar arrangements also existed with a couple of East African countries, the so called Arusha arrangements of 1969. Bilateral trade agreements between the EU and former Dutch colonies also existed, as well as the developing Commonwealth member's preferential market access into the UK, which were taken into account when the UK joined the EU in 1973. These schemes were all superseded by the first Lomé Convention that was signed in 1975.

2.3.1 The Lomé Conventions

The Lomé Convention was the most important preferential trade agreement that the EU had signed at that point in time. Compared to the former reciprocal agreements, not only did the Lomé Convention mean a quantitative change in the number of countries covered by the scheme, but also a qualitative change since, besides trade, major areas covered by the new agreement were aid, technical assistance and export stabilization programmes (Stabex and Sysmin). Furthermore, developing countries

---

[13]In September 2010, the draft agreement was under linguistic and legal review.

did not have to grant counter concessions for imports from the EU in contrast to the earlier reciprocal trade agreements.

The first Lomé convention was superseded by Lomé II and Lomé III and the last Lomé Convention, Lomé IV, was signed at Lomé in December 1989 and put weight on the link between aid and structural adjustment and on the consequences for the ACP of the establishment of the internal market in 1993. A review of Lomé IV in 1995 resulted in Lomé IV bis which distinguished itself by the importance accorded to decentralised cooperation and the role of civil society.

The scope of products that the trade preferences were going to cover was also an essential element of the Convention. Its basic features were that (1) industrial products originating in the ACP countries could be imported free of custom duties and quotas into the EU, (2) some agricultural products were to be imported free of duties and quotas and (3) special Protocols applied to Bananas, Rum and on Beef and Veal which sought to protect ACP suppliers from competition from third countries (EC 1992). Furthermore, under the sugar protocol, the EU agreed to buy, and 13 ACP agreed to sell, a certain quota of sugar, free of levies and duties, to a guaranteed price (EC 1992, Part Three, Title II, Chapter 2: Special undertakings on sugar).

2.3.2 The Cotonou Agreement

The fourth Lomé Convention was superseded by the ACP-EU Partnership Agreement (hereinafter the Cotonou Agreement), which was signed between the EC and the 77 ACP countries on 13 June 2000 and entered into force in April 2003.

Under the Cotonou Agreement's trade pillar, the ACP benefited from non-reciprocal trade preferences for the period 2001–2007.[14] The preferences were identical to those under the last Lomé Convention. Products originating in ACP countries were exempted from EU customs duties, while preferences for agricultural products were differentiated. For example, tropical products which did not compete with European products entered the EU market duty free. Temperate products faced an exemption or reduction of customs duties, while fruits and vegetables were subject to seasonal restrictions. For bananas, beef and veal and sugar, the EU continued to provide special market access and so-called commodity protocols.

Over the two decades preceding the signature of the Cotonou Agreement, many ACP countries had seen their share of exports on the EU market decline. Their general economic situation was also at the same level, if not worse, compared to the situation before the non-reciprocal preferences contained in the Lomé Conventions

[14]South Africa is a signatory to the Cotonou Agreement but its membership of the ACP Group is qualified (Protocol 3 on South Africa attached to the Cotonou Agreement). The provisions of the Trade, Development and Cooperation Agreement between the EC and South Africa take precedence over the provisions of the Cotonou Agreement. Cuba belongs to the ACP group of countries but is not a signatory to the Cotonou Agreement.

were introduced. The EU had subsequently started to take an increasing interest in the economic policies of the ACP and to question the relevance of unilateral trade preferences for the development of these countries (EC 1996).[15]

Meanwhile, non-ACP developing countries at the same development level as the ACP had not been granted the special treatment which ACP countries receive from the EU. This is in breach of the fundamental principle of the MFN treatment set out in Article I of the GATT. Because of this, the EU had had to seek a series of waivers from other WTO members to enable its special trade regime for the ACP to continue. The latest of these waivers was only agreed in Doha in 2001 with the express condition that the EU and ACP must agree new WTO compatible trade arrangements by the end of 2007 after which the waiver expired.

The negotiations on the last waiver were difficult.[16] Those who doubt the willingness of developing countries to question special treatment for other developing countries need look no further than the long and bitter "banana dispute" during which non-ACP countries challenged a series of frameworks established by the EU to provide special access to the market for ACP bananas. However, this issue was finally resolved towards the end of 2009 when it was agreed that the EU will gradually cut its import tariff on bananas from Latin America from 176 Euros per ton to 114 Euros.

The main feature of the Cotonou Agreement is that the Parties agreed to conclude new WTO-compatible trading arrangements, so-called EPA, which aim at progressively removing barriers to trade, enhancing co-operation in all areas relevant to trade and to smoothly and gradually integrate the ACP economies into the world economy.

2.3.3 Economic Partnership Agreements[17]

The purpose of the EPA is to promote sustainable development in the ACP, including regional integration within the ACP (based on existing initiatives) as well as poverty reduction. Through regional integration and integration between the EU and the ACP, the EPA are intended to act as a stepping stone to the gradual integration of the ACP countries into the world economy. The agreements will be consistent with WTO rules and in some respects go beyond.

---

[15]However, while recognizing that some ACP did benefit greatly from these preferences (e.g., Mauritius) even without visible progress in the figures and on the ground in many of the countries, one needs to consider that the ACP might have been worse off if the Lomé Convention never had come into effect.

[16]Several concessions were required to other developing countries to secure the waiver. Notably, additional market access in tuna for several Asian countries and in bananas for Latin America.

[17]Formal negotiations at the level of all ACP countries started in September 2002. In October 2003, regional negotiations got under way with West Africa and Central Africa, in February 2004 with Eastern and Southern Africa, in April 2004 with the Caribbean, in July 2004 with Southern African Development Community (SADC) and in September 2004 with the Pacific.

The Cotonou Agreement was under the cover of a WTO waiver approved at the Doha Ministerial Meeting, which expired on 31 December 2007 (WTO 2001). In order to be WTO compatible, EU trade relations with the ACP will move from a context framed by a GATT Article I waiver to one framed by the rules on FTAs and/or customs unions, i.e., Article XXIV of the GATT. This approach enables EU-ACP relationship to move to a structure which is WTO compatible and therefore free from the threat of challenge.

The EU liberalisation of trade will provide for free access to the EU market for the EPA signatories and improved rules of origin in areas of interest to the partner countries. It will thus be more far-reaching and also more rapid compared to the liberalisation undertaken by the ACP. Furthermore, the inclusion of services and the creation of transparent, predictable and regional rules on issues such as investment, public procurement and competition policy are essential to successful economic governance and key to attracting more local and foreign investment in the ACP and thus also to development.

These latter elements, which do not relate to the simple opening of markets through tariff reduction, have become increasingly important with the gradual lowering of tariff barriers over the last decades. It is important to note that the objective of the EU is not to enforce EU type rules in the ACP regions, but rather to foster agreement, especially within regional groupings, on certain minimum standards.

To date one comprehensive EPA, the Caribbean Forum of African, Caribbean and Pacific States (CARIFORUM) EPA has been signed and is applied, while some 20 African countries have initialled or signed interim EPA. In Eastern and Southern Africa (ESA), an interim EPA has been agreed with six ESA states and signed by four of them and with the Central African region, Cameroon has signed an interim EPA. In West Africa, interim EPA have been signed with Ivory Coast and initialled with Ghana. The five East African Community (EAC) countries have initialled an interim EPA and among the SADC, an interim EPA has been concluded with Botswana, Lesotho, Namibia, Swaziland and Mozambique and signed by all but Namibia. Finally, in the Pacific, Fiji and Papua New Guinea have signed an interim EPA.

2.4 European Union Imports and the Use of European Union Trade Preferences

The EU is the world's largest importers of goods from developing countries, absorbing close to 20% of their total exports. In 2008, some 800 billion Euros were imported from the GSP beneficiaries (see Table 2.1).[18] Out of these, less than

[18]Note that all developing countries are eligible for GSP preferences so that all country groupings (except Chile) form part of the GSP grouping. Note also that the group of ACP countries contains most of the LDC.

Table 2.1 European Union imports from developing countries by tariff regime (billion Euros) and preference utilization rate, 2008

Country/group	Imports (billion Euros)					
	Total	MFN-0	Dutiable	Pref. eligible	Pref.	Pref. util. rate
GSP	811.5	525.7	285.9	140.0	101.7	72.6
ACP[a]	51.9	42.1	9.7	9.7	9.0	92.4
LDC	24.2	15.4	8.8	8.7	7.3	83.6
Med. Countries	59.3	33.9	25.3	25.2	21.3	84.6
Mexico	13.0	7.9	5.2	5.2	3.8	73.9
South Africa	20.5	12.6	7.9	7.5	6.6	87.6
Chile	10.2	7.3	2.9	2.9	2.5	85.4

Source: Comext

[a]Excluding South Africa. All developing countries are in principle eligible for the EU's GSP scheme

Table 2.2 European Union imports from Generalized System of Preferences beneficiaries by main Harmonized System 2 digit categories (billion Euros) and preference utilization rate, 2008 (%)

Harmonized System Chapter	Imports (billion Euros)					
	Total	MFN-0	Dutiable	Pref. eligible	Pref.	Pref. util. rate
Total	811.5	525.7	285.9	140.0	101.7	72.6
27	305.5	278.9	26.6	26.6	10.3	38.9
85	80.6	49.8	30.8	8.8	5.3	60.6
84	67.0	44.6	22.4	8.5	5.9	69.2
72	28.0	22.9	5.1	3.7	3.5	96.3
61	21.2	0.0	21.2	10.3	8.8	85.2
62	24.2	0.0	24.2	10.1	7.1	70.8

Source: Comext

300 billion dollars were dutiable, that is subject to positive MFN duties. The share of non-dutiable (MFN-0) imports range from about 60% in the case of the LDC, the Mediterranean countries, Mexico and South Africa to more than 80% for the ACP with Chile in-between at some 70%.

Except for the GSP beneficiaries, for which about half of all dutiable imports are eligible for preferences, EU dutiable imports from the beneficiaries are in the main eligible for preferences. This reflects the more comprehensive scope of the EU's other preferential arrangements compared to the standard GSP. EU preferences are generally well used. The preference utilisation rate for the GSP group of countries (including all preferences available) is higher than 70%, while for the other preferential arrangements, it ranges from slightly more than 75% in the case of Mexico to some 85–90% for the rest of the countries.

Table 2.2 displays the five most important HS2 digit chapters in terms of EU imports and EU preference eligible imports from the GSP group of countries. Six HS2 categories make up 65% of all such imports. Five of the six most important HS2 chapters are also the ones which contain most preference eligible exports. The largest share of EU imports take place in HS27 (Mineral Fuels). This is also the HS chapter containing most EU imports eligible for trade preferences, some 25 billion

Euros or close to 20% and the one in which most preferential imports occur. However, the preference utilisation rate is low, just under 40%, which is most likely due to low MFN tariffs and thus low preferential margins for products included in this chapter.

EU imports of HS61 (Knitted apparel), 62 (non-knitted apparel), 84 (Machinery) and 85 (Electronics) are of similar magnitude in terms of how much is eligible of preferences, but the value of EU imports of the two latter categories are several times higher than EU imports of the two former ones. The EU also imports a fair share of HS72 (Iron and Steel), more than of both HS61 and 62. The preference utilisation rates are higher for all these HS2 chapters compared to HS27 (Mineral Fuels). It ranges from 60% in the case of HS85 to 96% for HS72.

Annex Tables 2.4–2.9 show corresponding figures for the other country groups. The pattern for the ACP (excluding South Africa) is similar. HS27 dominate with a share of total exports to the EU of above 60%, about ten times higher than the second most important chapter in terms of export value, HS18 (Cocoa). As far as preference eligible exports are concerned, HS03 (Fish) accounts for 25% of all such exports followed by HS17, 08, 18 and 27 with some 15–20% each. Again, for HS27, the preference utilisation rate is lower compared to the other HS chapters, about 60%, while the preference utilisation rate for the other main preference eligible categories is at 95% and above.

In case of the LDC, HS27 accounts for more than 45% of all exports, while five HS2 chapters account for almost 85% of all preference eligible exports. HS61 dominate with a share of more than 45% of preference eligible exports, followed by HS62 at around 20%, and HS3 and HS76 (Aluminium) at about 10% each. Preferences are used to more than 90% in HS61 and close to 100% for HS03 and HS76. However, the preference utilisation rates remain low for HS62 at about 46%. This is most likely be explained by the origin rule in HS62 which requires so called double transformation, that is, requiring clothing to be made up from yarn.

As for the other country groups, HS27 is the most important HS chapter exported making up for about 50% of all exports from the Mediterranean countries. Five main preference eligible HS2 categories, HS27, 62, 85, 61 and 28 (Inorganic chemicals) together account for more than 80% of the group's preference eligible exports. The use of preferences in HS27 is relatively low at some 45%, but as opposed to some of the other country groups, the use of preferences in HS62 (Non-knitted apparel) is high, 95%. This is likely either due to that yarn used to produce the clothing is imported from the EU and therefore qualifies as originating; alternatively, some of the Mediterranean countries may be large enough to support an efficient domestic textiles industry supplying the yarn. Use of preferences in the other main HS chapters is also high at 90% or more.

Chile's exports to the EU are dominated by HS74 (Copper) which accounts for 45% of the country's total exports to the EU. In terms of preference eligible exports, the top-five HS2 chapters make up 90% of Chile's preference eligible exports to the EU. Close to 40% of Chile's preference eligible exports take place in HS08, 17% falls in HS22 (Beverages), while about 10% are allocated to each HS03 and HS72

(Iron and steel). Except for HS08, for which the preference utilisation rate is 70%, the preference utilisation rate is often 95% and higher.

For Mexico, the most important exported products are found within HS27, which account for about 25% of the country's exports to the EU, followed by HS87 at about 20%. The latter is also by far the most important in terms of preference eligible exports, making up circa 60% of all preference eligible exports. HS87 together with HS85 and HS84 make up for about 85% of the country's preference eligible exports. However, while the preference utilisation rate is 95% in case of HS87, it reaches no more than 15% in HS85 and just above 50% in HS84. The most important products exported in HS85 are Boards, panels etc for electric control or the distribution of electricity (HS85371099) for which the MFN tariff is 2.1%. In combination with the fact that up to 70% domestic value added is required to give the product originating status; this may explain the low use of preferences for this product.

In the case of South Africa, exports of HS71 and 27 make up more than 40% of the country's exports to the EU, while HS84 and HS72 dominate preference eligible exports with share of about 35 and 30%, respectively. HS08 and HS87 follow with about 15% each. Together, the five main HS2 chapters containing preference eligible imports account for more than 95% of all preference eligible exports from the country. The preference utilisation rate varies between 80 and 95%. For HS22 (Beverages), it is however low at some 50%.

2.4.1 Small Trade Flows and Preference Utilization

Nilsson (2009) found that a significant number of preference eligible goods are imported into the EU from developing countries at relatively low values and that while the overall use of EU trade preferences is high, preference utilisation rates of these imports are markedly lower. For example, he found that 90% of the count of preferential import flows (defined as the number of EU imports by country and product disaggregated at 8 digit level) accounted for only 5% of the total value of EU preferential imports in 2008. Restricting the value of preferential import flows to 1 million Euros cut the preference utilisation rate in half compared to the full sample. Products imported to 10,000 Euros or less hardly used preferences at all.

The analysis was carried out at the Tarif Douanier Commun (TDC) section level of the HS. The result held for all country groups examined and for most of the TDC Sections.[19] Most affected by low preference utilisation rates in case of small trade

[19]The study covers the following country groups: ACP-LDC, ACP non-LDC (excluding South Africa), ASEAN (excluding Singapore, Myanmar, Lao, and Cambodia), Commonwealth of Independent States (CIS), excluding Belarus, developing country FTA (Mexico and South Africa), GCC, GSP Other (developing countries not classified under any other grouping), Latin America (excluding Chile and Mexico), LDC non-ACP (excluding Myanmar) and the Mediterranean countries (excluding Israel and Turkey).

Table 2.3 Preference utilization rates of top-5 preference eligible Harmonized System Chapters by preferential import value thresholds, Generalized System of Preferences beneficiaries, 2008 (%)

HS Chapter	Preferential import value threshold (Euros)			
	<10,000	<100,000	<1,000,000	All
27	19.4	33.8	49.0	38.9
61	39.0	49.7	58.5	85.8
62	37.9	48.3	54.8	70.8
84	15.3	24.4	36.0	69.2
85	13.4	24.4	36.4	60.6
Total	22.5	33.4	44.7	58.3

Source: Comext and own calculations

flows were TDC XVI (Machinery), that is HS84 and HS85. The effects were somewhat less pronounced in TDC I (Live Animals), TDC II (Vegetable Products) and TDC IV (Prepared Foodstuffs). The outcome did not seem to be explained by neither the preferential margin nor by rules of origin.

In order to analyse whether these results hold also at a lower level of aggregation, the TDC sections are broken down to HS2 chapter level. The preference utilisation rate of small flows for the five main preference eligible HS2 chapters (27, 61, 62, 84 and 85) of the GSP group of countries display a similar picture as for the TDC sections (see Table 2.3). As we impose a preferential import value threshold, the rate of preference utilisation generally decreases. It holds for all the five HS chapters examined and is particularly strong in HS84 and HS85 (which is in line with the result of Nilsson (2009)), while still present but less strong in HS61 and HS62. Note also that for HS27, restricting the preferential import value threshold to 1 million Euros *increases* the preference utilisation; still the preference utilisation rates drops again under the other thresholds and becomes lower compared to the full sample.

The pattern is similar for the most important preference eligible HS2 Chapters for the other country groupings, see Annex Tables 2.10–2.14.[20] For the ACP, it is much less pronounced however. Except for HS27, the preference utilisation rate does not drop further than to 60–70% even for lowest preferential import value threshold, down from close to full utilisation in the full sample.

What differ the LDC from the other groups here is that the use of preference in HS62 actually increases as the preferential import value threshold is lowered. Again, the use of preferences is fairly well held up as it does not drop lower than roughly 40–60%.

For the Mediterranean countries, the same story can be told. What is noteworthy here is that the preference utilisation rate for HS28 (Inorganic chemicals) does not continue to fall after the first drop from 97% in the full sample to less than 40% when the preferential import threshold is set at 1,000,000 Euros.

[20]The underlying data does not include Chile in the analysis on the grounds that it is not a beneficiary of the EU GSP. As far as the aspect of preference utilization and small trade flows is concerned, Chile is therefore excluded also from this analysis.

As far as Mexico is concerned, this is also true for the preference utilisation rate of HS84 which drops to some 20–25% from the full sample use of (only) 50%. For HS90 (Optical, photo etc) the preference utilisation rate increases from a meagre 7% in the full sample to some 25–30% in the restricted samples. The main reason for the low rate of preference utilization is likely to be that the MFN tariff of the most important product HS90328900 (regulating or controlling instruments) in the full sample of 2.8% is suspended making preferences for this product superfluous. For most of the HS90 products exported in the restricted sample, the MFN tariff of 2.8% still applies, which may explain that the utilisation rate, though still low, is higher than in the full sample.

Finally, in the case of South Africa, one may note that for HS08 and for HS87, preference utilisation rates drop from the full sample to half or less than half when the value of the import value thresholds is lowered. However, the preference utilisation rate hardly changes in HS22 (Beverages) with a lower threshold and in HS72 it drops to zero for preferential import values of 100,000 Euros and 10,000 Euros. The MFN rate for the main product concerned under the 10,000 Euros threshold is HS72012000 (Non-alloy pig iron) is 2.2% but the South African exporter shipping less than 5,000 Euros of the products does not make use of the preferences.

These results are slightly less clear-cut compared to the picture presented by Nilsson (2009), who found a clear and unambiguous decrease in preference utilisation rates as the preferential import value thresholds were lowered. However, that analysis was carried out at the more aggregated TDC section level which makes the results not strictly comparable. Nilsson (2009) argued that explanations to this phenomenon were to be found on the side of the exporting countries.

It could be that exporters (or importers) are simply not aware of the preferences offered.

Other possible explanations could be found by looking at the time dimension of products exported at low values. Could it be that these exports do not survive; that they are exported one year from one country but not the next? Do business associations in the exporting countries sufficiently inform about and promote the use of preferences? Some qualitative research on institutional/administrative matters at beneficiary country level could potentially be a way forward to solve this riddle. Agostino et al. (2010) (see Chapter 10), follow a similar line of reasoning and argue in their conclusions that the EU should reinforce initiatives to enhance human and institutional capacity to utilise the preferences.

2.5 Summary and Conclusions

EU trade preferences for developing countries have evolved significantly since the first GSP scheme was introduced in the early 1970s. Today, the GSP covers three separate schemes: the standard scheme, special incentive arrangements for sustainable development and good governance providing additional preferences compared to the standard scheme and a scheme for the LDC offering duty- and quota free access for all products but arms.

Similarly, the unilateral preferences for the ACP countries dating back to the first Lomé Convention in the mid-1970s and their successor the Cotonou Agreement are gradually being transformed into reciprocal free trade agreements – EPA – which go beyond conventional free-trade agreements, focusing on ACP development, taking account of their socio-economic circumstances and including co-operation and assistance to help them implement the agreements.

EU trade relations with developing countries are in general moving towards reciprocal relationships. This can e.g., be seen in the on-going FTA negotiations with India and some ASEAN countries and in the recently concluded negotiations with six Central American countries and with Colombia and Peru.

EU imports are to a large extent non-dutiable, that is, they are duty free on an MFN basis. More than half of EU imports from the GSP beneficiaries take place in non-dutiable goods. Remaining imports have seen tariff levels in the EU coming down through several rounds of multilateral trade liberalization and bilateral or regional free trade agreements. Preferential margins are thus shrinking. Nonetheless, while EU trade preferences are well used overall, there is some evidence that products imported in relatively low values make lesser use of preferences.

We have learned a great deal about the impact of EU trade preferences over the years. The gravity model, which is the work horse model used for analyzing the impact of trade preferences and of trade arrangements in general, has seen its theoretical underpinnings be strengthened over the past decades. The way the model is applied empirically has also developed over time. Its importance for trade policy evaluation can hardly be overestimated and it remains vital tool for many in this area of research.

With a changing international environment there are a number of questions relating to the impact of EU trade preferences on which some further light ought to be shed. For example, does the generally positive impact of EU trade preferences on imports from developing countries still hold in light of decreased preferential margins, be it through trade negotiations and, in the case of agriculture also through internal EU reform of the common agricultural policy? Against the fact that LDC have enjoyed far-reaching preferences on the EU market since the early 1990s, what has been the impact of the full liberalization introduced under the EBA initiative?

EU tariffs (available at 10-digit level) are updated daily, while EU import flows (publicly available at 8 digit level) are published monthly. While this primarily holds for a limited number of agricultural products it points to a potential problem of correctly defining preference margins and highlights the need to assess the impact of EU preferences (at least for some products) using more frequent trade data than annual flows. Furthermore, the estimation of the preferential margin can be difficult for some agricultural and fisheries products, especially for processed agricultural products and fresh fruit, not only because duties may vary depending on the date of entry of the product into the EU, but also because some duties are related to the ingredients of the good, such as the flower content. This remains a key matter.

Parts of the literature argue that a preferential margin of some 4% or more is needed for countries to make use of their trade preferences (see e.g., Carrère and de Melo 2007). Still, the most common tariff preference under the standard GSP scheme is a 3.5% point reduction of the MFN tariff and these preferences are generally well used. Hence, there appears to be scope for additional research, in particular as far as the use of "true" preferential margins are concerned, that is preferential margins also taking into account trade preferences offered to competitor countries.

Appendix

Table 2.4 European Union imports from the African Carribean and Pacific countries by main Harmonized System Chapter, tariff regime (billion Euros) and preference utilization rate, 2008 (%)

HS Chapter	Imports (billion Euros)					
	Total	MFN-0	Dutiable	Pref. eligible	Pref.	Pref. util. rate
Total	51.9	42.1	9.7	9.7	9.0	92.4
27	31.7	31.1	0.6	0.6	0.4	63.8
18	3.0	2.3	0.7	0.7	0.7	99.0
71	1.4	1.4	0.0	0.0	0.0	77.3
26	1.3	1.3	0.0	MFN-0	MFN-0	MFN-0
44	1.2	0.9	0.3	0.3	0.3	97.1
89	1.1	1.1	0.0	0.0	0.0	22.4
03	1.0	0.0	1.0	1.0	1.0	97.8
09	1.0	1.0	0.0	0.0	0.0	95.1
08	0.9	0.2	0.7	0.7	0.7	96.5
17	0.8	0.0	0.8	0.8	0.7	95.5

Source: Comext and own calculations

Table 2.5 European Union imports from the Least Developed Countries by main Harmonized System Chapter, tariff regime (billion Euros) and preference utilization rate, 2008 (%)

HS Chapter	Imports (billion Euros)					
	Total	MFN-0	Dutiable	Pref. eligible	Pref.	Pref. util. rate
Total	24.2	15.4	8.8	8.7	7.3	83.6
27	11.5	11.3	0.2	0.2	0.1	49.5
61	3.8	0.0	3.8	3.8	3.6	93.2
62	1.8	0.0	1.8	1.7	0.8	46.0
26	1.0	1.0	0.0	MFN-0	MFN-0	MFN-0
03	0.8	0.0	0.8	0.8	0.8	98.3
71	0.7	0.7	0.0	0.0	0.0	59.7
76	0.6	0.0	0.6	0.6	0.6	99.9
09	0.6	0.6	0.0	0.0	0.0	96.1
74	0.3	0.3	0.0	0.0	0.0	44.3
63	0.2	0.0	0.2	0.2	0.2	95.1

Source: Comext and own calculations

Table 2.6 European Union imports from the Mediterranean countries by main Harmonized System Chapter, tariff regime (billion Euros) and preference utilization rate, 2008 (%)

HS Chapter	Imports (billion Euros)					
	Total	MFN-0	Dutiable	Pref. eligible	Pref.	Pref. util. rate
Total	59.3	33.9	25.3	25.2	21.3	84.6
27	29.4	25.0	4.4	4.4	2.0	46.2
85	4.2	1.3	3.0	3.0	2.7	92.4
62	3.5	0.0	3.5	3.5	3.3	95.0
71	1.7	1.6	0.1	0.1	0.1	87.0
61	1.7	0.0	1.7	1.7	1.5	89.8
84	1.4	0.5	0.9	0.9	0.7	79.0
28	1.3	0.1	1.2	1.2	1.2	97.7

Source: Comext and own calculations

Table 2.7 European Union imports from Chile by main Harmonized System Chapter, tariff regime (billion Euros) and preference utilization rate, 2008 (%)

HS Chapter	Imports (billion Euros)					
	Total	MFN-0	Dutiable	Pref. eligible	Pref.	Pref. util. rate
Total	10.2	7.3	2.9	2.9	2.5	85.4
74	4.6	4.6	0.0	0.0	0.0	95.4
26	1.7	1.7	0.0	MFN-0	MFN-0	MFN-0
08	1.0	0.0	1.0	1.0	0.7	70.5
47	0.5	0.5	0.0	MFN-0	MFN-0	MFN-0
22	0.5	0.0	0.5	0.5	0.5	98.0
03	0.4	0.0	0.4	0.4	0.3	95.8
28	0.3	0.1	0.2	0.2	0.2	99.8
72	0.3	0.0	0.3	0.3	0.2	91.3

Source: Comext and own calculations

Table 2.8 European Union imports from Mexico by main Harmonized System Chapter, tariff regime (billion Euros) and preference utilization rate, 2008 (%)

HS Chapter	Imports (billion Euros)					
	Total	MFN-0	Dutiable	Pref. eligible	Pref.	Pref. util. rate
Total	13.0	7.9	5.2	5.2	3.8	73.9
27	3.2	3.1	0.1	0.1	0.1	100.0
87	2.5	0.0	2.5	2.5	2.4	94.9
85	2.0	1.4	0.6	0.6	0.1	15.7
90	1.2	1.1	0.1	0.1	0.0	7.6
84	1.1	0.6	0.5	0.5	0.3	53.4
72	0.5	0.5	0.0	0.0	0.0	81.4
29	0.2	0.1	0.1	0.1	0.1	94.2
22	0.2	0.2	0.0	0.0	0.0	65.0
39	0.2	0.0	0.2	0.2	0.1	78.2

Source: Comext and own calculations

Table 2.9 European Union imports from South Africa by main Harmonized System Chapter, tariff regime (billion Euros) and preference utilization rate, 2008 (%)

HS Chapter	Imports (billion Euros)					
	Total	MFN-0	Dutiable	Pref. eligible	Pref.	Pref. util. rate
Total	20.5	12.6	7.9	7.5	6.6	87.6
71	5.7	5.7	0.0	0.0	0.0	74.4
27	3.2	3.2	0.0	0.0	0.0	92.6
72	2.3	0.7	1.6	1.6	1.6	98.0
84	2.2	0.1	2.1	2.1	2.0	94.0
26	1.5	1.5	0.0	MFN-0	MFN-0	MFN-0
08	1.1	0.0	1.1	0.9	0.7	81.2
87	0.9	0.0	0.8	0.8	0.7	81.0
22	0.4	0.0	0.4	0.3	0.2	51.3

Source: Comext and own calculations

Table 2.10 Preference utilization rates by main preference eligible Harmonized System Chapters, African, Caribbean and Pacific countries, 2008 (%)

HS Chapter	Preferential import value threshold (Euros)			
	<10,000	<100,000	<1,000,000	All
03	72.4	80.5	85.4	98.1
08	60.5	70.3	73.6	96.5
17	64.0	64.8	45.3	98.0
18	60.1	64.9	56.9	99.0
27	0.2	29.2	62.1	61.0
Total	65.4	76.2	79.7	92.3

Source: Comext and own calculations

Table 2.11 Preference utilization rates by main preference eligible Harmonized System Chapters, Least Developed Countries, 2008 (%)

HS Chapter	Preferential import value threshold (Euros)			
	<10,000	<100,000	<1,000,000	All
03	62.6	75.9	83.0	98.3
61	52.4	54.1	58.7	93.5
62	48.5	61.5	62.4	44.8
63	56.2	68.2	66.0	95.1
76	35.2	45.2	15.1	99.9
Total	52.3	62.8	65.3	83.5

Source: Comext and own calculations

Table 2.12 Preference utilization rates by main preference eligible Harmonized System Chapters, Mediterranean countries, 2008 (%)

HS Chapter	Preferential import value threshold (Euros)			
	<10,000	<100,000	<1,000,000	All
28	40.9	36.5	37.5	97.8
39	42.1	66.3	65.3	95.0
61	43.8	62.1	75.2	91.3
62	40.7	57.5	69.1	95.1
85	17.8	33.3	50.6	92.7
Total	30.9	50.4	66.2	94.0

Source: Comext and own calculations

Table 2.13 Preference utilization rates by main preference eligible Harmonized System Chapters, Mexico, 2008 (%)

HS Chapter	Preferential import value threshold (Euros)			
	<10,000	<100,000	<1,000,000	All
39	21.2	35.1	47.1	78.2
84	22.1	24.2	20.0	53.4
85	15.7	29.8	24.6	15.7
87	17.2	20.4	42.1	94.9
90	29.8	29.4	25.3	7.6
Total	20.9	27.6	27.6	74.0

Source: Comext and own calculations

Table 2.14 Preference utilization rates by main preference eligible Harmonized System Chapters, South Africa, 2008 (%)

HS Chapter	Preferential import value threshold (Euros)			
	<10,000	<100,000	<1,000,000	All
8	48.8	42.0	58.0	81.2
22	55.7	52.0	44.1	51.3
72	0.0	0.0	5.5	98.0
84	18.1	19.9	37.9	94.0
87	46.8	32.9	35.4	81.0
Total	25.3	23.9	39.5	89.1

Source: Comext and own calculations

Chapter 3
European Union Preferential Margins: Measurement and Aggregation Issues

Maria Cipollina and Luca Salvatici

Abstract The main goal of this chapter is to define and measure the intensity of tariff preferences. Several definitions are feasible and have been used in the literature. Once the tariff margin is defined, it can be expressed in absolute or relative terms. These are not alternatives because they provide different information about trade policy. Nevertheless, however the tariff margin is defined and expressed, in the context of trade policy there are problems related to aggregation. Building on Anderson and Neary's (*Measuring the restrictiveness of international trade policy*, MIT Press, Cambridge, MA, 2005) work on theoretically grounded trade policy indexes, we define an aggregate measure (Mercantilistic Trade Preference Index – MTPI) of trade preferential margins. Because it focuses on export volumes, the MTPI enables a method of aggregation that is consistent with the main objective of preferential policies. We compute sectoral MTPI for European Union (EU) preferences granted to 167 exporters, to assess how preferential market access differs across sectors.

3.1 Introduction

There is no clear and unequivocal definition of a preferential tariff margin in the literature. This chapter summarizes and analyzes various definitions and attempts to provide a quantitative measure of the intensity of tariff preferences. Preferential tariffs include reduction or elimination of tariff barriers to imports from particular countries or regional groupings. Ostensibly, a country that enjoys trade preferences is at a competitive advantage relative to other exporters that are faced with higher duties.

M. Cipollina
Department of Economics, Management and Social Sciences, University of Molise, Via Francesco de Sanctis, 86100 Campobasso, Italy
e-mail: cipollina@unimol.it

L. Salvatici
Department of Economics, University Roma Tre, Via Silvio D'Amico, 77-00145 Roma, Italy
e-mail: lsalvatici@uniroma3.it

L. De Benedictis and L. Salvatici (eds.), *The Trade Impact of European Union Preferential Policies*, DOI 10.1007/978-3-642-16564-1_3,

How should the extent of a preference margin be computed? And, having reached different figures for bilateral margins for different countries, how should they be aggregated to provide an overall quantitative assessment of preferential policies?

First, we need a clear definition of "tariff margin": several definitions have been proposed in the literature. Tariff margins can be expressed in absolute or relative terms; both provide different information about trade policy. However, regardless of the definition used and the way that it is expressed, in the context of trade policy, there remains the problem of how tariff margins should be aggregated. National tariff schedules often have thousands of tariff lines, characterized by wide variations in tariff rates, with the added complexity that preferential trade policies vary across products and exporters. Thus, analyses of tariff margins need to be based on the most disaggregated data available. However, if the objective is to make comparisons across products, countries and over time, this requires measures that summarize the levels of the trade preferences implied by the various schemes applicable to different commodities and/or countries. Preferential schemes are defined at a very detailed level, which means that in order to compare across sectors and/or countries and over time data need to be aggregated, an exercise that in the context of trade policy is very challenging (Cipollina and Salvatici 2008).

In this chapter, we review some of the available absolute and relative tariff margin definitions and compute them in the case of the European Union (EU) policies. We continue by focusing on the aggregation problem and define an aggregate preference index – Mercantilistic Trade Preference Index (MTPI) – in the spirit of Anderson and Neary (2003). We compute MTPI for the preferences granted by the EU to various sectors using a partial equilibrium model based on Bureau and Salvatici (2004, 2005).

The chapter is structured as follows. Sections 3.2 and 3.3, respectively outline the measurement and aggregation issues. Section 3.4 describes the data, Section 3.5 presents the results and Section 3.6 concludes the chapter.

3.2 Preference Margins: Definition

Margins are calculated based on subtraction where both operands need to be expressed in the same metric, i.e. either *ad valorem* or specific. In the case of complex tariff structures it is necessary to compute some *Ad Valorem* Equivalents (AVE), which introduces several common methodological problems (Cipollina and Salvatici 2008).[1]

Assuming *ad valorem* tariffs and considering K possible goods (denoted by k where $k = 1, 2 \dots . K$), the absolute preferential margin (Pa_{ik}) granted by the EU to the imports of commodity k from country i at any given moment is equal to:

$$Pa_{ik} = \left(Tr_k - Ta_{ik}^v\right) \tag{3.1}$$

[1]This issue is dealt with in Chapter 9.

where Tr_k is the reference tariff applied to product k and Ta_{ik}^{v} is the preferential duty applied to imports of k from i. The superscript v refers to one of the preferential schemes available to the ith exporter, since overlapping preferences meaning, tariff lines may be eligible for several different treatments, are not uncommon.

Chapter 2 describes the evolution of EU trade policies. Fig. 3.1 in this chapter provides an overview of the EU's preferential agreements in 2004 and, although not exhaustive, and not illustrative of the variation across countries in of the product coverage of each agreement, it gives an idea of the complexity of these policies (Pishbahar and Huchet-Bourdon 2008). Discriminatory trade agreements are applied at product level; Fig. 3.2 shows that applying the lowest rate may lead to an overestimation of the preferential margins. For instance, Bureau et al. (2007) show that some schemes are systematically preferred over others due to compliance costs, which include non-price variables, such as the rules of origin attached to each agreement.

Problems related to the individuation of preferential margins are made more complex in the presence of Tariff Rate Quotas (TRQ). In Chapter 9 authors point out that when there are economies of scale, it is no longer the case that tariff rate equivalents vary according to which of the three elements of a TRQ regime (in-quota tariff, out-of-quota tariff, quota level) is binding. Due to the presence of fixed costs, if imports do not exceed quota, the tariff equivalent will be the in-quota tariff; alternatively, if imports exceed quota, then the tariff equivalent will be the weighted average of the two tariffs. Thus, preference margin computed on the basis of an

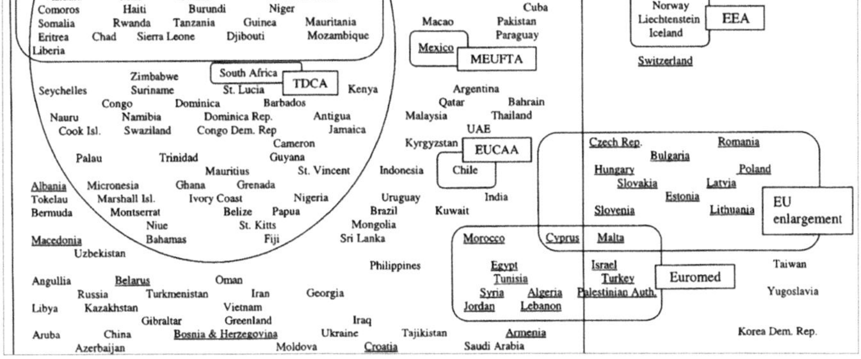

Fig. 3.1 European Union's trade agreements in 2004
Source: Pishbahar and Huchet-Bourdon (2008)

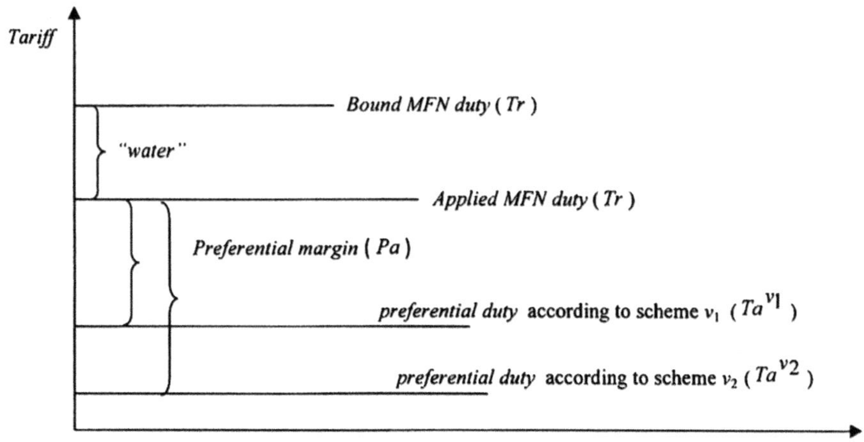

Fig. 3.2 Tariff structure
Source: Authors' elaborations

economies of scale-monopolistic competition framework will always be higher than the margin that is consistent with a perfect competition model.

In the case of a World Trade Organization (WTO) member country, the reference level or benchmark against which the preference is measured should be the bound Most Favored Nation (MFN) duty. However, there are two reasons why there may be a difference between bound and applied tariffs. One is the binding overhang, which describes the difference between bound and MFN applied tariffs (the so-called "water in the tariffs"), the other is based on the difference between the MFN and preferential tariffs. Since only the latter is relevant when computing the tariff margin, if the applied MFN tariff is lower than the bound, defining the preference margin based on the bound MFN duty leads to an obvious overestimation of the competitive advantages enjoyed by exporting countries. Even considering the applied MFN rather than the bound rates may lead to prohibitive duties, which in turn may lead to overestimate the margin (Fig. 3.2).

To emphasize the competitive advantage with respect to other exporters, and in order to avoid an overestimation, it is necessary to consider actual rather than potential exporters/competitors. A definition that focuses on actual preferences should use as the benchmark the duties imposed on actual exporters. However, since not all exporters have the same weight in terms of competitiveness, it may be preferable to use the (average) duties imposed on specific countries as the reference: e.g. the largest exporter(s) in the preference-granting market or worldwide. On the other hand, the impact of prohibitive tariffs may be underestimated if we consider actual rather than potential exporters.

More generally, the intensity of the preferential treatment depends both on the highest paid rate and on the share of exporters paying that rate. The basic intuition underlying "multilateral trade resistance" in gravity models (see Chap. 4) suggests that trade is influenced by the trade policies towards all the partners. In the current context, this means that bilateral trade depends on the whole structure of applied tariffs preferences as well as the country-pair specific margins. Accordingly, the reference tariff used to compute the margin enjoyed by exporter i on product k should be exporter-specific (Tr_{ik}) and computed as a (weighted) average of the duties paid for the given product by each exporter:[2]

$$Pa^1_{zk} = \left(\sum_{z \neq i} w_{ik} Ta_{zk} - Ta^v_{ik} \right) \tag{3.2}$$

where w_{ik} are the weights related to applied bilateral tariffs. The most commonly used weights are bilateral export flows, but, in the case of tariffs, trade-weighted averages create the well-known endogeneity bias: weighting by imports leads to underestimation of a country's protection level (Cipollina and Salvatici 2008). The negative correlation between tariff levels and import levels implies that a high (low) tariff generates limited (large) imports, reducing (increasing) its contribution to overall protection.

Returning to the simplest definition, the result of the subtraction in (3.1) means that the same absolute number can have very different implications according to the level of the reference duty. Taking the ratio between the absolute margin and the reference tariff gives the relative preference margin (Pr_{ik}):

$$Pr_{ik} = \frac{Tr_{ik} - Ta^v_{ik}}{Tr_{ik}} \tag{3.3}$$

This gives additional information about the intensity of the preferential policy, since it is straightforward to provide examples of cases where the same absolute margin implies very different relative margins, and *vice versa*.

Another relative measure is the preferential discount rate (Pdr_{ik}) defined as the absolute value divided by unity plus the applied duty (i.e. the tariff factor):

$$Pdr_{ik} = \frac{Tr_{ik} - Ta^v_{ik}}{1 + Ta^v_{ik}} \tag{3.4}$$

For many purposes, this second relative measure is a more economically meaningful measure of the intensity of the preferential policy. For a small country whose imports do not affect world prices, Pdr_{ik} measures the price reduction or the rent generated by the preference as a percentage of the imported product's domestic price. If the focus is on market access, it is not appropriate, for example, to treat half of a 2% tariff as equivalent to half of a 50% tariff. The latter would allow a 20% improvement in the (after tariff) price received by the importer, while the former would provide an improvement of less than 1%.

[2]This is in the spirit of the *adjusted preferential access measure* suggested by Carrère et al. (2008).

The Pdr_{ik} is embedded in the preferential factor defined as:

$$pref_{ijk} = 1 + Pdr_{ik} = \frac{1 + Tr_{ik}}{1 + Ta^{v}_{ik}} \tag{3.5}$$

This is the preference margin definition that is going to be used in Chap. 6.

3.3 Preferential Margins: Aggregation

National tariff schedules can have thousands of tariff lines, and wide variations in tariff rates. Preferential trade policy agreements also vary widely across products and exporters. Therefore, analyses of preferential tariff margins should use the most disaggregated data available. However, for comparisons across products, countries and over time it is necessary to construct measures that summarize the levels of trade preferences implied by the various schemes, for different commodities and/or countries. Because of the wide variation in preferential margins across products and countries, margins need to be aggregated in order to provide an overall measure, and for trade policy analysis it is important to use the correct aggregation method.

Several forms of aggregation are used in the literature, but few are theoretically based, and often lead to biased results (Cipollina and Salvatici 2008). *Ad hoc* or purely statistical measures can be used to resolve the aggregation problem, but they do not provide any clarity about what is being measured. We need a conceptual framework that takes account of the *level* and the *effects* of preferential policy combined; this is provided by new approaches to the problem of aggregation, which are based on rigorous theoretical foundations.

A *simple average* of the preferential margins implies the same weight for each tariff line regardless of the importance of the product for which preference is granted. Clearly, this approach makes poor use of information. Some products have a larger trade share than others. Also, this approach is potentially subject to manipulation. For example, in an extreme case it would be possible to have zero preferences for a relatively small number of tariff lines covering the most "sensitive" products, and hundreds of tariff lines with large preferential margins. The simple average would be quite high, which would grossly overestimating the real degree of preference being granted.

Thus, trade policies should be weighted according to their impact. The simplest and most frequently-used method is to use trade volumes as weights. However, as mentioned earlier, in the context of tariffs *trade-weighted averages* have some major deficiencies due to the endogeneity bias. As the tariff on a good increases, the level of its imports falls, so the highest tariffs are weighted lowest. For high tariffs, the reduction in weight may be so large that the index is decreasing in the tariff rate. This does not apply to preferential margins, since higher margins typically are associated with higher trade values.

Trade-weighted preferential margins avoid the most obvious shortcoming associated with the use of trade weights: weights are not biased downwards by preferences, and the index is always increasing in each individual preferential margin. However, the case for using it is not compelling, given the lack of an explicit theoretical basis. For instance, import volumes might be much larger than under an MFN regime because preferences are high, or they are imposed on highly elastic goods. A central theme of the economic approach to index numbers is that the choice between alternative index-number formulas should be based primarily not on informal issues of plausibility, but on the extent to which they approximate some "true" or benchmark index, which responds to some well-defined economic question (Diewert 1976). According to Anderson and Neary (1996), a general definition of a policy index is as follows: depending on a pre-determined reference concept, any aggregate measure is a function mapping from a vector of independent variables – defined according to the policy coverage – to a scalar aggregate. The reference concept allows computation of an index of restrictiveness which is "equivalent" to the actual policy in terms of the chosen impact and drives the computation of the weights used in the aggregation process.

These types of indexes are equivalence measures since they provide results that are equivalent to the original data in terms of the information we are interested in; several possible reference concepts – such as welfare, income, output – have been proposed in the literature (Cipollina and Salvatici 2008). Since foreign exporters are concerned with domestic market access, it makes sense to aggregate preferences in such a way that volume of imports holds as the reference standard.

3.3.1 The Mercantilistic Trade Preference Index

Our policy index is based on the mercantilistic trade restrictiveness index introduced by Anderson and Neary (2003). Taking import flows as the start point, the question: "How does one measure trade preferences?" can be answered by computing the uniform preferential margin, which, if applied to all goods and/or partners, would be equivalent to the actual preferential policies, in the sense of yielding the same volume of imports. Based on the notations in the previous section we can define the reference tariff as the maximum applied rate (τ^{max}) and the bilateral applied duties (t) as the lowest available for each product:

$$\mathrm{Pr}_{ik} = \frac{Tr_{ik} - Ta_{ik}}{Tr_{ik}} = 1 - \frac{Ta_{ik}}{Tr_{ik}} = 1 - \frac{t_{ik}}{\tau_{ik}^{\max}} = 1 - \alpha_{ik}^{i} \tag{3.6}$$

The MTPI is defined as the uniform relative margin $(1 - \alpha)$, which yields the same volume (at world prices) of tariff-restricted imports as the initial vector of (non-uniform) relative preferential margins. In other words, the uniform reduction percentage (α) generates a counterfactual preferential tariff vector ($\tau = \alpha\tau^{max}$) that yields the same volume of imports as generated by the initial tariff vector. This can be expressed formally using the import demand functions M, while holding the balance of trade function constant at level B^0:

$$\alpha : M\left[(1 + \alpha\tau^{\max})p^*, B^0\right] = M^0 \tag{3.7}$$

where p^* denotes the international prices vector of the K goods $k = (1, \ldots, K)$ and M^0 is the value of imports (at world prices) in the reference period.

Define the scalar import demand summing over the i exporters:

$$M(p, p^*, B^0) \equiv \sum_i \sum_k p_{ik} I_{ik}^m \tag{3.8}$$

where I^m denotes the uncompensated (Marshallian) import demand function and p is the domestic price vector. Thus, the MTPI can be computed by solving the following equation for α:

$$\sum\nolimits_i \sum\nolimits_k p_{ik}^* I_{ik}^m \left[p_{ik}^*(1 + \alpha\tau_k^{\max}), B^0\right] = \sum\nolimits_i \sum\nolimits_k p_{ik}^* I_{ik}^m \left[p_{ik}^*(1 + \alpha_k\tau_k^{\max}), B^0\right] \tag{3.9}$$

Indexes such as the MTPI have a solid theoretical foundation, although their definition relies on several restrictive assumptions, including the existence of a competitive equilibrium, a single representative consumer, and fixed world prices (i.e. the small country assumption). The assumption of fixed world prices is particularly questionable, since our empirical analysis deals with the EU, which is a large trader. However, assuming a small country helps to guarantee the existence and uniqueness of the indexes, and rules out counterintuitive "second best" results. It is consistent, therefore, with a *ceteris paribus* approach (Bureau and Salvatici 2004).[3]

After defining the MTPI, for the empirical implementation we follow Bureau and Salvatici (2005) and model demand assuming a Constant Elasticity of Substitution (CES) functional form. This function imposes well-known restrictive assumptions about separability and, since if there is either no or little trade in the base period there will be no or little trade impact of reducing tariffs, it does not properly account for the presence of prohibitive tariffs. In our case, this may lead to an underestimation of the counterfactual uniform percentage reduction, which will lead to an overestimation of the preferential indexes. In any case, it should be noted that such underestimation is a consequence of the functional form actually used, rather than being a limitation of the index. Notwithstanding these shortcomings, the CES functional form has several empirical advantages that explain its application for in modelling import demand (Winters 1984).

[3]Anderson and Neary (2003) argue that there is a rationale for a ceteris paribus trade restrictiveness index that fixes world prices even when these prices are in fact endogenous. This rationale may be that by keeping world prices constant, we focus on the component of protection explained by national policies, not by the national degree of market power.

The MTPI (1 – α_j) for each sector j is found by setting the value of the import volume function with the uniform preferential margin equal to the initial value of imports (evaluated at world prices, p_{kj}^*):

$$\sum\nolimits_k p_{kj}^* \beta_{kj} \left(\frac{P_j^\tau}{p_{kj}^*(1 + \alpha_j \tau_j^{\max})} \right)^{\sigma_j} e_j^0 = \sum\nolimits_k p_{kj}^* I_{kj}^0 \tag{3.10}$$

where the parameters β_{kj} are calibrated to the initial values of the expenditure shares in the base data when all domestic prices are set to 1; $\sigma_j = 1/(1 - \rho_j)$ denotes the elasticity of substitution within the j group; e_j^0 is the initial total expenditure (expenditure on both domestic production and imports in j); I_{kj}^0 is the volume of imports in the initial period (i.e. 2004 in our application), and P_j^τ is the price index:

$$P_j^\tau = \left(\beta_{dj}(p_{dj})^{1-\sigma_j} + \sum\nolimits_k \beta_{kj}(p_{kj}^*(1 + \alpha_j \tau_j^{\max}))^{1-\sigma_j} \right)^{-\sigma_j} \tag{3.11}$$

The uniform preferential margins for each aggregate commodity j are computed using the GAMS package (Brooke et al. 1998), solving for α_j in (3.10) and (3.11). The overall MTPI can be obtained by summing all J sectors. The MTPI indexes on their own are relevant to the analysis of trade policy. In addition, they can be used as inputs to analyses using a commodity aggregation and import demand structure that are consistent with our assumptions. However, it must be remembered that they are approximations only of the "true" (i.e. general equilibrium) MTPI indexes.

3.3.2 *Potential Mercantilistic Trade Preference Index*

In the policy literature dealing with preferential policies, four issues stand out (Hoekman and Ozden 2005):

- Preferential margins: the difference between the MFN and preferential tariffs applied to each product;
- Potential coverage: the ratio between the value of products covered by a preferential scheme and the value of dutiable imports originating in beneficiary countries;
- Utilization: the ratio between the value of imports receiving preferential treatment, and eligible imports covered in principle;
- Utility: the ratio of the value of imports that receive preferences and all dutiable imports from the same exporter.

In terms of the *preferential margin*, we compute the margin for each product on a bilateral basis as the difference between the maximum duty applied by the EU across all exporters, and the actual duty imposed on each exporter. We are not concerned with the difference between multilateral bound tariffs and bilateral applied duties; rather our focus is on actual preferential margins with respect to potential competitors.

We do not deal with the *potential coverage* of each and every preferential scheme, but are able to assess the overall *utility* of EU trade preferences since the MTPI calculation takes into account the volume of trade that actually benefits from the preferences. To shed further light on the relevance of the utilization issue, we compute a *potential-MTPI* which assumes that all imports pay the preferential duty. This represents an (admittedly) rough estimate of the possible value of the granted preferential margins were they to be fully utilized. In fact, preferences often are limited to certain quantities and always have some strings attached in terms of implementations costs, such as rules of origin. By comparing potential and actual MTPI we can assess the extent to which exporters are constrained by non-price factors in exploiting preferences.

3.4 Data

We consider 4,879 products at the 6 digit level Harmonized System (HS) classification level, from 167 exporters to the EU (25 countries). Tariffs are taken from the most recent version of the MAcMap-HS6 database.[4] Trade flows are from the Eurostat Comext database.[5] Information on elasticities of substitution and domestic expenditure is from Version 7 of the Global Trade Analysis Project (GTAP) dataset (Narayanan and Walmsey 2008). All data – i.e. tariffs, trade and domestic expenditure, elasticities – refer to 2004.

We aggregate the 187,544 EU tariff lines associated with positive trade flows up to the 42 commodity sectors included in the GTAP database. Note that the number of tariff lines in each commodity aggregate is very uneven. We cannot justify our reliance on GTAP elasticities, but providing new estimates is beyond the scope of the current study. We did conduct sensitivity tests to examine the effects of different elasticity values on the measurement of the MTPI.

The Eurostat Comext database contains trade data distinguished by tariff regimes, as reported by EU member states. Based on these data, the applied duty (t) used to compute the MTPI is equal to the "MFN (applied) tariff" when imports enter under MFN arrangements, and equal to the "preferential (bilateral) tariff" when imports are registered as preferential flows. Thus, our MTPI calculation takes account of the actual volume of trade that benefits from the preference.

Table 3.1 shows that more than 60% of our tariff lines with positive trade flows enjoy preferential access (mostly duty-free), and around 80% of these are actually used; 18% of tariff lines are MFN-duty free.

---

[4]MAcMap provides a consistent assessment of protection across the world, including AVE rates of applied tariff duties and TRQ at the 6 digit level of the HS (http://www.cepii.fr/).

[5]The Comext database (http://fd.comext.eurostat.cec.eu.int/xtweb/) contains detailed foreign trade data distinguished by tariff regimes as reported by EU member states.

Table 3.1 Share of European Union tariff lines by type of tariff regime (year 2004)

GTAP sector	Obs.	% of MFN duty-free tariff lines	% of MFN duty tariff lines (no preference)	% of Preferential duty-free tariff lines		% of Preferential duty tariff lines	
				Potential	(Used)[a]	Potential	(Used)[a]
All products	187,560	18	14	55	(38)	14	(38)
Agricultural sector							
Animal prod.	753	80	7	9	(35)	4	(19)
Beverages and tobacco prod.	1,431	33	19	26	(36)	22	(33)
Bovine cattle, sheep and goats, horses	35	46	3	29	(70)	23	(25)
Bovine meat prod.	217	9	47	21	(50)	23	(14)
Cereal grains n.e.c.	183	5	35	17	(32)	43	(9)
Crops nec	2,568	30	11	40	(42)	20	(40)
Dairy prod.	284	0	44	11	(40)	46	(20)
Fishing	1,079	15	17	43	(57)	25	(47)
Food prod.	8,612	3	21	33	(54)	42	(46)
Forestry	816	72	3	19	(47)	6	(37)
Meat prod.	379	8	45	21	(24)	26	(16)
Oil seeds	362	100	0	0	(0)	0	(0)
Paddy rice	64	0	86	3	(50)	11	(29)
Plant-based fibers	105	100	0	0	(0)	0	(0)
Processed rice	80	0	94	6	(60)	0	(0)
Raw milk	7	0	43	57	(25)	0	(0)
Sugar	227	0	75	16	(39)	9	(43)
Sugar cane, sugar beet	71	0	55	24	(12)	21	(33)
Vegetable oils and fats	903	17	24	32	(49)	27	(40)
Vegetables, fruit, nuts	3,422	14	14	32	(52)	41	(45)
Wheat	42	0	52	12	(20)	36	(7)
Wool, silk-worm cocoons	67	100	0	0	(0)	0	(0)
Non-agricultural sector							
Chemical, rubber, plastic prod.	24,005	17	15	58	(37)	9	(29)
Coal	110	100	0	0	(0)	0	(0)
Electronic equipment	6,348	53	8	30	(21)	8	(14)
Ferrous metals	4,428	79	3	16	(40)	1	(53)
Gas	20	100	0	0	(0)	0	(0)
Leather prod.	3,607	0	14	70	(45)	15	(36)
Machinery and equipment n.e.c.	41,239	12	13	71	(29)	4	(29)
Manufactures n.e.c.	9,806	22	13	63	(37)	3	(31)
Metal prod.	11,007	8	14	73	(38)	4	(37)
Metals n.e.c	3,822	34	17	33	(46)	16	(39)
Mineral prod.	6,927	9	14	64	(44)	13	(39)
Minerals n.e.c.	1,951	93	2	5	(47)	0	(0)

(*continued*)

Table 3.1 (continued)

GTAP sector	Obs.	% of MFN duty-free tariff lines	% of MFN duty tariff lines (no preference)	% of Preferential duty-free tariff lines		% of Preferential duty tariff lines	
				Potential	(Used)[a]	Potential	(Used)[a]
Motor vehicles and parts	3,120	2	11	77	(33)	10	(23)
Oil	31	100	0	0	(0)	0	(0)
Paper prod., publishing	4,137	97	0	2	(36)	0	(18)
Petroleum, coal prod.	326	40	11	49	(45)	0	(0)
Textiles	20,386	2	17	50	(49)	31	(43)
Transport equipment n.e.c.	2,661	3	16	70	(26)	11	(32)
Wearing apparel	17,486	1	13	59	(47)	27	(38)
Wood prod.	4,420	30	8	56	(39)	6	(37)

[a]The numbers in parenthesis indicate the percentage of preferential tariff lines that enter in EU under a preferential scheme

Note: data refer to tariff lines with positive trade flows

Some GTAP sectors[6] do not include positive duties: since in these sectors all preferential margins are (obviously) equal to zero, they are not reported in the results tables.[7]

Taking into account the duty actually paid (Table 3.2) we can see that in several instances average paid rates are closer to MFN than preferential tariffs. This applies especially to grains, meat, wheat and various non-agricultural products such as chemicals and electronics. This suggests that in these sectors, traders are not taking advantage of the right to sell into the EU market at reduced duty because of restrictions on rules of origin or the high level of the administrative costs involved in securing preferential treatment relative to the cost of paying the MFN tariff. To shed more light on the relevance of utilization, we compare MTPI with *potential-MTPI* computed under the assumption that all eligible imports are subject to the preferential duty.

Table 3.3 presents simple averages of the absolute and relative margins calculated using the benchmark of MFN or the highest applied duty. It emerges clearly that the preference measure is very sensitive to its definition and, obviously, using MFN duty always implies higher margins than those obtained if we consider actual exporters/competitors.

[6]Coal; Gas; Oil; Oil seeds; Plant-based fibers; Wool, silk-worm cocoons.

[7]The results tables do not include sectors with small numbers of products (and therefore observations), or very small trade flows (e.g. bovine meat products; dairy products; processed rice; raw milk; sugar; sugar cane, sugar beet).

Table 3.2 European Union tariff structure (year 2004)

GTAP sector	MFN duty (simple mean, %)	Preferential duty[a] (simple mean, %)	Paid duty[b] (simple mean, %)
All products	5.7	2.3	4.3
Agricultural sector			
Animal products nec	4.0	1.4	3.4
Beverages and tobacco products	17.3	9.1	14.7
Bovine cattle, sheep and goats, horses	24.7	8.8	15.7
Cereal grains nec	35.8	29.8	34.0
Crops nec	4.4	1.3	3.0
Fishing	8.1	2.9	5.1
Food products nec	18.7	10.7	14.5
Forestry	1.0	0.3	0.7
Meat products nec	22.1	16.8	20.9
Paddy rice	78.7	75.9	77.4
Vegetable oils and fats	13.4	8.9	11.2
Vegetables, fruit, nuts	13.7	6.6	10.3
Wheat	22.5	19.1	21.8
Non-agricultural sector			
Chemical, rubber, plastic products	4.2	1.1	3.0
Electronic equipment	2.2	0.8	1.9
Ferrous metals	0.7	0.1	0.5
Leather products	7.9	2.2	5.3
Machinery and equipment nec	2.0	0.4	1.5
Manufactures nec	2.5	0.5	1.7
Metal products	2.9	0.6	2.0
Metals nec	3.5	1.2	2.5
Mineral products nec	4.0	1.1	2.8
Minerals nec	0.2	0.1	0.2
Motor vehicles and parts	5.7	1.3	4.4
Paper products, publishing	0.1	0.0	0.1
Petroleum, coal products	0.6	0.1	0.3
Textiles	7.5	3.1	5.4
Transport equipment nec	2.9	0.8	2.3
Wearing apparel	10.9	3.9	7.7
Wood products	2.5	0.5	1.6

[a]Preferential duty granted by EU
[b]Paid duty according to tariff regime used

When comparing absolute and relative measures, it should be remembered, that the same relative margin implies very different duty reductions depending on the initial tariff levels.

Table 3.3 shows that these two measures appear to be inversely related (MFN benchmark) or to be uncorrelated (highest duty benchmark). In (absolute) percentage points, the margin is higher for the agricultural than the industry sectors; in relative terms the preference is lower for the agricultural sector.

Table 3.3 Simple average preferential margins (year 2004)

GTAP sector	Benchmark: MFN duty		Benchmark: the highest paid duty	
	Absolute	Relative	Absolute	Relative
All products	3.9	72.9	1.9	28.3
Agricultural sector				
Animal products nec	3.6	60.0	1.7	22.2
Beverages and tobacco products	11.9	61.4	6.3	35.1
Bovine cattle, sheep and goats, horses	26.3	78.4	12.1	46.6
Cereal grains nec	18.7	39.7	14.5	29.8
Crops nec	3.0	71.5	1.4	30.0
Fishing	5.2	65.5	3.1	36.6
Food products nec	12.3	57.0	8.4	33.5
Forestry	0.7	75.3	0.3	34.6
Meat products nec	14.6	43.5	10.4	21.1
Paddy rice	21.3	22.8	19.9	20.9
Vegetable oils and fats	10.3	56.5	8.0	30.0
Vegetables, fruit, nuts	11.4	62.4	7.6	34.0
Wheat	5.7	34.8	3.0	15.4
Non-agricultural sector				
Chemical, rubber, plastic products	3.1	76.0	1.3	28.0
Electronic equipment	1.4	72.1	0.3	14.5
Ferrous metals	0.6	81.7	0.2	33.1
Leather products	5.7	77.2	2.6	34.2
Machinery and equipment nec	1.6	82.4	0.5	23.9
Manufactures nec	2.0	82.2	0.8	30.2
Metal products	2.3	82.4	0.9	31.2
Metals nec	2.3	64.2	1.0	28.8
Mineral products nec	2.9	77.8	1.3	33.6
Minerals nec	0.3	74.4	0.2	47.7
Motor vehicles and parts	4.4	81.9	1.3	26.6
Paper products, publishing	0.1	76.1	0.0	27.1
Petroleum, coal products	0.4	81.3	0.2	36.5
Textiles	4.4	58.1	2.1	28.3
Transport equipment nec	2.1	78.8	0.6	21.0
Wearing apparel	7.1	65.3	3.2	29.9
Wood products	2.0	83.6	0.9	32.7

3.5 Results

Table 3.4 compares the MTPI margin results for different sectors. The trade-weighted average clearly outperforms the simple average (last column in Table 3.3) in terms of its ability to mirror the MTPI results. This is consistent with the results in Anderson and Neary (2003, 2005) and Bach and Martin (2001), which show that the trade-weighted average tariff is a linear approximation of the tariff aggregator based on the expenditure function, while the simple mean is a pure statistical construct.

As expected (Bureau and Salvatici 2005), the MTPI and the trade-weighted average are closer when the number of tariff lines in the aggregate is small, or when

Table 3.4 Mercantilistic trade preference index margins

GTAP sector	MTPI $(1-\alpha)$ (%)	Potential MTPI $(1-\alpha)$ (%)	Weighted mean margin (%)
All products	25.8	38.7	31.7
Agricultural sector			
Animal products nec	21.6	39.8	27.0
Beverages and tobacco products	54.5	56.6	55.7
Bovine cattle, sheep and goats, horses	47.3	63.5	54.7
Cereal grains nec	10	13.4	11.9
Crops nec	37.5	–	43.9
Fishing	40	45.1	41.5
Food products nec	40.7	57	43.0
Forestry	30.3	45.1	31.2
Meat products nec	34.2	36.8	40.8
Paddy rice	10.9	15.7	12.5
Vegetable oils and fats	13.2	16.1	13.3
Vegetables, fruit, nuts	39.4	49.8	42.1
Wheat	16	16.1	16.8
Non-agricultural sector			
Chemical, rubber, plastic products	25	45.9	27.5
Electronic equipment	7.4	–	10.0
Ferrous metals	61.3	78.1	63.0
Leather products	17.2	24.8	19.7
Machinery and equipment nec	23.8	36.2	25.5
Manufactures nec	19.9	30.1	21.3
Metal products	27	34.7	29.3
Metals nec	51.8	70.4	56.3
Mineral products nec	30.1	–	32.7
Minerals nec	52.1	–	52.7
Motor vehicles and parts	18.4	30.6	20.7
Paper products, publishing	67.1	74.5	68.9
Petroleum, coal products	44.4	82.6	45.0
Textiles	34.8	53.3	41.0
Transport equipment nec	6.8	18.5	7.9
Wearing apparel	27.3	–	33.4
Wood products	31.5	55.8	33.9

the dispersion in the margins within an aggregate is small; larger differences emerge when the number of tariff lines is higher (see e.g. textiles and textile articles). In line with Anderson and Neary (2003), the MTPI uniform percentage reductions (α_j) always exceed the trade-weighted reductions. In terms of preferential margins, this means that the trade-weighted average always overpredicts the MTPI value, with differences ranging from 0.1 (in the case of vegetable oils and fats) to 7.4 (in the case of bovine cattle, sheep and goats, horses) percentage points.

The overall MTPI margin granted by the EU is around 26%, but there are large differences across sectors. In the agricultural sector the MTPI margins range between 10%, in the case of cereal grains, and 54.5% in the case of beverages and tobacco. The industrial sector, on the other hand, shows greater variability with a minimum of around 7% in the cases of electronic and transport equipment, and a maximum of 67.1% for paper products. This is an interesting result since agricultural products are often the most important exports for the developing countries and attract much higher duties (see Table 3.2).

Table 3.4 also reports the results for the potential MTPI margins. Although this index is likely to underestimate the impact of regulations that do not allow full exploitation of the existing preferences, because potential trade volumes may be larger than the actual trade, comparison with the MTPI margins is informative. The largest differences are found in the animal and food products sectors, which have the strictest standards (e.g. sanitary and phyto-sanitary measures). Other sectors that show large differences are some traditional manufactures (e.g. textiles and apparel) and more advanced sectors such as chemical, rubber and plastic products. This may be due to quantitative restrictions and/or rules of origin requirements.

In order to assess the sensitivity of our results to the choice of the parameters for the CES function, we computed the MTPI making different assumptions about the values of the substitution elasticities. Even though the elasticities extracted from the GTAP dataset are widely used for applied analysis, their relevance is questionable. For instance, we believe that GTAP elasticities are low compared to what would be consistent with recent econometric estimates of import elasticities (see e.g. Erkel-Rousse and Mirza 2002; Hummels 1999).

So how do assumptions about the values of the substitution elasticities affect the MTPI computation? Although the sector rankings do not change, the MTPI are obviously sensitive to the degree of substitution between products, a finding that is consistent with the results in Bureau and Salvatici (2005). An increase in the elasticity of substitution from one-third to three times the original values leads to lower values of the overall-MTPI index, which decreases from 29.5 to 17%, since when products are more similar from the consumer's point of view, lower margins are required to generate the same trade volumes.

3.6 Conclusions

Since 2000, there has been increased interest in the problem of how to measure the openness of developed country markets *vis-à-vis* developing country exports. In this chapter, we provide a summary measure of EU preferential policies, that takes account of the different margins for a large number of tariff lines. Several characterizations of preferential tariffs are proposed in the literature, but there is no clear, unequivocal definition.

Margins are the result of a subtraction in which both operands are expressed in the same metric. The choice of a reference level with respect to the preference being measured is important. The applied MFN rate is preferred to the bound MFN duty, since the latter may lead to overestimation in the margin computation. However, to emphasize competitive advantage gained with respect to other exporters, we need to consider actual rather than potential exporters/competitors. Not all exporters have the same weight in terms of competitiveness; as a consequence many authors use as a reference simple or weighted average duties imposed on all (or a subset of) the other exporters.

In choosing the preferential rate, overlap in the preferential schemes needs to be considered. Individual products may be eligible for more than one preferential regime. In the case of overlapping preferences, many companies could import the same good under different agreements. In the case of overlapping preference schemes, the preferential rate considered here is the lowest available to each exporter, which can lead to overestimation of the preferential margins. Moreover, in the case of complex policy instruments, such as TRQ, computation of the relevant tariff depends on the assumed market structure. Finally, actual margins can be expressed in absolute or relative terms, of a combination of both through the preference discount rate.

In this chapter, we built on the work of Anderson and Neary to develop an MTPI, grounded in economic theory. The MTPI is defined as complementing one of the uniform scaling factors applied to the maximum tariffs levied to produce the same effect on the volume of trade as the importing country's preferential tariff structure. The computation follows Bureau and Salvatici (2005) and makes some simplifying assumptions, but does not require a Computable General Equilibrium (CGE) model.

Methodologically, the MTPI uniform preferences and the trade-weighted margins are more strongly aligned when the number of commodities and the, margin dispersion are small. However, the trade-weighted aggregator overestimates the true preferential margin as measured by the MTPI.

The overall margin granted by the EU is around 26%, with large differences across sectors, from high percentages in the cases of beverages and tobacco, and livestock (54 and 47%, respectively) to around 7% in the cases of electronic and transport equipment and 67.1% for paper products. Comparison with potential-MTPI shows that the largest differences are in sectors with the most stringent standards (e.g. animal and food products), quantitative restrictions (e.g. textiles) and/or rules of origin requirements (e.g. chemicals).

Our results show that theoretically consistent preferential policy aggregation is possible if some structure is imposed on the importing country's behaviour. Nevertheless, the results are inherently sensitive to assumptions regarding the elasticity of substitution, on which reliable information remains scarce.

Acknowledgments We acknowledge financial support from the "New Issues in Agricultural, Food and Bio-energy Trade (AGFOODTRADE)" (Small and Medium-scale Focused Research Project, Grant Agreement no. 212036) funded by the European Commission, and the "European Union policies, economic and trade integration processes and WTO negotiations" research project funded by the Italian Ministry of Education, University and Research (Scientific Research Programs of National Relevance 2007). We are grateful to Luca De Benedictis and David Laborde for the comments and the many conversations on the topic. Any remaining errors are solely our responsibility and the views expressed in this paper are those of the authors and do not necessarily reflect those of the European Commission.

Chapter 4
The Gravity Model in International Trade

Luca De Benedictis and Daria Taglioni

Abstract Since Jan Tinberben's original formulation (Tinbergen 1962, *Shaping the World Economy*, The Twentieth Century Fund, New York), the empirical analysis of bilateral trade flows through the estimation of a gravity equation has gone a long way. It has acquired a solid reputation of good fitting; it gained respected micro foundations that allowed it to move to a mature stage in which the "turn-over" gravity equation has been replaced by a gravity model; and it has dominated the literature on trade policy evaluation. In this chapter we show how some of the issues raised by Tinbergen have been the step stones of a 50-year long research agenda, and how the numerous empirical and theoretical contributions that followed dealt with old problems and highlighted new ones. Some future promising research issues are finally indicated.

4.1 Introduction

When in 1962 Jan Tinbergen, the future winner of the first 1969 Alfred Nobel Memorial Prize for economics, was sketching the empirical analysis for a report financed by a New York-based philanthropic foundation, his mind was back at his college years. In 1929, he had received his PhD in physics from Leiden University, the Netherlands, with a thesis entitled *Minimum Problems in Physics and Economics* under the supervision of Paul Ehrenfest, a close friend of Albert Einstein's (Szenberg 1992, p. 276; Leen 2004). Theoretical physics was his bread and butter,

L. De Benedictis
Department of Economic and Financial Institutions, University of Macerata, Via Crescimbeni 20, 62100 Macerata, Italy
e-mail: debene@unimc.it

D. Taglioni
World Bank, Washington DC, USA and Centre for Economic and Trade Integration at The Graduate Institute of International and Development Studies, Rue de Lausanne 132, 1211 Geneva, Switzerland
e-mail: dtaglioni@worldbank.org

L. De Benedictis and L. Salvatici (eds.), *The Trade Impact of European Union Preferential Policies*, DOI 10.1007/978-3-642-16564-1_4,

before the concern for the causes of poverty of the local working class pressed him to switch to economics. Therefore, it must not come as a surprise that, when he had to propose to the team of fellow colleagues of the Netherlands Economic Institute an econometric exercise "to determine the normal or standard pattern of international trade that would prevail in the absence of trade impediments," he came out with the idea of an econometric model formulated along the lines of Newton's law of universal gravitation[1], where trade flows are directly related to the economic size of the countries involved, and inversely related to the distance between them.

All simple and successful ideas have a life of their own, and their paternity can be attributed to multiple individuals. Before Tinbergen, Ravenstein (1885) and Zipf (1946) used gravity concepts to model migration flows. Independently from Tinbergen, Pöyhönen (1963), inspired by Leo Tornqvist,[2] published a paper using a similar approach.[3] Tinbergen's student and team-member of the Netherlands Economic Institute, Hans Linnemann, published a follow-up study (Linnemann 1966) which extended the analysis and discussed the theoretical basis of the gravity equation using the Walrasian model as a benchmark.[4] By the 1970s the gravity equation was already a must. The famous international trade book by Edward Leamer and Robert Stern included almost an entire chapter on it (Leamer and Stern 1970, pp. 157–170), based on the contribution of Savage and Deutsch (1960). Leamer and Stern's book introduced trade economists to the term resistance, that entered their glossary as a synonym for distance and other trade impediments. To make a long story short, from the first conceptualisation of Tinbergen (1962) the gravity equation has been used time and again to empirically analyse trade between countries. It has been defined as the workhorse of international trade and has been considered as a "fact of life" in this field of research (Deardorff 1998). The gravity equation's ability to correctly approximate bilateral trade flows makes it one of the most stable empirical relationships in economics (Leamer and Levinsohn 1995).

In Tinbergen's version of the gravity equation, X_{ij}, the size of the trade flow between any pair of countries is stochastically *determined*[5] by: (1) M_i, the amount

---

[1]The description of the econometric analysis was included in Appendix IV to the *Shaping the World Economy* report (Tinbergen 1962, pp. 262–293). Tinbergen himself described the summary of the results in Chapter 3 of the same report (Tinbergen 1962, pp. 59–66).

[2]Leo Tornqvist, was a famous Finnish statistician teaching at the University of Helsinki and father of the Tornqvist Price Index.

[3]Describing the exchange of goods between countries in matrix form, Pöyhönen (1963) makes it evident how international trade flows also depend on *internal trade*, a point also briefly covered by Tinbergen in the main text of his book (Tinbergen 1962, pp. 60–61).

[4]Linnemann quotes Zipf's work (Zipf 1946) and referring to Isard and Peck (see the impressive figure 1 on page 101 of Isard and Peck (1954)) surprisingly states that "Some authors emphasize the analogy with the gravitation law in physics . . . we fail to see any justification for this." He was not prophetic, but he was basing this statement on the fact that the elasticity of trade flows to distance were never found equal to 2.

[5]All words and phrases in *italics* are Tinbergen's. We will use them as milestones in our selective grand tour of the gravity model in international trade. This does not mean that all the main issues in this field of research were already pointed out by the author of the first path breaking contribution.

of exports a country i is able to supply to country j, depending on its economic size measured in terms of GNP *converted* in US dollars; (2) M_j, the size of the importing market, measured by its GNP, also converted in US dollars; (3) ϕ_{ij}, the geographical distance between the two countries in 1,000 nautical miles, as *a rough measure* of transportation costs or an index of information about export markets. The *model* was expressed in a *log–log* form, so that the elasticity of the trade flow was a constant (a_1, a_2, and a_3) with respect to the three explanatory variables. Actually, trade flows were *measured* both in terms of exports and imports of *commodities* and only *non-zero trade flows* were included in the analysis.[6] Results turn out to be not much different using exports or imports. *Adjacent countries* were assumed to have a more intense trade than what distance alone would predict; the adjacency was indicated by the dummy variable N_{ij}, that took the value 1 if the two countries were sharing a common land border. Finally, the equation was augmented with political or *semi-economic* factors: a dummy variable V_{ij} indicated that goods traded received a preferential treatment in the importing country if they belonged to the British Commonwealth system of preferences.[7] As customary, a gravitational constant G and a i.i.d. stochastic term ε_{ij} were also included. In equation-form:

$$\ln X_{ij} = \underbrace{\ln G}_{a_0 \equiv \text{constant}} + \underbrace{a_1 \ln M_i + a_2 \ln M_j}_{\text{economic attractors}} + \underbrace{a_3 \phi_{ij} + a_4 N_{ij}}_{\text{distance}} + \underbrace{a_5 V_{ij}}_{\text{policy}} + \underbrace{\varepsilon_{ij}}_{\text{iid}} \tag{4.1}$$

Elasticities were estimated by means of an Ordinary Least Squares (OLS) *cross-country regression* on 1,958 trade flows data for 18 countries, as a first trial, and for 42 countries, as a robustness check.[8]

The relationship between trade and the dummy policy variable V_{ij} can be seen in a simple graphical illustration of this relationship, conditional on distance, as in Fig. 4.1. The linear prediction for trade flows reported in the chart is obtained by replicating Tinbergen's first exercise with data on trade, Free Trade Agreements

However, many open questions were already intriguing researchers fifty years ago. A surprising persistence that we think is worth pointing out.

[6]For an early discussion of the zero trade flows see Linnemann (1966, p. 64).

[7]A dummy variable was also included for Benelux and, in a larger subsample to a broad variable identifying preferential agreements. The strategy of considering the effect of Preferential Trade Agreements (PTA) through the use of dummy variable has been prominent in the literature. Only recently the alternative strategy of explicitly including the preferential margin guaranteed by the agreement has been taken into account (see Chapter 3). We will come back to this issue in Section 4.4.2.4.

[8]The countries included in the first exercise were mainly developed countries: Brazil, Venezuela, South Africa, Japan, Canada, USA, Austria, Belgium-Luxembourg, Denmark, France, Germany (FR), Italy, Netherlands, Norway, Sweden, Switzerland, UK, and Australia. For a complete list of the 42 countries included in the second exercise see Tinbergen (1962, p. 274). The Benelux preference (between Belgium, Luxembourg and the Netherlands) was also represented by a dummy variable.

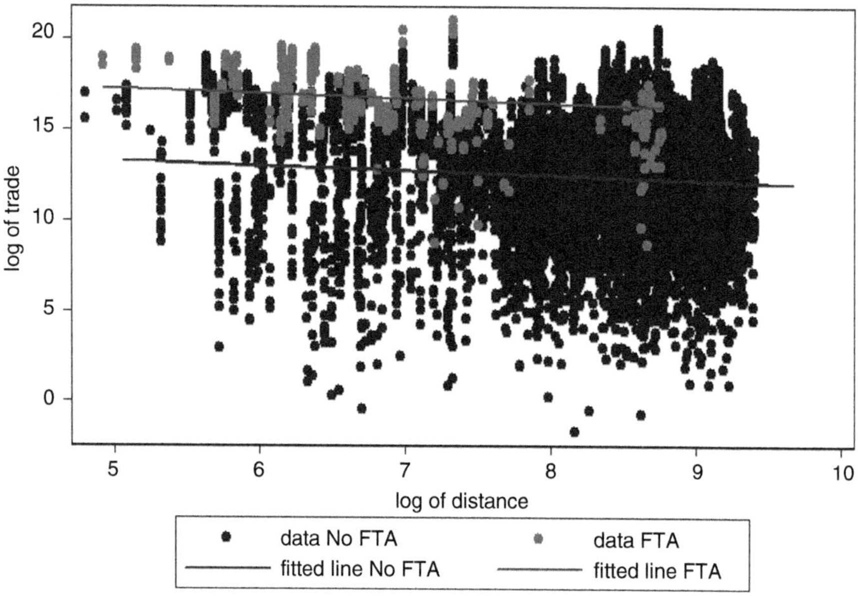

Fig. 4.1 Distance and trade preferences

(FTA) and distance, from Subramanian and Wei (2007). It reproduces the negative marginal effect of distance, conditional on the preferential treatment granted by FTA.[9] The positive effect of trade preferences is visible in Fig. 4.1 as the vertical distance between the two parallel regression lines. Things get less clear cut when we also include other covariates in the regression.

In the original estimation by Tinbergen (1962), the coefficients of GNP and distance had what became "the expected sign" in all subsequent analyses – the coefficients of the economic attractors were positive and the one of distance was negative – and resulted relevant and significant.[10] Moreover, the fit of the estimation was found to increase when the data sample was increased from 18 to

[9]The resulting estimation reproduces fairly well Tinbergen's original one. We did not have data on Benelux and also the trade data for South Africa was largely missing. We used data for 1960 and replaced GNP with GDP.

[10]In his comments to the regression's functional form, Tinbergen explained that in his view the economic size (GNP) of the importing country played a twofold role: it indicates its demand – external and internal – and its degree of diversity of production. In principle, the sign of the coefficient could have been positive (demand) or negative (self-sufficiency). For Tinbergen it was a surprise that the coefficient was positive. It was also a surprise to observe that countries "trading less than normally" (below the regression line) were the bigger and the richer countries. Though the second evidence – small countries trade more with the rest of the world – has been explored theoretically (Anderson and Yotov 2010) and empirically (Alesina et al. 2005; Rose 2006), the role played by self-sufficiency has been largely neglected by the literature.

42 countries; on the other hand, the coefficient for adjacency was never significant and the one for trade preference was borderline. Although its functioning wasn't perfect, Tinbergen, who was a *correlation hunter* (Szenberg 1992, p. 278), succeeded in identifying a specification whose key variables explained a very high percentage of variability in the data, with a multiple correlation coefficient, R^2, of 0.82. This result led the way to the application of the log-linearized version of Newton's universal law of gravity to social and economic activities. Since then, the equation was viewed as a big success in enlightening "... the dominant role played by ... exporters' and importers' GNP and distance in explaining trade flows" (Tinbergen 1962, p. 266).

The specification however, left room for improvement, and the positive but relatively small role of trade preferences was an issue that stimulated further inquiry. In this chapter we will address one at the time some of the main open issues – associated to Tinbergen's original wording, that we have highlighted by marking the text in *italics*. We will review, briefly, the theoretical and, more extensively, the empirical trade literature on the gravity equation and we will indicate some of the promising avenues for future research.

4.2 Estimating Gravity

Let's start from the first term highlighted in the introduction: *determined*. Bilateral trade flows are determined by the variables included in the right-hand-side of the gravity equation. This implies a clear direction of causality that runs from income and distance to trade. This direction of causality is nowdays largely theory-driven and based on the assumption that the gravity equation is derived from an micro-economic model where income and tastes for differentiated products are given. Empirically, the causality (as if in a randomized quasi-experimental setting[11] *à la* Rubin) of the gravity equation, as described in (4.1), is more difficult to establish: the equation as it stands represents a regression of endogenous variables on endogenous variables. As a consequence, the parameter of the gravitational constant G is not constant: it varies by trade partner and over time and is correlated with many, if not all, policy variables affecting trade (which are rarely considered as the equivalent of a treatment in a random trial experimental setting). Failure to acknowledge this leads to an estimated impact of the policy variables likely to be biased and often severely so.

[11]In this setting researchers are interested in the causal effect of a treatment that takes the form of binary trade policy intervention (when the treatment is a dummy variable) or an ordered or continuous trade policy intervention (when considering trade preferential margins). Units, in this case countries or specific sectors of a country, are either exposed or not exposed to the treatment. Even if the effect of the treatment can be potentially heterogeneous across units, usually researchers focus on the identification of an average treatment effect (see Angrist and Pischke 2008 for a discussion of quasi-experimental settings).

We are in the realm of omitted variable biases. To simplify, let's assume away GDP and distance and focus on the policy variables. The estimated gravity equation will have the following structure:

$$\ln X_{ij} = \underbrace{\ln G}_{a_0 \equiv \text{constant}} + \underbrace{a_5 V_{ij}}_{\text{policy}} + \underbrace{\varepsilon_{ij}}_{\text{iid}} \tag{4.2}$$

while the true structural model is:

$$\ln X_{ij} = \underbrace{\ln G}_{a_0 \equiv \text{constant}} + \underbrace{a_5 V_{ij}}_{\text{policy}} + \underbrace{a_6 \ln Z_{ij}}_{\text{omitted varible}} + \underbrace{\varepsilon_{ij}}_{\text{iid}} \tag{4.3}$$

We can write Z_{ij} as a function of V_{ij} in an auxiliary regression:

$$\ln Z_{ij} = \underbrace{b_0}_{\text{constant}} + \underbrace{b_1 V_{ij}}_{\text{policy}} + \underbrace{u_{ij}}_{\text{iid}} \tag{4.4}$$

Without being aware of it, we have estimated the following equation:

$$\ln X_{ij} = \underbrace{(a_0 + b_0\, a_6)}_{\text{constant}} + \underbrace{(a_5 + a_6\, b_1) V_{ij}}_{\text{policy}} + \underbrace{(\varepsilon_{ij} + a_6\, u_{ij})}_{\text{iid}} \tag{4.5}$$

Therefore, unless $b_1 = 0$, $\mathrm{E}(\hat{a}_5) = a_5 + \underbrace{a_6 \left[\frac{\sum V_{ij} Z_{ij}}{\sum V_{ij}^2}\right]}_{\text{bias}}$. Accordingly, the bias depends on the correlation between the policy variable and the omitted variable, and can have a positive or negative sign. Furthermore, the mis-specification also affects the standard errors, which would result in a positive bias (Wooldridge 2002, Chapter 4).

The omitted variable problem in the gravity equation has been dealt through different approaches. The first has been to include in the equation one or more proxy variables correlated with the omitted variable. We will discuss this strategy in the context of the effect of distance on trade. A second approach has been to include a time-dimension in the analysis and to move from cross-country analysis to panel data analysis, since one of the most likely sources of omitted variables is country heterogeneity, an issue that is not likely or easy to account for in a cross-country setting. While we will tackle the aspects related to a correct specification in the following example, where we show that the biases from mispecification are non-trivial, here we would like to focus on the choice between cross-section and panel estimations. Even though elements such as distance and size are best captured by cross sections with the panel not adding much content in short horizons, in most cases panel specifications should be preferred to cross-section specifications because of the inability of the latter to properly account for the omitted variables bias. On the other hand, policy effects, such as the trade promotion of free trade agreements or custom unions, are always better identified in panels, through the time series dimension. Indeed, in the cross-section specification they are highly collinear with distance.

With these issues in mind, in the next two sections we first empirically show the potential biases from a bad specification and then provide a synthetic discussion of how to specify a theoretically sound gravity equation. The aim is to give the reader an informed perspective of what theory-based specifications can be applied to address the various empirical questions posed to the gravity equation.

4.2.1 How Big Are the Biases?

In order to show how big are the biases from mis-specifying the gravity equation, we re-run Tinbergen's regression as a benchmark, for the same subset of 42 countries and for data taken at intervals of five years, from 1960 to 2005. We will show that the trade policy variable coefficient is very sensitive to the specification. In particular, we show the effect of introducing different types of fixed effect controls and of using real-vs-nominal GDP.[12] Results are reported in Table 4.1 below.

Columns (1) and (2) report the base regression as in Tinbergen (1962), with only two differences. First, instead of GNP we use GDP (in column (1) real GDP and in column (2) nominal GDP). Second, our policy variable of interest is whether a country pair is in an FTA relationship. Columns (3) and (4) reports results where time dummies are added to the regression, to account for the changing nature of the relationship over time, with the difference between column (3) and (4) being the real-vs-nominal GDP choice. Column (5) and (6) report results with time invariant importer and exporter fixed effects on top of the time dummies. Column (7) shows results for time varying exporter and importer fixed effects. Lastly, column (8) presents a specification where time invariant pair effects are also added.

In spite of Fig. 4.1, the baseline Tinbergen-like specification seems to suggest that being in an FTA does not have any statistically significant effect on trade if we use real GDP, but a positive and statistically robust effect if we use nominal GDP (columns 1 and 2). Similarly, adjacency (i.e. sharing a border) does not seem to be trade-enhancing when we use real GDP figures, and positive and significant when we use nominal GDP figures. All other variables have the expected sign and are statistically significant, with both GDP specifications. Adding time fixed effects (columns 3 and 4) and time-invariant importer and exporter fixed effects (columns 5 and 6) however has the surprising effect of reversing the sign of the FTA

[12] The use of nominal GDP (instead of real GDP) is theoretically more sound. We will come back to this issue in Section 4.5.3.

Table 4.1 The gravity equation with different fixed effects

Variables	(1) *ln imports*	(2) *ln imports*	(3) *ln imports*	(4) *ln imports*	(5) *ln imports*	(6) *ln imports*	(7) *ln imports*	(8) *ln imports*
ln $rgdp_i$	1.027***		1.077***		1.449***			
	(0.01)		(0.01)		(0.08)			
ln $rgdp_j$	1.115***		1.169***		1.375***			
	(0.01)		(0.01)		(0.08)			
ln gdp_i		0.704***		0.957***		0.803***		
		(0.01)		(0.01)		(0.05)		
ln gdp_j		0.777***		1.051***		1.003***		
		(0.01)		(0.01)		(0.06)		
ln distance	−1.227***	−0.897***	−1.225***	−1.014***	−1.045***	−1.067***	−1.089***	
	(0.03)	(0.03)	(0.03)	(0.02)	(0.03)	(0.03)	(0.03)	
sharing a border dummy	0.0780	0.406***	0.115	0.537***	0.608***	0.587***	0.564***	
	(0.09)	(0.10)	(0.09)	(0.08)	(0.09)	(0.09)	(0.09)	
FTA dummy	−0.0490	0.146**	0.214***	−0.172***	−0.396***	−0.632***	−0.717***	0.266***
	(0.06)	(0.07)	(0.06)	(0.06)	(0.07)	(0.07)	(0.07)	(0.06)
Constant	−17.61***	−16.64***	−18.37***	−25.54***	−32.26***	−19.85***	28.56***	13.02***
	(0.346)	(0.384)	(0.335)	(0.355)	(2.536)	(2.241)	(0.319)	(0.377)
Observations	10,781	10,831	10,781	10,831	10,781	10,831	10,831	10,831
R-squared	0.656	0.550	0.692	0.732	0.785	0.785	0.815	0.928
Time effects	No	No	Yes	Yes	Yes	Yes	No	No
Exporter and importer time invariant fe	No	No	No	No	Yes	Yes	No	No
Exporter and importer time-varying fe	No	No	No	No	No	No	Yes	Yes
Time invariant pair fe	No	No	No	No	No	No	No	Yes

Note: robust standard errors in parentheses. (*) significant at 10% level; (**) significant at 5% level; (***) significant at 1% level. fe stands for fixed effect(s).

coefficient in three out of the four cases. Notwithstanding the sign of the coefficient, the fact that the FTA coefficient acquires statistical significance and that its point estimates increase with the inclusion of time dummies, suggests the existence of a significant time trend non-orthogonal to the FTA dummy. Interestingly, while the FTA coefficient is negative, the coefficient for sharing a border is positive and strongly significant. The two results in combination lead us to formulate the hypothesis that the two variables might be correlated with each other. If this the case, entering the exporter and importer fixed effects in a time-varying way does not help achieving a sound specification.[13] Hence the only solution remains changing slightly the focus of our research question, by asking, what is the effect of entering in a FTA relationship for bilateral trade? With this different angle, we can formulate a gravity specification where we add time invariant pair effects on top of time-varying importer and exporter fixed effects to address pair-specific invariant omitted variables. The outcome is an FTA coefficient positively signed and statistically significant. The coefficient is now to be interpreted as the effect of entering in an FTA instead of being part of it, i.e. with this specification a country-pair that was part of a bilateral agreement throughout the period of observation would not be picked up by the FTA dummy.[14]

Given the evidence of how important it is to properly specify the gravity equation to account for country heterogeneity, we now turn to provide the reader with an informed perspective on the empirical issues associated with the estimation of the gravity equation. We do this by discussing how to achieve theoretically sound gravity specifications. In other words, abandoning for a while Tinbergen's wording, we link the gravity equation to the gravity model.

4.3 Theory-Based Specifications for the Gravity Model

For Tinbergen (1962, p. 263) the gravity *equation* was a "turnover relation," where no separate demand and supply were considered, no prices were specified, and no dynamics was taken into account. This doesn't mean that there was no model under the equation. The exporter's and importer's GNP captured, respectively the effect of production capacity and of demand and distance was a measure of the trade

[13]Another source of bias in the regression could come from self-selection, i.e. nations that choose to be in a given trade policy regime are not randomly chosen. Geographical proximity, common language, common border, former colonial status, size and wealth of a nation are likely to strongly influence the decision to enter or not in given policy regimes. This causes a selection problem. Matching methods have been used to control for self-selection (see Persson (2001) for an early application and Millimet and Tchernis (2009) for a discussion of the methodology). However, solving for self-selection needs to be done on a case by case basis.

[14]Fixed effects specifications require getting rid of RHS variables that are accounted for by the fixed effects. This explains why we have no entries for GDP, distance and border in columns (5) to (8).

feasibility set. Assumptions were not spelled out and restrictions were not explicitly imposed, but a model was already *in nuce*. Surprisingly, all developments up to the early 1980s concerned the empirics of the relationship, while the theoretical basis remained underdeveloped.[15] Since then, things have changed radically. Three decades of theoretical work has shown that the gravity equation can be derived from many different – and sometimes competing – trade frameworks. In 1979, James Anderson proposed a theoretical explanation of the gravity equation based on a demand function with Constant Elasticity of Substitution (CES) *à la* Armington (1969), where each country produces and sells goods on the international market that are differentiated from those produced in every other country. Later work has included the Armington structure of consumer preferences in (1) monopolistic competition frameworks (Krugman 1980; Bergstrand 1985, 1989; Helpman and Krugman 1985), (2) models *à la* Heckscher-Ohlin (Deardorff 1998), or (3) models *à la* Ricardo (Eaton and Kortum 2002). The catalyst of the more recent wave of theoretical contributions on gravity is the literature on models of international trade with firm heterogeneity, spearheaded by Bernard et al. (2003) and Melitz (2003).

Given the plethora of models available, the emphasis is now on ensuring that any empirical test of the gravity equation is very well defined on theoretical grounds and that it can be linked to one of the available theoretical frameworks. Accordingly, the recent methodological contributions brought to the fore the importance of defining carefully the structural form of the gravity equation and the implications of mis-pecifying (4.1). In this context, two broad sets of key issues have been identified. A first important range of contributions is related to the multilateral dimension of the gravity model. Anderson and van Wincoop (2003) – building on Anderson (1979) – showed that the flow of bilateral trade is influenced by both the trade obstacles that exist at the bilateral level (Bilateral Resistance) and by the relative weight of these obstacles with respect to all other countries (what they called the Multilateral Resistance). After this contribution, the omission of a Multilateral Resistance term is considered a serious source of bias and an important issue every researcher should deal with in estimating a gravity equation. The second main area of methodological concern is related to the selection bias associated to the presence of heterogeneous firms operating internationally. Contrary to what is implied by models of monopolistic competition *à la* Krugman, not all existing firms operate on international markets. In fact, only a minority of firms serves foreign markets (Mayer and Ottaviano 2008; Bernard et al. 2007). Moreover, not all exporting firms export to all foreign markets as they are generally active only in a subset of countries.[16] The critical implication of firm heterogeneity for modeling the gravity

[15]Alan Deardoff refers to the gravity model as having "somewhat dubious theoretical heritage" (Deardorff 1998, p. 503). Similar assessments can be found in Evenett and Keller (2002) and Harrigan (2001).

[16]The heterogeneity in firm behavior is due to fixed costs of entry which are market specific and higher for international markets than for the domestic market. Hence, only the most productive firms are able to cover them. Firm productivity is furthermore correlated with a large array of other

equation is that the matrix of bilateral trade flows is not full: many cells have a zero entry. This is the case at the aggregate level and the more often this case is seen, the greater the level of data disaggregation. The existence of trade flows which have a bilateral value equal to zero is full of implications for the gravity equation because it may signal a selection problem. If the zero entries are the result of the firm choice of not selling specific goods to specific markets (or its inability to do so), the standard OLS estimation of the gravity equation would be inappropriate: it would deliver biased results (Chaney 2008; Helpman et al. 2008).

Irrelevant of the theoretical framework of reference, most of the modern mainstream foundations of the gravity equation are variants of the demand-driven model described in the appendix of Anderson (1979). Hence, in the following paragraphs, we summarise the key theoretical points of this common framework. We will mainly rely on the Anderson and van Wincoop (2003) and Baldwin and Taglioni (2006) derivations, using standard notation to facilitate the exposition. We will obviously mention where and in what way the supply-driven models *à la* Eaton and Kortum (2002) differ.

The starting point of Anderson and van Wincoop (2003) is a CES demand structure, with the assumption that each firm produces a unique variety of a unique good. Since trade data are collected in value terms it is convenient to work with the CES expenditure function rather than the CES demand function. The solution to the utility maximisation problem tells us that spending on an imported good that is produced in nation i and consumed in nation j is:

$$x_{ij} \equiv \left(\frac{p_{ij}}{P_j}\right)^{1-\sigma} M_j \quad \text{where} \quad \sigma > 1 \tag{4.6}$$

where x_{ij} is the expenditure in destination country j on a variety made in country i, P_j is nations-j's CES price index, σ is the elasticity of substitution among varieties assumed greater than one, and M_j is nation-j expenditure, and p_{ij} is the consumer price in nation j of goods produced in nation i

$$p_{ij} = \mu_{ij} p_i \phi_{ij} \tag{4.7}$$

In this equality, p_i is nation i's domestic price, μ_{ij} is the bilateral price mark-up (which depends on the assumed market structure) and ϕ_{ij} is the bilateral "trade costs," which is one plus the *ad valorem* tariff equivalent of all natural and manmade barriers, i.e. whatever cost-factor that introduces a wedge between domestic and foreign goods' prices, conditional on market structure. This is the pass-through equation. Combining this with (4.6) gives us the per-variety

observable firm characteristics. Hence firms that serve both domestic and foreign markets are not only more productive but also larger, more innovative and more intensive in human and physical capital. By contrast firms that only serve the domestic market are less productive, smaller, less innovative, and labor intensive.

relationship. Aggregating over all varieties exported from country i to country j (assuming that all varieties produced in nation i are symmetric) yields aggregate bilateral trade:

$$X_{ij} = \sum_{i} x_{ij} = n_{ij}\left(\mu_{ij} p_i \phi_{ij}\right)^{1-\sigma} \frac{M_j}{P_j^{1-\sigma}} \tag{4.8}$$

where X_{ij} indicates the value of the aggregate trade flows (measured in terms of the numeraire), and n_{ij} indicates the number of nation-i varieties sold in nation-j.[17]

Let us stress the point that our derivation of the gravity equation is based on an expenditure function. This explains two key factors. First, destination country's GDP enters the gravity equation (as M_j) since it captures the standard income effect in an expenditure function. Second, bilateral distance enters the gravity equation since it proxies for bilateral trade costs which get passed through to consumer prices and thus dampens bilateral trade, other things being equal. The most important insight from the above mathematical derivation is that the expenditure function depends on relative and not absolute prices. This allows factoring in firms' competition in market j via the price index P_j. Hence, (4.8) tells us that the omission of the importing nation's price index P_j from the original gravity equation described in (4.1) leads to a mis-specification. It should further be noted that the exclusion of dynamic considerations is problematic: Although we omitted time suffixes for the sake of simplicity, the reader should be aware that P_j is a time-variant variable, so it will not be properly controlled for if one uses time-invariant controls, unless the researcher is estimating cross-sectional data.

Having shown why destination-country GDP and bilateral distance enter the gravity equation, we turn next to explaining why the exporter's GDP should also be included. The explanation is Tinbergen's: it reflects the export capacity or the supply available on the side of the exporter. While the way it enters the equation is the same across theoretical frameworks, the interpretation of the role it plays depends on the specificities of the underlying theory. The Anderson-van Wincoop derivation is based on the Armington assumption of competitive trade in goods differentiated by country of origin. In other words, each country makes only one product, so all the adjustment takes place at the *price* level. This implies that nations with large GDPs export more of their product to all destinations, since their good is relatively cheap. This equates to saying that their good must be relatively cheap if they want to sell all the output produced under full employment. Helpman and Krugman (1985) make assumptions that prevent prices from adjusting (frictionless trade and factor price equalisation), so all the adjustment happens in the number of varieties that each nation has to offer. This implies that nations with large GDP export more to all destinations, since they produce many varieties. Since each firm produces one variety and each variety is produced only by one firm, stating that the

[17]Anderson and van Wincoop (2003, p. 174) assume that this number is equal to 1 for all origin and destination markets.

adjustment takes place at the level of varieties equates to stating that the number of firms in each country adjust endogenously. This is enough to lead to the standard gravity results.

Turning back to Anderson and van Wincoop and how the exporter's GDP should enter the gravity equation, the idea is that nations with big GDPs must have low relative prices so to sell all their production (market clearing condition). To determine the price p_i that will clear the market, we sum up nation i's sales over all markets, *including its own market*, as Tinbergen originally pointed out (Tinbergen 1962, pp. 60–61) and set it equal to overall production. This can be written as follows: $M_i = \sum_j n_{ij}x_{ij}$ which equates to

$$M_i = p_i^{1-\sigma} \sum_j n_{ij} \left[\left(\mu_{ij}\phi_{ij} \right)^{1-\sigma} \frac{M_j}{P_j^{1-\sigma}} \right], \tag{4.9}$$

where the second equality follows from the substitution of the expression for x_{ij}, that is produced in turn by the substitution of (4.7) into (4.6). Solving (4.9) for $p_i^{1-\sigma}$ yields:

$$p_i^{1-\sigma} = \frac{M_i}{\Omega_i}$$

$$\Omega_i = \sum_j \left[n_{ij} \left(\mu_{ij}\phi_{ij} \right)^{1-\sigma} \frac{M_j}{P_j^{1-\sigma}} \right] \tag{4.10}$$

where Ω_i represents the average of all importers' market demand – weighted by trade costs. It has been named in many different ways in the literature, including market potential (Head and Mayer 2004; Helpman et al. 2008), market openness (Anderson and van Wincoop 2003) or remoteness (Baier and Bergstrand 2009).

Using (4.10) in (4.8) yields a basic but correctly specified gravity equation

$$X_{ij} = n_{ij} \left(\mu_{ij}\phi_{ij} \right)^{1-\sigma} \frac{M_j}{P_j^{1-\sigma}} \frac{M_i}{\Omega_i} \tag{4.11}$$

If we suppose that each country only produces one product, as in Anderson and Van Wincoop (2003), i.e. n_{ij} $(=1)$, and assume that the markup μ_{ij} depends upon the distance between the two trading partners, we arrive to the most familiar specification of the gravity equation:

$$X_{ij} = \phi_{ij}{}^{1-\sigma} \frac{M_j}{P_j^{1-\sigma}} \frac{M_i}{\Omega_i} \tag{4.12}$$

Hence, we just showed that origin country's GDP enters the gravity equation since large economies offer goods that are either relatively competitive or abundant in variety, or both. The derivation also shows that the exporting nation's market potential Ω_i matters, and that the misspecification in the gravity equation would be more serious the bigger the asymmetry among countries.

Equation (4.12) is identical to (4.9) in Anderson and van Wincoop (2003, p. 175). But it is not identical to their final expression. As shown by Baldwin and Taglioni (2006), Anderson and van Wincoop (2003) assume that $\Omega_i = P_i^{1-\sigma}$ for all nations, since it is a solution to the system of equation that defines these two terms. There are three critical assumptions behind this. First, they assume that trade costs are two-way symmetric across all pairs of countries. This assumption however is automatically violated in the case of preferential trade agreements. Second, they assume that trade is balanced, i.e. $X_{ij} = X_{ji}$, also an hypothesis that is often violated in practice. Finally, they assume that there is only one period of data. Were the above three conditions verified, we could refer to the product of the two terms Ω_i and $P_i^{1-\sigma}$ as to a single country geography index, with the term of *multilateral resistance*; which can be empirically controlled for by a time-invariant country-fixed effect.[18] In fact, a more general case is that Ω_i and $P_i^{1-\sigma}$ are proportional, i.e. that $\alpha\Omega_i = P_i^{1-\sigma}$ and that there is a different α per year. If this point is acknowledged, it is simple to see that the gravity model in (4.1) is missing a time-varying dimension and that Ω_i and $P_i^{1-\sigma}$ must be accounted for with separate terms. An easy and practical solution to match the theory with the data is to introduce time-varying importer and exporter fixed effects. Obviously, in cross-sections, the Anderson van Wincoop specification is sufficient owing to the lack of time dimension. Often however, the need of correcting for omitted variables biases clashes with problems of collinearity with the other variables. Hierarchical Bayesian methods may be able to assist in reducing the resulting overparametrization problem (Guo 2009), but not in solving it. Alternatively, more sophisticated terms that account for Ω_i and $P_i^{1-\sigma}$ but that are orthogonal to the other variables in the equation must be computed, or strategies to control for potential collinearity have to be devised case-by-case.

A final aspect to consider is firm heterogeneity and the connected issue of zeroes in the trade matrix. In models with identical firms, in the absence of natural and man-made trade costs, countries either trade or they are in autarky. If they do trade, every firm in a country exports to every country in the world. Introducing firm heterogeneity in models of international trade however allows for a more realistic representation of reality, namely one where not all firms in a country export, not all products are exported to all destinations and not all countries in the rest of the world are necessarily served. Moreover, as trade barriers move around, the set of exporters will change, and this additional margin of adjustment – the extensive margin – will radically change the aggregate trade response to the underlying geographical and

[18]Obviously, some econometric fixes have been found. In particular, the practice introduced by Harrigan (2001) and popularized by Feenstra (2003), to control for Multilateral Resistance through the use of country fixed effects in the econometric estimation. Incidentally, the country fixed effect practice diverted the analysis from the causes of multilateral resistance to the effects of multilateral resistance. The latter remains a promising area of analysis, especially in the context of policy evaluation.

policy variables. Helpman et al. (2008), from a demand side, and Chaney (2008), from a supply side, have both introduced heterogeneity in gravity models, allowing for the more general derivation of gravity with heterogeneous firms.

Consider a world with many countries and same CES preferences across countries with elasticity of substitution $\sigma > 1$. Country i has a given number N_i of potential producers, i.e. entrants. These entrants draw their unit input requirement a from a distribution $G(a) = (a/\bar{a})^k$, where $k > \sigma - 1$ and $0 \leq a \leq \bar{a}$. The term k denotes the productivity distribution parameter that governs the entry and exit of firms into the export markets. Hence k indicates the degree of firm heterogeneity and σ the degree of differentiation across products. The same distribution $G(a)$ holds across countries, but the cost of the input bundle w_i is country-specific. Trade costs ϕ_{ij} for trade between countries i and j are composed of a variable and a fixed part. The variable component is $\tau_{ij} \geq 1$, a per-unit iceberg trade cost. The fixed component is $f_{ij} > 0$. These costs include also serving the domestic market where $i = j$ and where one can assume that $\tau_{ii} = 1$ and that f_{ij} includes overhead fixed costs.

If a producer in country i with unit cost a exports to j, it will set a price $p_{ij}(a)$ and generate export sales $x_{ij}(a)$ and export profits $\pi_{ij}(a)$:

$$p_{ij}(a) = \frac{\sigma}{\sigma - 1} w_i \tau_{ij} a \tag{4.13}$$

$$x_{ij}(a) = \frac{M_j}{P_j^{1-\sigma}} p_{ij}(a)^{1-\sigma} \tag{4.14}$$

$$\pi_{ij}(a) = \frac{1}{\sigma} x_{ij}(a) - w_i f_{ij} \tag{4.15}$$

As before M_j and $P_j^{1-\sigma}$ are expenditure and price index, respectively in importer country j. The cut-off for profitable exports from i to j which we define a_{ij} is determined by $\pi_{ij}(a_{ij}) = 0$. In other words, we assume that $\bar{a}$ is high enough to allow that $a \leq \bar{a}$ for every pair of countries i and j.

Given this, aggregate bilateral trade from i to j is then

$$X_{ij} = N_i \int_0^{a_{ij}} x_{ij}(a) dG(a) \tag{4.16}$$

If one defines $M_i = \sum_j X_{ij}$ as the value of country i's aggregate output, where trade with every country in the world including self is accounted for, then – after some algebraic transformations – the aggregate bilateral trade from i to j can be written as follows:

$$X_{ij} = \tau_{ij}{}^{-k} f_{ij}^{-\frac{k-\sigma+1}{\sigma-1}} \left(\frac{M_j}{P_j^{1-\sigma}} \right)^{\frac{k}{\sigma-1}} \frac{M_i}{\Omega_i}, \tag{4.17}$$

where $\Omega_i = \tau_{ij}{}^{-k} f_{ij}^{-\frac{k-\sigma+1}{\sigma-1}} \sum_j \left(\frac{M_j}{P_j^{1-\sigma}} \right)^{\frac{k}{\sigma-1}}$.

The gravity specification with firm-heterogeneity differs from previous specifications in two broad ways, which we summarise below. While some of the points we will make are already clear from (4.17), the interested reader is referred to Chaney (2008) which demonstrates explicitly each of the issues that we raise below. He does so by decomposing (4.17) by the two margins of trade, solving for each expression and expressing each margin in elasticities.

To start with, the per-unit trade costs are shown to affect both the intensive and the extensive margin of trade. However, they do so with some important differences. First, per-unit trade costs τ_{ij} are subject to firm heterogeneity (as indicated by the superscript k) and no longer to product differentiation (i.e. the parameter $1 - \sigma$ in 4.12). This is due to the fact that, with Pareto or Frechet distributed productivity shocks, the effect of σ on the intensive and extensive margin cancels out, so that in aggregate the elasticity of trade flows with respect to the per-unit trade costs only depends on k. Nevertheless, when per-unit trade costs move, both the intensive and the extensive margin of trade are affected and σ, the degree of competition in the market, plays an important role in the dynamics. The intensive margin of trade responds to changes in variable trade costs as in traditional specifications: i.e. the elasticity of incumbent exporters with respect to τ_{ij} is $(\sigma - 1)$, hence each firm faces a constant elasticity residual demand, and therefore when goods are very substitutable, the export of incumbents is very sensitive to trade costs. The extensive margin, on the other hand, behaves idiosyncratically. When per-unit trade costs move, some of the less productive firms start exporting, but their impact on aggregate flows is inversely proportional to σ. As goods become more substitutable (high σ), the market share of the least productive firms shrinks compared to the market share of the more productive firms and the change in trade costs has a decreasing impact on aggregate trade flows. Finally, fixed costs only matter for the extensive margin of trade, since those exporters that have already decided to enter a market are not going to change their decision. This effect is clearly visible with a first order approximation, as the derivative of trade flows to fixed costs posts zero elasticity for the intensive margin. A second important set of implications of firm-heterogeneity for gravity models arises because the importer CES market demand effect is amplified by the upshot of demand on the extensive margin of trade $k/(\sigma - 1) > 1$. By contrast, the exporter's market potential is computed as in previous models, given however differences in trade costs and the existence of importer fixed effects. Having shown how to handle firm heterogeneity in gravity models from a theoretical point of view,[19] in the following sections of the chapter we will now come back to Tinbergen's wording and discuss the empirical strategies that allow making use of the information contained in the trade model founding the gravity equation.

[19]From a practical point of view, it is not necessary to rely on firm-level data to consider the effect of firms heterogeneity. Given the productivity distribution of domestic firms, the aggregate volume of trade defines the volume of trade of the marginal exporting firm – the one with the productivity exactly equal to the cut-off point of the productivity distribution.

4.4 A Piecewise Analysis of the Gravity Equation

4.4.1 Dependent Variable

To put things in context, there are three issues associated with the left-hand side variable of the gravity equation. The first has to do with the issue of *conversion* of trade values denominated in domestic currencies and with the issue of deflating the time series of trade flows. The second is associated with the effect of the inclusion or exclusion of *zero-trade flows* from the estimation. Finally, the third issue is related with the *typology* of goods or economic activities to be included in the definition of trade flows: imports, exports, merchandise trade or any other possible candidate for a trade link between country *i* and country *j*. In the current section we will discuss the third and the first issues while leaving the problem of zero-trade flows for a more focused discussion in Section 4.5.1.

Starting with the issue of *typology*, in the large majority of studies the dependent variable is usually a measure of bilateral merchandise trade.[20] Three choices of trade flow measures are available to the researcher for the dependent variable of a classical gravity equation on goods trade: export flows, import flows or average bilateral trade flows. The choice of which measure to select should be driven first and foremost by theoretical considerations which mostly imply privileging the use of unidirectional import or export data. Sometimes however, considerations linked to data availability or differences in the reliability between exports and imports data may prevail. For example, a common fix to poor data is to average bilateral trade flows in order to improve point estimates. This is done because averaging flows takes care of three potential problems simultaneously: systematic under reporting of trade flows by some countries, outliers and missing observations. Although there are better ways of dealing with those problems,[21] it is common practice to justify the use of this procedure using the above arguments. This notwithstanding, caution should be applied in averaging bilateral trade. First of all, averaging is not possible in those cases where the direction of the flow is an

[20]Nevertheless, gravity models have also been employed for examining the determinants of trade in goods and services, other than merchandise. The gravity model offers a high probability of a good fit, but what we mentioned for trade in merchandise is also true for all other left-hand side variables: there is no reliable gravity equation without a supporting theoretical model. If one wants to explore a gravity model on Foreign Direct Investments (FDI), it is better to have a theory to refer to (as in Carr et al. 2001; or in Baltagi et al. 2007). The need for a theory is even more compelling if one wants to account for the many alternative strategies that heterogeneous firms have at their disposal to serve foreign markets, i.e. trade and FDI (and even differentiating further between offshoring or joint-ventures).

[21]It is true that reliability of the data varies significantly from country to country. But if this corresponds to a national characteristic that is considered to be constant along time, the country-specific quality of the data can be controlled for, as any other time-invariant country characteristic or country fixed effects.

important piece of information. Second, if carried out wrongly, averaging leads to mistakes.

Average bilateral trade is constructed by averaging the exports of country i to country j with the exports of country j to country i. Since each trade flow is observed as exports by the origin nation and imports by the destination country and most countries do both import and export from the same trade partner, typically four values are averaged to get the undirected bilateral trade that then needs to be log-linearised:[22]

$$T_{ij} = \mathrm{E}(x_{ij}, x_{ji}, m_{ij}, m_{ji}) \tag{4.18}$$

A bias may arise if researchers employ the log of the sum of bilateral trade as the left-hand side variable instead of the sum of the logs. Many published studies in the field of trade analysis, including some very recently published works, carry this bias. The mistake will create no bias if bilateral trade is balanced. However, if nations in the treatment group (i.e. the countries exposed to the policy treatment which average effect is being estimated) tend to have larger than usual bilateral imbalances – this is the case for trade between EU countries and also for North-South trade – then the misspecification leads to an upward bias of the treatment variable. The point is that the log of the sum (wrong procedure) overestimates the sum of the log (correct procedure). This leads to an overestimated treatment variable, as shown in Baldwin and Taglioni (2006). At any rate, the mistake implies that the researcher is working with overestimated trade flows within the sample.

Turning to *conversion*, the first item listed at the beginning of the section, trade should enter the estimation in nominal terms and it should be expressed in a common *numeraire*. This stems from the fact that the gravity equation is a modified expenditure equation. Hence, trade data should not be deflated by a price index. Deflating trade flows by price indices not only is wrong on theoretical grounds but it also leads to empirical complications and likely shortcomings, due to the scant availability of appropriate deflators. It is practically impossible to get good price indices for bilateral trade flows, even at an aggregate level. Therefore, approximations may become additional sources of spurious or biased estimation. For example, if there is a correlation between the inappropriate trade deflator and any of the right-hand side variables (the trade policy measures of interest), the coefficient will be biased, unless the measures are orthogonal to the deflators used.

---

[22]In constructing average trade, the researcher should make sure that the observations are statistically independent. Hence, if the two trade partners import and export from each other caution should be taken to cluster the four single observations in one single data point. We will come back to the issue of independence latter on.

As far as accounting conventions are concerned, trade data can be recorded either Free On Board (FOB) or gross, i.e. augmented with the Cost of Insurance and Freight (CIF).[23] Using CIF data may lead to simultaneous equation biases, as the dependent variable includes costs that are correlated with the right hand side variables for distance and other trade costs. If FOB data are not available, "mirror techniques," matching FOB values reported by exporting countries to CIF values reported by importing countries, can be used. These techniques however, remain to a large extent unsatisfactory due to large measurement errors (Hummels and Lugovskyy 2006). Hence, the suggestion as to this point is to be aware of whether CIF or FOB data are being used and interpret the results accordingly. If moreover the researcher is constructing a multi-country dataset, she should care for choosing data that are uniform, i.e. either all CIF or all FOB, controlling for measurement errors.

4.4.2 Covariates

As indicated above, a well specified gravity equation should include the "un-constant" terms Ω_i and $P_j^{1-\sigma}$. While several attempts at explicitly accounting for these terms have been made, including by means of structural assumptions on the underlying model and the use of non-linear methods of estimations, the practice has increasingly moved towards the use of simple-to-use fixed effects for these terms. As discussed earlier, however, fixed effects methods sometimes cannot be applied due to problems of overparametrization and correlation with the variable of interest.

[23]Most common sources of trade data include the following. International Monetary Fund (IMF) DOT statistics (http://www2.imfstatistics.org/DOT/) provides bilateral goods trade flows in US dollar values, at annual and monthly frequency. UN Comtrade (http://comtrade.un.org/) provides bilateral goods trade flows in US dollar value and quantity, at annual frequency and broken down by commodities according to various classifications (BEC, HS, SITC) and up to a relatively disaggregated level (up to 5 digit disaggregation). The CEPII offers two datasets CHELEM (http://www.cepii.fr/anglaisgraph/bdd/chelem.htm) and BACI (http://www.cepii.fr/anglaisgraph/bdd/baci.htm) which use UN Comtrade data but fill gaps. corrects for data incongruencies and CIF/FOB issues by means of mirror statistics. WITS by the World Bank provides joint access to UN Comtrade and data tariff lines collected by the WTO and ITC. The most timely annual, quarterly and monthly data are available from the WTO Statistics Portal. Similarly, the CPB provides data for a subset of world countries at the monthly, quarterly and annual frequency as indices. Series for values, volumes and prices are provided along with series for industrial production. Finally, regional or national datasets provide usually more detail. Notable examples are the US and EUROSTAT (EU27) bilateral trade data available in values and quantities up to the 10 digit and 8 digit level of disaggregation respectively. Australia, New Zealand and USA also collect consistent CIF and FOB values at disaggregate levels of bilateral trade. Interesting is also the case of China, It is interesting to note that China, besides providing SITC classifications also provides data series for processing trade.

4.4.2.1 Fixed Effects Specifications

The advantage of using fixed effect specifications lies in the fact that they represent by far the simplest solution to testing a gravity equation: they allow using OLS econometrics and do not require imposing ad-hoc structural assumptions on the underlying model. Specifications that make use of fixed effects are also very parsimonious in data needs: they only require data for the dependent variable and good bilateral values to estimate trade friction ϕ_{ij}.

Some caution however should be applied when using fixed effects on panel data. Importer and exporter fixed effects should be time-varying, as they capture time varying features of the exporter and importer, as discussed in the theory section above. Similarly, if data are disaggregated by industry, country-industry specific time-varying fixed effects should be applied. With very large panels, this may lead to computational issues. Whatever the solution the researcher devises, it is a necessary condition to control for the omitted time-varying terms Ω_i and $P_j^{1-\sigma}$ and to avoid large biases on the estimates of the other explanatory variables. Therefore, if computational complications arise, the researcher is recommended to find a way to solve the computational issues rather than giving up on properly specifying fixed effects. One final note of caution is in order: the use of exporter and importer fixed effects is suitable only if the variable of interest is dyadic, i.e. for ϕ_{ij}. If by contrast, the latter is exporter or importer specific, exporter and importer specific variables should be introduced explicitly and other means of avoiding the omitted variables bias (i.e. of controlling for Ω_i and $P_j^{1-\sigma}$) should be devised. Finally, pair (exporter–importer) fixed effects can also be used, if appropriate and if their introduction does not generate problems of collinearity with other explanatory variables.

4.4.2.2 Attractors

In line with the theoretical specification, attractors should reflect expenditure in the country of destination and supply in the country of origin. GDP, GNP and Population are all measures that have been used as proxies of the above terms. Per capita GDP (Frankel 1997) and measures for infrastructural development (Limao and Venables 2001) have also been used. Again, the appropriate measure should be selected on the basis of theoretical considerations.[24] As in the case of the dependent variable, these measures should enter in nominal terms. At any rate, deflating them would have no impact if one includes time fixed effects, which would swipe them away.

Many studies, the large part of them in a cross-sectional setting, augment the gravity equation with variables that could ease trade relations. Sharing a common

[24]This is true not only for variables to be included but also for restrictions on coefficients. From (4.14) the coefficient of M_i and M_j must be constrained to be one (this is why Anderson and van Wincoop (2003) estimated the gravity equation using $\frac{X_{ij}}{M_i \cdot M_j}$ as the left-hand side variable). With heterogeneous firm, as in (4.17), this is not required.

language, common historical events – such as colonial links, common military alliances or co-membership in a political entity – common institutions or legal systems, common religion, common ethnicity or nationality (through migration), similar tastes and technology, and input–output linkages enhance international trade. Many of those issues are of interest *per se* and are worth to be explored. An example in point is Head et al. (2010) who, while examining the effect over time of the independence of post-colonial trade between the colonized country and the former colonizer, conclude that trade flows are associated to some sort of relational capital that deteriorates with time if it is not renewed. They do so by showing that on average there is little short-run effect of the change in colony-colonizer relationship on trade: the reduction takes place progressively, over time, but trade does not stop suddenly, even in cases of hostile separation.

The researcher should be aware that most attractors have in general very low time variability. For this reason the researcher should pay particular caution in introducing them in fixed effects specifications. Should a specific attractor represent the core of the analysis, a safer option would be to avoid fixed effects estimations. This can be done by introducing measures of the exporter's market openness Ω_i and importer's CES price index, $P_j^{1-\sigma}$ along with the trade partners' GDPs. However, exporter's market openness and, even more so, importer's CES price index are difficult to construct. Once more, case-by-case solutions may be needed in controllig for the omitted variable bias.[25]

4.4.2.3 Trade Frictions

Distance matters! As Waldo Tobler's first law of geography states: "Everything is related to everything else, but near things are more related than distant things." The question is: why? As we emphasized in the introduction, Tinbergen's idea is that physical distance is *a rough measure* of transportation or information costs about foreign markets - already too many things for one single rough (and robust!) measure. Econometric estimates of the constant elasticity of trade to distance range within an interval of -0.7 and -1.2 (Disdier and Head 2008) and distance appears to be very persistent over time (Brun et al. 2005).

In the early years of the empirical analysis on bilateral trade flows, many researchers focused on producing better approximations for trade distance than simple Euclidean distance between the two poles of economic attraction of the two trade partners (respective capitals, main city in term of population or local production, main port or airport). To do so, some choose to estimate wedges between CIF

[25]It is difficult to give further details here, as the solutions should be devised case by case, based on the nature of the data at hand and on the research question. Nevertheless, options include introducing fixed effects at a different frequency than the attractors (Ruiz and Villarubia 2008; De Benedictis and Vicarelli 2009; Cardamone 2011) or to only look at entries and exits in a different (policy) regimes as we have done in Section 4.2.1.

and FOB data. Others used great-circle or orthodromic formulas.[26] Nowadays, all most common distance measures across virtually all country pairs in the world are freely available online[27] or can be obtained from the applets of the most important geo-representations available on the web. The issue is therefore not anymore how to calculate physical distance between two countries in the most appropriate way, but how to interpret the distance coefficient and if distance has a linear effect on trade.

Starting from the second issue, there is no reason to believe that distance should be related to trade in a linear manner. Trade costs are much dependent on the characteristics of specific goods, such as fragility, perishability, size or weight. In aggregate terms, trade cost would be country specific, depending on country's remoteness and sectoral specialization. In the absence of hard theoretical priors it is better to be agnostic and let the data speak. This is what has been done by Henderson and Millimet (2008). Using nonparametric techniques they found that the linearity assumption was supported by the data. We interpret this result as being clear evidence of variable trade costs being linear in distance for the average country. But what about fixed costs?

From the literature on heterogeneous firms and trade we know that fixed costs affect only the extensive margin of trade (Chaney 2008). Lawless (2010), extends the strategy proposed by Bernard et al. (2007), and decomposes the dependent variable of the gravity equation (export flows to each different foreign market) into the number of firms exporting (the extensive margin) and average export sales per firm (the intensive margin). Although, the proxy chosen for the intensive margin is not ideal in representing firm heterogeneity in exports, Lawless shows that distance has a negative effect on both margins, but the magnitude of the effect is considerably larger and significant for the extensive margin. Furthermore, the variables capturing the fixed cost (i.e. language, internal orography, infrastructure and import barriers) work through the extensive margin. Even Tinbergen (1962), in formulating the gravity equation as in (4.1) distinguished between variable costs (distance) and fixed costs. He approximated fixed costs by the cost-reducing effect of the *adjacency* dummy. We are therefore back to square one to the question of what lies behind the distance coefficient.

Let's tackle this issue from a very general point of view. In modern econometric terms, the concept of *distance as a rough measure of trade costs* (broadly defined as every cost that generates a conditional wedge between domestic and foreign prices) can be translated in the presence of a measurement error in the distance variable.

---

[26]The great-circle, or orthodromic, formula is the formula used for calculating the distance between longitude-latitude coordinates of the polar city of two countries is based on the spherical law of cosines is: $\phi_{ij} = a\cos\left(\sin(lat_i)\cdot\sin(lat_j) + \cos(lat_i)\cdot\cos(lat_2)\cdot\cos(long_j - long_i)\right)\cdot R$; where $R = 6{,}371$ is the radius of the earth, in km.

[27]CEPII generated a positive externality for all researchers by making freely available their measures of distance (see http://www.cepii.fr/anglaisgraph/bdd/distances.htm). Jon Haveman, Vernon Henderson and Andrew Rose were pioneers in this matter. Haveman's collection of International Trade Data and his "Useful Gravity Model Data" can be freely downloaded from, the FREIT. database http://www.freit.org/TradeResources/TradeData.html#Gravity.

It is well known that a measurement error in an explanatory variable, such as ϕ_{ij}, does result in a bias in the OLS estimates of a_3 in (4.1).

Following on that, we can write the measured value of ϕ_{ij} as the sum of the true unobserved value of the trade cost ϕ_{ij}^{*} plus a measurement error e_{ij} that is an i.i.d. normally distributed random variable:

$$\phi_{ij} = \underbrace{\phi_{ij}^{*}}_{\text{true unobserved measure}} + \underbrace{e_{ij}}_{\text{classical measurement error}} . \qquad (4.19)$$

Consider now a simplified version of the gravity equation described in (1), where trade flows depend only on distance:

$$\ln X_{ij} = a_3\phi_{ij}^{*} + \varepsilon_{ij} = a_3\phi_{ij} + (\varepsilon_{ij} - a_3 e_{ij}). \qquad (4.20)$$

The presence of e_{ij} in the error term generates a mechanical correlation between the error term, $(\varepsilon_{ij} - a_3 \cdot e_{ij})$, and the explanatory variable $\phi_{ij} = \phi_{ij}^{*} + e_{ij}$. It can be shown (Wooldridge 2002, p. 75) that $\hat{a}_3$ converges in probability to a fraction $\frac{\text{var}(\phi_{ij}^{*})}{\text{var}(\phi_{ij}^{*})+\text{var}(e_{ij})} < 1$ of the true a_3. This bias is called attenuation bias, since $\hat{a}_3$ is biased towards zero, irrespectively of whether a_3 is positive or negative. The magnitude of the attenuation bias is linked to the so called *signal-to-noise ratio* since $\text{var}(\phi_{ij}^{*})$ is the variance of the correct signal while $\text{var}(e_{ij})$ is the variance of the noise. The larger the latter relative to the former, the larger is the magnitude of the attenuation bias, i.e. if half the variance of $\text{var}(\phi_{ij})$ is noise, the bias would be 50%.[28]

If the distance variable is measured with error, we should expect an attenuation bias in the relevant coefficient. There is a general consensus that the distance coefficient is instead too high and the fact that it is highly persistent and also increasing over time (Disdier and Head 2008) is at odds with the evidence reported by Hummels and Lugovskyy (2006) of a decreasing pattern in freight costs. Many have offered possible explanations; we will point out to a simple mechanical one. If the error-in-variable is not of the classical kind but is instead positively correlated with the distance variable ϕ_{ij}, the bias would tend to be positive and the magnitude would still depend on the signal-to-noise ratio.

Many authors have implicitly worked on the minimization of the signal-to-noise ratio, better defining the relevant meaning of "distance." Some worked along the lines of distance as a proxy for transport costs, and it is surprising to observe (Anderson and van Wincoop 2004) how little is known on transport costs and their different modes, their magnitude and evolution, and their determinants. Hummels and Skiba (2004) focus on the implications of differences in transport

[28]It is worth noting that in a multivariate regression we do not have such a clear and simple result, but the bias will also depend on the correlation between ϕ_{ij} (measured with error) and other covariates. The problem is even more serious with estimates in first-differences, whose aim is to eliminate a possibly omitted fixed effect (Griliches and Hausman 1986). The traditional solution is to find an instrument correlated with distance but not with the error term.

costs across goods on trade patterns, challenging the conventional Samulson's iceberg assumption that transport costs are linear in distance. They show that actual transport costs are much closer to being per unit than iceberg, and they derive clear implications for trade: imports from more distant locations will have disproportionately higher FOB prices. Harrigan (2010) separates air and surface transport costs. Using a Ricardian model with a continuum of goods which vary by weight and hence transport cost, he shows that comparative advantage depends on relative air and surface transport costs across countries and goods. He tests the implication that the US should import heavier goods from nearby countries, and lighter goods from faraway countries, using detailed data on US imports from 1990 to 2003. Looking across US imported goods, nearby exporters have lower market share in goods that the rest of the world ships by air. Looking across exporters for individual goods, distance from the US is associated with much higher import unit values. The effects are significant and economically relevant. Jacks et al. (2008) work in the opposite direction, deriving distance measures from a Anderson-van Wincoop type gravity equation,[29] and finding that the decline in this inherent measure of trade cost explain roughly 55 percent of the pre–World War I trade boom and 33 percent of the post–World War II trade boom, while the rise in that very measure explains the entire interwar trade bust. This stream of research requires a leap of faith on the data-generating process of the trade cost measure and the acceptance that trade costs are the trade empirics equivalent of the Solow's residual: a measure of our ignorance.

Others have worked on Tinbergen's idea that distance could be more than transport costs, moving from spatial distance to economic distance. In analogy with the inclusion of further attractors as explanatory variables, the gravity equation has been therefore augmented with many dyadic variables that could reduce trade (trade policy aside). These variables are mainly associated with a common history of conflict, and are generally found to be highly significant (Martin et al. 2008a, b).

The border between two nations is an equilibrium concept. It is the remaining evidence of the solution of a bargaining process concluding an international conflict and is the fossil of historical events. Since the seminal works of McCallum (1995) and Helliwell (1998), trade economists have wondered how borders could generate a home bias in consumption. Using data on interprovincial and international trade by Canadian provinces for the period 1988–1990, McCallum (1995) showed that, other things being equal, the estimated interprovincial trade was more than 20 times larger than trade between Canadian provinces and US states. The result was striking and largely unbelievable. Anderson and van Wincoop (2003), controlling for multilateral resistance, reduced the border effect by half. Wei (1996), developing a procedure to calculate a country's *trade with self* – a measure rarely reported by official statistics, and relevant on a theoretical basis (being part of the consumer expenditure) – obtained the same reduction for OECD countries and much more for European countries. His estimate of the ratio of imports from self to imports from

[29]See also Novy (2010) for a distance measure derived from heterogeneous firms trade models.

other European countries was 1.7. But he was not controlling for multilateral resistance and was using aggregate data. Disregarding the role of sectoral specialization would attenuate the border effect. Head and Mayer (2000) found that in 1985, Europeans purchased 14 times more from domestic producers (for the average industry) than from equally distant foreign ones. The border effect varies from sector to sector and is related more to consumer tastes than to trade barriers.

We would like to conclude this section on distance by mentioning that over the years, the gravity equation has been applied with great success also to issues which are only marginally related to the cost of physical distance. Blum and Goldfarb (2006) show that gravity holds even in the case of digital goods consumed over the Internet and that do not have trading costs. This implies that trade costs cannot be fully accounted by the effects of distance on trade.[30] Using bilateral Foreign Direct Investment (FDI) data, Daude and Stein (2007) find that differences in time zones have a negative and significant effect on the location of FDI. They also find a negative effect on trade, but this effect is smaller than that on FDI. Finally, the impact of the time zone effect has increased over time, suggesting that it is not likely to vanish with the introduction of new information technologies. Portes and Rey (2005) show that a gravity equation explains international transactions in financial assets at least as well as goods trade transactions. In their analysis, distance proxies some information costs, information transmission, an information asymmetry between domestic and foreign investors. Tinbergen would have been happy to know it, since he proposed information as a possible further explanation of the role of distance (Tinbergen 1962, p. 263). Guiso et al. (2009) go even further, finding that lower bilateral trust leads to less trade between two countries, less portfolio investment, and less FDI. The effect strengthens as more trust-intensive goods are exchanged.

4.4.2.4 Trade Policy

As we pointed out in the introduction, the original use of the gravity equation by Tinbergen was "to determine the normal or standard pattern of international trade that would prevail in the absence of trade impediments," which resulted in the evaluation of the effect of the British Commonwealth and of other FTA. The wider use of the gravity equation has still remained the same: the ex post evaluation of the trade-enhancing effect of preferential trade policy.

The mainstream approach to preferential trade policy evaluation still follows Tinbergen's original strategy, defining the presence of FTA or Custom Unions (CU) or any specific preferential trade policy regime [i.e. Generalised System of

---

[30]Blum and Goldfarb (2006) also show that Americans are more likely to visit websites from nearby countries, even controlling for language, income, and immigrant stock. For taste-dependent digital products, such as music, games, and pornography, a 1% increase in physical distance reduces website visits by 3.25%. On the contrary, for non-taste-dependent products, such as software, distance has no statistical effect.

Preferences (GSP), African, Caribbean and Pacific (ACP) Partnership, Everything But Arms (EBA), in the case of the European Union (EU)] with positive realization of a Bernoully process. In all these cases, as in Fig. 4.1, the trade effect of the preferential trade policy is the marginal effect of a dummy variable that takes the value of one if the preferential trade policy affects the imports of country *i* from country *j* (in sector *s* at time *t*). The advantage of this strategy is in the ease of implementation. The list of existing FTA, CU, or specific preferential trade policies is generally available online[31] and subsets are included in many datasets used and made available by experts in the field.[32] The disadvantages are that the dummy identification for policy measures implies that all countries included in a treated group are assumed to be subject to the same dose of treatment, which may be correct in the case of non discriminatory policy (e.g. the Most Favored Nation (MFN) clause of the GATT/WTO agreement) but which is false in the case of non reciprocal preferential agreements. In addition, the treatment gets confounded with any other event that is specific to the country-pair and contemporaneous to the treatment (De Benedictis and Vicarelli 2009). Moreover, questions related to the effect of a gradual liberalization in trade policies cannot be answered using dummies, and the trade elasticity to trade policy changes cannot be estimated. Since this is the most common event (trade policy *non facit saltus*, at least not all the times shifts from zero to one) the use of a dummy for preferential trade policy can be a relevant shortcoming.

An alternative exists, and it is largely explored in this volume. It consists in switching from a dummies strategy to a continuous variables strategy, quantifying the preferential margin that the preferential agreement guarantees. This alternative strategy has been fruitfully used by Francois et al. (2006), Cardamone (2007) and Cipollina and Salvatici (2010). It opens an interesting research agenda and also offers some methodological challenges and some puzzling results.[33] These issues are discussed at length in Chapter 3.

Some issues are however worth discussing also in this context. The first is related to the choice of the dependent variable and its consequences. Generally, the stream of literature adopting a dummy strategy focuses on aggregate effects, uses aggregated data, while all papers adopting the alternative strategy of preferential margins

[31] The WTO collects all Trade Agreements that have either been notified, or for which an early announcement has been made, to the WTO (http://rtais.wto.org/UI/PublicMaintainRTAHome.aspx). The World Bank – Dartmouth College Tuck Trade Agreements Database can also be consulted at http://www.dartmouth.edu/~tradedb/trade_database.html.

[32] Andrew Rose's homepage (http://faculty.haas.berkeley.edu/arose/RecRes.htm) is a great example of data sharing. It has encouraged new research and promoted the good practice of replicability in empirical research.

[33] Francois et al. (2006) estimate of the trade policy elasticity has a huge variance and also include some *negative* cases. This result is by no means exclusive to this stream of literature. Also some dummy strategy papers find negative coefficients to preferential dummies (Martínez-Zarzoso et al. 2009).

variables focus on disaggregated data on trade.[34] This alternative strategy expands the panel data along the sectoral dimension, and is therefore more demanding in terms of specific knowledge required, data mining, accuracy in the derivation of the preferential margin,[35] and caution in the aggregation of tariff/products lines, from high level of product disaggregation (often at the 8th or even higher number of digits) to more aggregated data. Inaccurate aggregation could lead to a serious bias. But if precautions are taken on all the complications implicit in this approach, the higher level of information would increase the chance of more precise estimation of causal effect of trade policy. This is currently the most challenging problem of this literature.

The second issue is related to the exogeneity of trade policy. Baier and Bergstrand (2004, 2007) convincingly argue that the chance that the trade policy variable could be highly correlated with the error term is not irrelevant. The possible reverse causation between trade and trade policy could generate an endogeneity bias in the OLS estimates due to self-selection.[36] The same can happen if trade policy is measured with error (as certainly is in the dummy strategy case) or if it does not include relevant missing components (non-tariff barriers) that will end up in the error term. All this calls for an instrumental variable approach. And this is true for both the dummy and preferential margin strategies.

As suggested by Baier and Bergstrand (2007) and others, a possible solution to the omitted variable bias is the use of panel data techniques, that allow to control for time-varying unobserved country heterogeneity, and time-invariant country-pair unobserved characteristics. When instruments are rare this can be a proficuous alternative. On the other hand, the selection bias can be controlled for using a Heckman correction (Helpman et al. 2008; Martínez-Zarzoso et al. 2009).

We would like to conclude this section with a short mention of the role of counterfactuals and control groups in trade policy evaluation. While there is widespread consensus on the relevance of the modern literature on program evaluation (Imbens and Wooldridge 2009), its application to trade policy issues is still rare. Since the gravity equation appears to be appropriate to estimate the causal effect on trade volumes of an average trade policy treatment, some effort should be devoted to the appropriate definition of the treatment (especially in the case of preferential margin), the timing of the treatment, the suitable control group, the counterfactual and the share of the population affected by the treatment when an instrumental variable method is used to estimate average causal effects of the

[34]See Chapter 5 of this volume for a Meta Analysis of the literature on EU preferential trade policy.

[35]See Chapter 3 of this volume. Chapter 10 also shows that the different formula adopted to derive the preferential margins matter significantly for the assessment of the existence and extent of preference erosion for developing countries.

[36]It is difficult to argue that countries enter a preferential agreement at random. Whereas it is hard to observe the original motives that lead to the signing of the agreement, it is reasonable that those motives could be correlated with trade volumes. This gives rise to the selection bias. In particular, the estimated trade policy coefficient will be upward biased if the omitted variables guiding the selection and the trade policy variable are positively correlated.

treatment. Propensity score matching estimators have been used by Persson (2001) and, showing that, in both cases, the relevant policy coefficient is substantially reduced. This literature is still in an embryonic phase, and the one explored by Millimet and Tchernis (2009) through propensity score is by no means the only possible weighting scheme to apply to the gravity equation (Angrist and Pischke 2008). Future research along these lines is required, and from a policy point of view, any step from the analysis of the average treatment effect towards the identification of heterogeneous treatment effects among the countries in the treatment group has to be encouraged.

4.5 "New" Problems and New Solutions

Having described the main components of the gravity equation, there are still some issues – potentially problematic – that deserve mention before bringing this chapter to a close. Some of these issues are well known, others are less so. The literature offers some possible solutions, some of which are firmly established, others are still under debate. We list them for the sake of the reader that wants to explore them further.

4.5.1 The Zero Problem and the Choice of the Estimator

One well recognized problem in empirical trade is that trade datasets often contain zeroes: the cross-country trade matrix is sparse. The conceptual reason why this is the case is exposed at length in Section 4.3. From an empirical point of view, the number of zeroes in the matrix increases with the increase in the level of disaggregation of the data and with the inclusion of smaller and poorer countries. At the aggregate country level, for the year 2000, only about 50 percent of the trade cells had a positive entry. The traditional *log–log* form of the gravity equation calls for particular caution in dealing with zeroes. Since it is not possible to raise a number to any power and end up with zero, the log of zero is undefined, and zero-trade flows cannot be treated with logarithmic specifications. At the same time, they need to be dealt with since they are non-randomly distributed. They indicate absence of trade, hence suggesting that barriers to trade are prohibitive to allow a particular trade relationship to take place at a given demand and supply.

What to do with the zeroes? A number of methods have been explored and proposed by the literature. Here we provide a summary of the most popular of these methods. A first possibility is to ignore the zeroes. However, this would be acceptable only if zeros were the result of an approximation of small trade flows. In this case, the zero-value has no specific meaning and is not a symptom of a self-selection process, as in the presence of distortions due to heterogeneity in exports. By contrast, if the zeros are a sign of selection, a second solution is available to the researcher: to replace them with a very small positive trade flow, i.e. replace all observations in the data-series by $x_{ij} + 1$. However, this apparently innocuous procedure leads to an inconsistent estimator. Third, assuming that the problem is not of selection but truncation (censored data), the Tobit estimator may be used, provided that the truncation value is known. If this is not the case, the inconsistency of the estimator cannot be avoided. Finally, one can control for the selection bias by means of a Heckman procedure. Indeed, the most popular way to correct for the selection bias is the Heckman 2-stages least squared estimation that introduces in the specification the inverse of the so-called Mills ratio (Heckman 1979).[37] However, in order to do so one needs variables that may explain the selection (zero or positive trade) but not the value of traded good, when this is positive. The exclusion restriction is crucially relevant in this case, and if the variable included in the selection equation also affects the outcome variable, it can lead to the researcher preferring simple OLS to the Heckman procedure (Puhani 2000). Helpman et al. (2008) for example, propose as selection variable the use of the regulation cost of firm's entry. This is a variable collected and analysed by Djankov et al. (2002). This choice is theory-driven, since, as aforementioned the fixed cost of entry only affects the extensive margin of trade under models of firm heterogeneity. Unfortunately, due to the limited data coverage, the costs in terms of sample size reduction are heavy. Hence, even Helpman et al. (2008) in their main results opt for an alternative measure: common religion. The problem with this choice however is that, from previous analyses we know that this type of attractor affects both the extensive and the intensive margin, so that the exclusion condition is violated. In conclusion, the question of the most appropriate selection variable is still open and more research on the topic is needed.

The evidence on the non-triviality of zero-trade flows in data and the growing importance of micro-foundations based on international trade models with firm heterogeneity have pushed researchers to seek solutions. Given the inability of log-linear models to efficiently account for zeroes, the emphasis has moved from OLS estimators to non-linear estimators. In an influential paper, Santos-Silva and Tenreyro (2006) propose an easy-to-implement strategy to deal with the inconsistency occurring when the gravity equation is estimated with OLS using a *log–log* functional form, in the presence of heteroskedasticity and zero trade flows. When the cross-country trade matrix is sparse, the assumption in (4.1) of a (log) normally distributed error term ε_{ij} is violated. In such cases, Santos-Silva and Tenreyro recommend the use of a Poisson Pseudo Maximum-Likelihood (PPML) estimator, using a log-linear function instead of log–log one. A sequel of contributions centered on the relative performance of different nonlinear estimators has followed. The econometric literature on count data (Cameron and Trivedi 2005), applied to non-negative integer values, offers different Poisson-family alternatives to PPML (Burger et al. 2009). How to choose among them is not always straightforward and

[37]The inverse Mills ratio, named after the statistician John Mills, is the ratio of the probability density function over the cumulative distribution function of a distribution.

the practitioner should always be guided by the structure of the data, the level of overdispersion and the assumptions she is willing to impose on the data. As an example, the Poisson model imposes some conditions on the moments of the distribution assuming equidispersion: the conditional variance of the dependent variable should be equal to its conditional mean (and equal to the mean occurrence rate). This is often a too strong assumption, mostly because it is equivalent to say that the occurrence of an event in one period of time (a zero in the trade flow matrix) is independent of its occurrence in the previous period. Is this reasonable?

If the data is characterized by overdispersion, it is possible to correct for between-subject heterogeneity using a Negative Binomial Regression Model (NBPML). NBPML is essentially a Poisson model with the same expected value of the dependent variable as before, but with a variance that takes the form of an additive (quadratic) function of both the conditional mean and a dispersion parameter capturing unobserved heterogeneity. Therefore, not correcting for overdispersion will still lead to consistent estimates of the dependent variable but to a downward bias in the standard errors of the variables of interest. By using NBPML and allowing the dispersion parameter to be different from zero, one can obtain correct standard errors and can properly test if a NBPML estimator is to be preferred to a PPML estimator.[38]

When the number of zeroes is much greater than what is predicted by a Poisson or Negative Binomial distribution (as it is often the case with disaggregated data) it is possible to rely on Zero-Inflated Poisson Model (ZIPPML) or Zero-Inflated Negative Binominal Model (ZINBPML). Both models assume that excess of zeros in the data is generated by a double-process (as in hurdle models), a count process (as in PPML and NBPML) supplemented by a binary process. If the binary process takes a value of zero then the dependent variable assumes a value zero. If the binary process takes a value one then the dependent variable takes count values 0, 1, 2, ... coming from a Poisson density or a negative binomial density. In both cases zeroes occur in two ways: as a realization of the binary process and as a realization of the count process when the binary random variable takes a value of one.

This choice is not harmless because the estimate of the first moment of the distribution changes between PPML and ZIPPML (as for the negative binomial case). The issue leads to a problem of inconsistency on top of the problem of efficiency. Using a count regression when the zero-inflated model is the correct specification implies a misspecification, which will lead to inconsistent estimates.

Opting for a ZIPPML or a ZINBPML estimation offers some advantages since it allows to study separately the probability of trade to take place, from the volume of trade, giving insights both into the intensive and the extensive margin of trade. At the same time, the two-part modeling, because of the form of the conditional mean specification, makes the calculation of marginal effects more complex.

---

[38] Cameron and Trivedi (2005 p. 676) suggest using a likelihood ratio test on the dispersion parameter to test whether it is equivalent to use a NBPML or a PPML estimator.

To conclude, the literature offers two main strategies to deal with the zeroes problem: a Heckman two-step procedure (controlling for heteroskedasticity) or count data (two-part) modeling. Both strategies need to take seriously the exclusion restriction. In both cases the researcher should pose herself a simple and difficult question: where are all those zeros coming from? Answering convincingly (Cipollina et al. 2010) is the prelude of a correct estimation strategy.

4.5.2 Dynamics

Dynamics is largely a missing piece in the gravity model story. Since Tinbergen (1962, p. 263) "... no attention is paid to the development of exports over time." By and large, this candid admission is still the norm (Eichengreen and Irwin (1995) are an exception). However, there are at least two good reasons to take dynamics into consideration. The first one is a direct consequence of deriving the gravity equation from a micro-founded trade model with heterogeneous firms. As shown in (4.17), if the decision of the firm to sell its products abroad (intensive margin) depends on the firm's ability to cover the sunk cost of entry in the foreign market, it would imply that the firm's decision today will be dependent on its past decisions. Therefore, the export process should be autoregressive. To put it differently, trade models with firm heterogeneity tell us that trade is essentially an entry and exit story. Firms enter and exit from the international markets as a consequence of a selection process on productivity, a learning mechanism, and according to the nature of exogenous shocks on the cost of distance. Some promising attempts (Costantini and Melitz 2008) are already underway.

The second reason is in the empirical counterpart of this proposition. Bun and Klaassen (2002), De Benedictis and Vicarelli (2005) and Fidrmuc (2009) all find strong persistence in aggregate trade data, and countries that trade with each other at time $t-1$ also tend to trade at time t. This evidence has also been reframed by Felbermayr and Kohler (2006) and Helpman et al. (2008, p. 443) that emphasised that "... the rapid growth of world trade from 1970 to 1997 was predominantly due to the growth of the volume of trade among countries that traded with each other in 1970 (the intensive margin) rather than due to the expansion of trade among new trade partners (the extensive margin)."

The introduction of dynamics in a gravity panel setting raises serious econometric problems due to the inconsistency of the estimators generally used in static panel data. If country specific effects are unobserved, the inclusion of the lagged dependent variable on the right-hand side of the equation leads to correlation between the lagged dependent variable and the error term that makes least square estimators biased and inconsistent.[39]

---

[39]See De Benedictis and Vicarelli (2005) for a discussion of the issue in the context of the gravity model.

Dynamic panel data models offer different options to the practitioner (Matyas and Sevestre 2007). The ones explored so far are the Blundell-Bond system GMM estimator (De Benedictis and Vicarelli 2005; De Benedictis et al. 2005) and the full set of panel cointegration estimators (i.e. the Fully Modified OLS estimator or the Dynamic OLS) that control for the endogeneity of dependent variables (Fidrmuc 2009). Both kind of contributions are exploratory in nature, and much more can be done along these lines of research.

4.5.3 Interdependence and Networks

The last topic we want to raise in these pages is interdependence. Anderson and van Wincoop (2003) have clearly made the case that the role played by the multilateral dimension of trade in the analysis of bilateral trade flows should not be disregarded, due to both theoretical and empirical reasons. Empirically, it was already mentioned in Section 4.4.2.1 that Multilateral Resistance is controlled for by means of (time-varying) country fixed effects. This simple procedure is correct, but it has often diverted the attention of the empirical researcher from two related issues. First, the fact that country i and country j are not independent. Second, the role of the third-country in the choices of i and j, where the notion of the third-country can be extended to the complete structure of trade links in which i and j are involved.

Dealing with the first issue, we know from disciplines that make frequent use of relational data, such as sociology and psychology, that dyadic observations typically violate the assumption of independence of observations, i.e. i and j should be considered as being part of a group g. This implies that we cannot rely anymore, as in (4.1) on the assumption of an i.i.d. stochastic term ε_{ij} (Lindgren 2010).

The traditional robust standard errors procedure is not sufficient to correct the error structure and may lead to biased estimated errors and erroneous statistical inference. Recent work by Cameron et al. (2010) shows that the appropriate way to control for such interdependence is to consider the potential correlation within group g in the covariance matrix, clustering the errors around g. This practice has now become more frequent, and many recent empirical estimates of the gravity equation report standard errors clustered at the country-pair level. This implies that, when a cluster is identified, standard errors need to be clustered. Indeed, it is not sufficient to include in the regression a fixed-effect parameter for each cluster a country-pair dummy since the fixed-effect centers each cluster's residual around zero but it does not affect the intra-cluster correlation of errors.

While the concept is relatively simple to grasp, the practice is more complicated. In the gravity equation there may be several choices for clustering. As for more general cases, in a panel data framework each single country can be considered as a cluster along the time dimension. Therefore, we shall cluster the errors by i if we believe that countries have a memory of their past decisions and project it onto the future. Moreover, if the two countries belong to the same preferential trade agreement V_{ij} we shall cluster by it as well. When average trade flows are used, as in eq. 4.18, exports of country i to country j are not anymore independent from exports of country j to country i. Hence, the two observation must be clustered in one single data point. If a hierarchical structure exists, we can nest the level of clustering choosing the most aggregate level. The caveat to keep in mind is that the number of clusters should be sufficiently large and sufficiently balanced. Researchers are therefore invited to use two-way or multi-way clustering, clearly discussing the adopted clustering structure instead of leaving the clustering procedure as a side note to the summary table of regression's results.

As far as the role of the third-country in the choices of i and j is concerned, their relevance has been widely recognized in trade theory, but only recently the empirical literature (see Baier and Bergstrand 2004 and Magee 2003, 2008 on FTA) has started considering how to include interdependence in the analysis. Baltagi, Egger and Pfaffermayr (2008) use a spatial lag panel data model to estimate the effect of regional trade agreements on inward FDI from Western European countries. They use the spatial weighting matrix to capture interdependence in a panel setting. The inclusion of this matrix is crucial for their results. First of all, they find spatial correlation in the data, leading to transmission effects of the 1990s preferential trade liberalization between the European Union and the Central and Eastern European Countries (CEEC). They find that the so-called Europe Agreements had a negative impact on Western Europe inward FDI, both in 1995 (when four agreements were ratified) and in 1999 (when only a single was ratified). At the same time, the CEEC experienced on average the strongest positive effects. Finally, they also find that the negative effects on FDI flowing into Western Europe is largely offset by the positive effects on FDI going to Central and Eastern European countries. This empirical work clearly shows that the analysis of the third-country effect is crucial in determining the relocation of FDI from Western European host countries to Eastern European host countries flowing from the Europe Agreements.

Both Egger and Larch (2008) and Chen and Joshi (2010) focus on the formation of an FTA given the existence of previous FTA. The general prediction of the three-country oligopolistic model of Chen and Joshi is that the role played by third countries is fundamental in understanding the formation of FTA. Just to give an example: if country i has an FTA with country j, but a third country, say k does not, country i and country k are more likely to establish an FTA when country i has a sufficiently large market size and high marginal cost of production relative to country j and the transport cost between the two is relatively low. This proposition is confirmed by the data on 78 countries between 1991 and 2005. The contribution by Chen and Joshi opens a promising research agenda on the role of third-country effects in trade policy, but the empirical analysis should be confirmed after a proper clustering of the error structure.

The relevant role played by the third-country in shaping the decision of country i and country j put in to question the fact that the role of countries interdependence could be relegated to the inclusion of the Multilateral Resistance term in the gravity equation.

In (4.10), Ω_i represents the average of all importers market demand – weighted by trade costs, while firms competition in market j is factored in via the price index P_j, which is also an average value. Therefore the Multilateral Resistance term includes in the gravity equation the *average* third-country effect. Which is perfectly sound from a modeling perspective, given the strong symmetry at the sectoral and country level assumed in the gravity model. On the other hand, the strong asymmetry revealed by the data cast some doubts on the fact that the average third-country effect should be a sufficient statistic to capture complex interdependence. Along these lines, De Benedictis and Tajoli (2010) generalise the third-country effect using network analysis (Jackson 2008). They focus on the interconnected structure of trade flows describing the changing topological property of the world trade network along time. They further focus on the extensive margin of trade, considering trade flows as a binary variable that takes the value 1 when trade occurs, and zero otherwise. They also calculate some network statistics to measure the level of interconnection of each country and the level of relative centrality of a country with respect to the whole trade network. The inclusion of these statistics in a gravity equation turns out to be significant with a positive and economically relevant coefficient, even when the standard errors were bootstrapped to take into account the correlation in the error structure (Davison and Hinkley 1997). This approach to interdependence in trade relations is in its infancy, and it may be fruitful to delve into the full implications of the multilateral dimension of the gravity model.

4.6 Conclusions

This chapter has shown how the 50-year long progress in the research agenda on gravity equation revolves around issues that were already raised in Tinbergen's original formulation of the relationship. The numerous empirical and theoretical contributions however, have allowed over the years to bring new, more efficient solutions to the old problems and to generate consensus around some new key issues. For example, it is now widely accepted that nominal variables should be used. Similarly panel estimations are to be preferred to cross-section estimates in most cases and fixed effects should be selected not blindly but with a view at how to best isolate developments in the variable of interest. Moreover, it is now widely accepted that distance is only an imperfect proxy for trade costs, that its effect on the extensive and intensive margin of trade differs from each other and that zero values contain information that should not be neglected.

Despite the fact that the state of the art on gravity equation has become very sophisticated, there are still many areas where further research is warranted. The analysis of gravity models on firm data is a promising avenue of research, as shown among others by Bernard et al. (2007). The changing nature of trade relationships calls for a re-evaluation of gravity specifications in particular contexts. For example, Baldwin and Taglioni (2010) show that the gravity equation breaks down when trade in parts and components is important. Structural estimations of gravity are also becoming very popular. Egger et al. (2010) and Anderson and Yotov (2010) are two important examples of this promising literature. Finally the increasing widespread availability of data is making quasi-natural experiments more common also in the evaluation of trade impediments (Feyrer 2009).

All the progress made from Tinbergen on to clarify the mysterious fitting power of the gravity equation is now at the disposal of a new generation of correlation hunters, wishing to move towards a better causal evaluation of trade enhancing policies.

Acknowledgments This essay has been written while Luca De Benedictis was visiting ARE at the University of California, Berkeley and EIEF in Rome. He gratefully acknowledges UCB and EIEF for the great hospitality. Luca De Benedictis also acknowledges the financial support received by the Italian Ministry of Education, University and Research (Scientific Research Program of National Relevance 2007 on "European Union policies, economic and trade integration processes and WTO negotiations" – PUE & PIEC). We are grateful to Davide Castellani, Michele Di Maio, Lucia Tajoli, Claudio Vicarelli and especially Luca Salvatici for the comments and the many conversations on the topic. Any remaining errors are solely our responsibility.

Chapter 5
Trade Impact of European Union Preferential Policies: A Meta-Analysis of the Literature

Maria Cipollina and Filomena Pietrovito

Abstract The gravity model is used frequently to estimate the impact of European Union (EU) Preferential Trade Agreements (PTA) on trade flows. Because of differences in the datasets, sample sizes and independent variables employed, existing studies report very different estimates. This chapter reviews and analyses a large number of results using Meta-Analysis (MA) to provide pooled estimates of the effect of PTA on bilateral trade, based on fixed and random effects models. We test the estimation results for sensitivity to alternative specifications and different control variables. After filtering out potential biases, the MA confirms our expectations of a robust and positive effect of PTA.

5.1 Introduction

It is generally assumed that Preferential Trade Agreements (PTA) have a positive effect on trade for the between countries or groups of countries involved. However, there is no clear empirical evidence of this effect on trade growth. This chapter reviews a range of empirical studies using the gravity model approach to estimate the impact of European Union (EU) PTA on trade.[1] Methodologically, we focus on those papers that estimate standard gravity equations, augmented by PTA as dependent variable:

$$\ln T_{EU,c} = \beta_0 + \beta_1 \ln(Y_{EU}) + \beta_2 \ln(Y_c) + \beta_3 \ln(Dist_{EU,c}) + \beta_4 X_{EU,c} + \gamma PTA_{EU,c} + \varepsilon_{EU,c} \tag{5.1}$$

[1]Comprehensive surveys are provided by Nielsen (2003) and Cardamone (2007). Our approach complements these qualitative analyses with a more fine-granted quantitative synthesis. The use of MA has increased in economics; Cipollina and Salvatici (2010b) provide an MA of the literature on the impact of reciprocal trade agreements on trade flows between partners.

M. Cipollina and F. Pietrovito
Department of Economics, Management and Social Sciences, University of Molise, Via Francesco de Sanctis, 86100 Campobasso, Italy
e-mail: cipollina@unimol.it; filomena.pietrovito@unimol.it

L. De Benedictis and L. Salvatici (eds.), *The Trade Impact of European Union Preferential Policies*, DOI 10.1007/978-3-642-16564-1_5,

where EU denotes an EU member, $T_{EU,c}$ is the trade flow between the EU and country c; $Y_{EU(c)}$ is the gross domestic product (GDP of the EU or country c; $Dist_{EU,c}$ is the distance between the EU and country c; $PTA_{EU,c}$ is a variable for the existence of a PTA between the EU and country c; $X_{EU,c}$ are control variables; and $\varepsilon_{EU,c}$ is the error term.

The impact of PTA on trade can be measured in different ways depending on how PTA are measured. Employing Meta-Analysis (MA) allows us to distinguish among studies using a dummy variable for PTA, and quantitative indicators to measure PTA between countries. Most of the studies in our sample use a dummy variable for PTA which is equal to 1 if there is a preferential arrangement between EU and the country in question (Oguledo and MacPhee 1994; Nilsson 2002; Péridy 2005; Caporale et al. 2009; Martínez-Zarzoso et al. 2009). However, as Cardamone (2007, 2011) highlights, using a dummy to capture the impact of PTA on trade is not adequate because: (1) it captures all the other factors that are specific to the country-pair and contemporaneous with the PTA; (2) it does not discriminate among the instruments adopted for preferential trade policy; and (3) it does not indicate the level of the trade preferences. The only published studies that do not use this dummy are Francois et al. (2006) and Cipollina and Salvatici (2010a), which compute preferential margins, and Manchin (2006) which uses the potential value of the preferential scheme had all eligible trade received preferential treatment. Several working papers also focus on explicit measures of PTA (Cardamone 2011; Demaria 2009; Nilsson and Matsson 2009; Aiello and Cardamone 2010; Aiello and Demaria 2009; Cipollina et al. 2010).

Most work that employs a dummy variable conducts empirical analysis on aggregate data, while papers that employ quantitative variables focus on disaggregated data on trade. Most published studies using dummy variables and aggregated data confirm the role of preferences in fostering trade, based on highly significant positive coefficients ranging between 1% and over 400%. However, some also find significant negative coefficients, implying a decline in trade of between 3% and over 50% (Nilsson 2002; Martínez-Zarzoso et al. 2009). The literature that employs quantitative variables for preferential policies and disaggregated data find elasticity coefficients of between 0.004 and 15.9, i.e., an increase of 10% in preferences determines an increase in trade of between 0.04 and 159%. An exception here is Francois et al. (2006) study which also shows some negative coefficients.

It is difficult to define the impact of the EU Generalized System of Preferences (GSP) scheme, estimated at the aggregate level, since in the studies reviewed, the dummy coefficients range between 1 and 290% (Oguledo and MacPhee 1994; Nilsson 2002). Also, Nilsson (2002) finds a significant negative effect of the GSP ranging between 3 and 50%. The impact of the GSP-Plus scheme on trade, which has been analysed in a few unpublished papers (Demaria 2009; Aiello and Demaria 2009), has been shown to be both positive and negative over the period 2001–2004. Martínez-Zarzoso et al. (2009) find mixed effects of the Euro-Mediterranean Partnership (Euro-Med) on exports to the EU, depending on specification and the sample. Other unpublished works find that the Everything But Arms (EBA) initiative and the Euro-Med scheme boost Least Developed Countries (LDC) exports

(Demaria 2009; Aiello and Cardamone 2010; Aiello and Demaria 2009) and exports from Mediterranean countries (Demaria 2009; Nilsson and Matsson 2009; Aiello and Demaria 2009) quite considerably, although some specifications report highly negative coefficients for both schemes. Positive results have been obtained for the African, Caribbean, and Pacific (ACP) countries, with elasticity coefficients ranging between 0.04 and 0.18 (Francois et al. 2006; Manchin 2006).

Finally, several studies that do not distinguish among agreements analyse the impact of PTA on trade generally, and find positive coefficients of the dummy variables for preferences ranging between 2% and over 400% (Nilsson 2002; Péridy 2005; Caporale et al. 2009), while Cipollina and Salvatici (2010a) estimate preference elasticities for different sectors ranging between 4 and 16.

Some authors focus on specific products and/or sectors, using highly disaggregated data. For example, Cardamone (2011) find that the GSP scheme seems to be effective in increasing exports of apples and mandarin oranges to the EU, while the Cotonou agreement seems to positive affect EU imports of fresh grapes and mandarin oranges from LDC. Regional trade agreements seem to increase EU imports of all fruits except oranges. Cipollina and Salvatici (2010a) find that the largest coefficients of the impact of PTA on trade are for the tropical products, beverages and tobacco sectors.

It can be seen that these results vary very widely: estimates for $\hat{\gamma}$, the coefficient of the variable for PTA, show huge variation across studies and some rather worrying differences in the rankings of PTA. It is not possible, therefore, just to summarize the results of this large literature in order to assess the impact of PTA on trade.

In order to analyse all the trade effects highlighted in the literature we apply MA.[2] It is a useful technique for evaluating the empirical results from different studies (Rose and Stanley 2005). The central concern in MA is to test the null hypothesis that different point estimates, treated as individual observations i of the jth study ($\hat{\gamma}_{ji}$), are equal to zero when all the findings in the particular area of research are combined.

In Sect. 5.2, we describe how the sample was constructed and present the MA regression and explanatory variables. Section 5.3 provides some comments on the main results and Sect. 5.4 outlines our conclusions.

5.2 Meta-Analysis Model

5.2.1 Meta-Analysis Sample

Evaluating and combining empirical results risks analysis of different outcome variables and different explanatory variables (the "apples and oranges problem"

[2]Empirical economic studies are using MA methods increasingly, in different fields of economic research. A Special Issue of the *Journal of Economic Surveys* (2005, Vol.19, No. 3) was dedicated to MA.

referred to in Glass et al. 1981). Thus, the first step in MA, which consists of constructing a database, is the most important. For the analysis in this chapter, we select only papers written in English, via an extensive search in Google Scholar and the EconLit, Web of Science and Scopus databases. The Google Scholar search produced papers published in academic journals as well as working papers and unpublished studies. EconLit provides coverage of the economics literature since 1969, and includes 750 journals. The Web of Science provides access to current and retrospective multidisciplinary information from approximately 8,700 of the most prestigious, international, high impact research journals (199 journals in the field of economics), covering 1992–2010. Scopus includes the abstracts and references for 15,000 peer-reviewed journals from more than 4,000 international publishers, which ensures broad interdisciplinary coverage. We also traced some specific papers that other work cross-referenced. We searched on the keywords "preferential trade agreements," "gravity equation" and "gravity model" in the title, abstract or text. These identified papers dealing with PTA, and papers that use a gravity approach. From the first group we selected papers analysing PTA and focusing on trade flows to the EU; in the second group, we selected those studies that had PTA as a key explanatory variable in the gravity equation.

Our final sample includes 36 papers (10 published in an academic journal and 26 working papers or unpublished studies), providing 638 point estimates based on a dummy variable for PTA and 388 point estimates based on quantitative variables for PTA, that is, the coefficient γ in (5.1) (see Table 5.1 for details).

Table 5.2 presents the structure of the dataset for our MA. It accounts for number of estimates of the impact of preferential schemes on sectoral trade, and total trade. For each group we distinguish the number of the estimated coefficients of the trade policy dummies and the measures for preference margins. Studies that focus on sectoral trade mostly provide estimates of the preference effect using an explicit measure of the margin for specific agreements, while studies that estimate the preference impact on total trade use dummy variables as a proxy for trade policy.

The estimates provide information that allows us to test the sensitivity of our to alternative specifications and differences in the control variables considered, and the impact of the publication selection process. We provide pooled estimates, obtained from fixed and random effects models of the size of the PTA effect on EU imports. The hypothesis that PTA have no effect on trade is rejected robustly at standard levels of significance.

5.2.2 *Meta-Regression Analysis*

Several of the sample in our study provide multiple estimates of the effect under consideration. Pooling different estimates to provide a large sample for MA raises questions about within-study versus between-study heterogeneity. To take account of this we employ fixed and random effects models: the former assumes that differences across studies are due only to within-variation; the latter considers

Table 5.1 Papers included in the Meta-Analysis

Authors and references	No. of estimates	Mean	Min	Max
Published studies using dummy variable				
Agostino M, Demaria F, Trivieri F (2010). J. of Agricultural Economics 61	27	0.19	−0.30	0.80
Caporale GM, Rault C, Sova R, Sova A (2009). Rev. of World Economy 145	7	0.21	0.67	15.9
De Benedictis L, De Santis R, Vicarelli C (2005). The European J. of Comparative Economics 2	1	0.11	−0.48	0.68
Martínez-Zarzoso I, Nowak-Lehmann DF, Horsewood N (2009). North Ame. J. of Econ. and Finance 20	14	0.02	−0.68	1.68
Nilsson L (2002). Appl. Economics 34	142	0.25	1.37	1.37
Oguledo VI, MacPhee CR (1994). Appl. Economics 26	1	1.37	0.12	1.65
Péridy N (2005). J. of Asian Economics 16	6	0.5	0.12	1.65
Published studies using preference margins				
Cipollina M, Salvatici L (2010a). J. of Econ. Policy Reform 13	10	5.32	−1.40	0.18
Francois J, Hoekman B, Manchin M (2006). The World Bank Econ. Rev. 20	4	−0.53	0.00	0.12
Manchin M (2006). The World Economy 29	28	0.05	−0.35	0.30
Working papers and unpublished studies using dummy variable				
Amurgo-Pacheco A (2006). Graduate Institute of International Studies, Geneva. HEI Working Paper n. 18/2006	6	0.18	−0.01	0.01
De Santis R, Vicarelli C (2006). Mimeo	22	0.40	0.15	0.58
De Santis R, Vicarelli C (2007). Istituto di Analisi Economica, Working Paper n. 79, March 2007	4	0.41	−50.9	20.46
De Wulf L, Maliszewska M (2009). Center for Social and Economic Research. Final report, September 2009.	8	0.08	−5.99	4.07
García-Alvarez-Coque JM, Marti Selva ML (2006) MPRA Working Paper n. 4124	54	−1.58	−0.29	1.08
Gasiorek et al., (2010). Report for the European Commission	11	1.07	2.97	−5.60
Gaulier G, Jean S, Ünal-Kesenci D (2004). CEPII Working Paper n. 2004–16, November	10	0.43	−1.83	−1.58
Gradeva K, Martinez-Zarzoso I (2009). Ibero America Institute for Econ Research (IAI) Discussion Paper n. 197, August 2009	5	−1.65	−1.77	1.93
Leite JC (2008). Dessarrollo y Sociedad, Primier semester 2008	112	0.25	0.00	0.63
Nilsson (2005). Mimeo	8	0.52	−0.70	0.88
Nilsson (2009). European Commission, Directorate General for Trade	12	0.20	−0.26	5.41
Nugent JB, Yousef TM (2005). EUI Working Paper RSCAS n. 2005/26	6	−0.55	−3.31	0.52

(continued)

Table 5.1 (continued)

Authors and references	No. of estimates	Mean	Min	Max
Persson E (2008). Bachelor thesis University of Lund - Department of Economics	40	−0.49	−0.67	0.74
Persson M, Wilhelmsson F (2005). Lund University, Sweden	32	0.16	−0.69	0.43
Persson M, Wilhelmsson F (2006). Lund University, Sweden	25	0.07	−1.51	−0.30
Pishbahar E, Huchet-Bourdon M (2007). Working Paper presented at PhD Workshop, EAAE 2007, Rennes, France	6	−0.99	0.09	0.73
Pusterla F (2007). IDB-SOE Working Paper, January 2007	9	0.39	−0.82	0.47
Ruiz JM, Vilarrubia JM (2007). Banco de Espana. Documentos de Trabajo n. 0720	25	−0.08	−0.94	1.96
Verdeja L (2006). Working Paper presented at ETSG 2005 in Dublin, Ireland	45	0.38	−0.94	1.06
Unpublished studies using preference margins				
Aiello F, Demaria F (2010). Università della Calabria. Dipartimento di Economia e Statistica. Working Paper n. 02/2010	75	0.00	−0.41	0.52
Aiello F, Cardamone P (2010). Analysing the effectiveness of the EBA initiative by using a gravity model. Pue&Piec Working Paper n. 10/7	94	0.02	−0.20	0.09
Cipollina M, Laborde D, Salvatici L (2010). Working Paper presented at ETSG 2010 in Lausanne, Switzerland	18	0.33	−0.13	0.61
Cipollina M, Salvatici L (2007). TradeAg Working Paper n. 2007/11	32	1.36	0.11	0.11
Demaria F (2009). On the impact of the EU GSP scheme. Dissertation, Università della Calabria	71	−1.47	−0.50	0.75
Manchin M (2004). Tinbergen Institute Discussion Paper 2004 - 132/2	40	0.12	0.23	0.78
Nilsson L, Matsson N (2009). European Commission, Directorate General for Trade	16	1.70	−1.34	0.97

Table 5.2 Structure of the database

Trade/policy (number of estimates)	Specific agreements		PTA	
	Dummy variable	Preference margin	Dummy variable	Preference margin
Sectoral trade	164	217	83	0
Total trade	330	38	144	50

both within-study and between-study variability, assuming that the estimates are a random sample from the universe of all possible results (Sutton et al. 2000).

Following Higgins and Thompson (2002), the fixed effects model calculates the "true" effects ($\hat{\gamma}_F$) underlying our studies, as the weighted average of all the study estimates, using their precisions as weights:

$$\hat{\gamma}_F = \frac{\sum_j \sum_i \hat{\gamma}_{ji} w_{ji}}{\sum_j \sum_i w_{ji}} \tag{5.2}$$

where $\hat{\gamma}_{ji}$ is the reported estimate i of the PTA effect in the jth study and the weights, w_{ji}, are inversely proportional to the square of the standard errors, so that studies with smaller standard errors have a greater weight than studies with larger standard errors. However, an area that is characterized by such high heterogeneity cannot be summarized by a fixed effects estimate which assumes that there is a single "true" effect underlying every study. Thus, a fixed effects estimator is inconsistent and the random effects model seems to be more appropriate. The random effects model assumes that there are real differences among studies in terms of the magnitude of the PTA effect. The random effects model does not assume that each study is estimating a true single effect size, but rather that the true effects are derived from the sample distribution of the effects that are assumed to be Normal with mean 0 and variance σ^2. The weights incorporate an estimate of between-study heterogeneity, σ^2, so that the random effects estimate ($\hat{\gamma}_F$) can be written as (Higgins and Thompson 2002):

$$\hat{\gamma}_R = \frac{\sum_j \sum_i \hat{\gamma}_{ji} w^*_{ji}}{\sum_j \sum_i w^*_{ji}} \tag{5.3}$$

where the weights are $w^*_{ij} = (w_{ij}^{-1} + \hat{\sigma}^2)^{-1}$. Allowing for between-study variation has the effect of reducing the relative weighting given to the more precise studies. Hence, the random effects model produces a more conservative confidence interval for the pooled effects estimate.

There is a general assumption that publication bias arises where researchers, referees, or editors have a preference for statistically significant results, and publication bias can affect the magnitude of the estimated effect. Several meta-regressions and graphical methods have been proposed to differentiate genuine empirical effects from publication bias (Stanley 2005). The simplest method conventionally used to detect publication bias is a funnel graph diagram, which is a scatter diagram in which the vertical axis provides a measure of the sample size or precision of the estimate, and the horizontal axis provides the size of the measured effect. The most common method used to measure precision is inverse standard error. Asymmetry indicates publication bias: in the absence of this bias, the estimates will vary randomly and symmetrically around the true effect. The diagram should resemble an inverted funnel, wide at the bottom encompassing the small-sample studies, and narrowing towards the top.[3]

Meta-Regression Analysis (MRA) is another method that can be used to investigate and correct publication bias. The model regresses the estimated coefficients ($\hat{\gamma}_{ji}$) on their standard errors (Card and Krueger 1995; Ashenfelter et al. 1999). Since the studies in the literature differ greatly in terms of datasets, sample size, and independent variables, the variance in these estimated coefficients may not be the same. This means that meta-regression errors are likely to be heteroschedastic, although Ordinary Least Square (OLS) estimates of the MRA coefficients will be unbiased and consistent. A Weighted Least Squares (WLS) estimate can be used to correct the MRA for heteroschedasticity. The regression equation then becomes:

$$\frac{\hat{\gamma}_{ji}}{Se_{ji}} = t_{ji} = \beta_0 + \beta_1 \frac{1}{Se_{ji}} + e_{ji} \tag{5.4}$$

where t_{ji} is the conventional t-value for $\hat{\gamma}_{ji,}$ the intercept and slope coefficients are reversed, and the independent variable becomes the inverse of Se_{ji}. The potential for heteroschedasticity directs the attention of the meta-analyst to the reported t-statistics (Stanley and Jarrell 2005). Equation (5.4) is the basis for the Funnel Asymmetry Test (FAT), and can be estimated using OLS. In the absence of publication selection the magnitude of the reported effect will be independent of its standard error and β_0 will be zero. Although the peer-review process can influence the magnitude of the estimated effect, whether or not this influence should be considered a bias is a moot point. Since in MA, notwithstanding the wide variation in the quality of the point estimates included in the study, each estimate in the sample is weighted equally, it could be argued that there is a *nonpublication bias* due to the lower quality of the unpublished research. For these reasons, in the following, we assess the consequences of the peer-review process, but refer to a general "publication impact" (rather than a "bias") (Cipollina and Salvatici 2010b).

The standard meta-regression model includes a set of explanatory variables (X) that integrate and explain the diverse findings in the literature:

$$\frac{\hat{\gamma}_{ji}}{Se_{ji}} = t_{ji} = \beta_0 + \beta_1 \frac{1}{Se_i} + \sum_{k=1}^{K} \frac{\alpha_k X_{jik}}{Se_{ji}} + e_{ji} \tag{5.5}$$

where β_1 expresses the true value of the parameter of interest, X_{jik} is the independent variable, which measures the relevant characteristics (k) of the empirical study and explains its systematic variation from the other results in the literature, α_k is the regression coefficient, which reflects the biasing effect of the characteristics of a particular study, and ε_{ji} is the disturbance term.

[3]Another graphical method is the Egger test, which detects funnel plot asymmetry by determining whether the intercept significantly deviates from zero, in a regression of the standardized effects estimates against their precision.

5.2.3 Explanatory Variables

The set of explanatory variables X in (5.5) fall into two groups: the first includes dummies explaining the diversity of the results from a methodological point of view; the second includes dummies for the structural features of the studies considered. The methodological dummies included in the MRA are based on a recent survey by Baldwin and Taglioni (2006) of the errors in the empirical literature based on gravity equations.

The classic (or "gold medal") gravity model mistake arises from correlation between possible omitted variables and the trade-cost terms, which leads to endogeneity and, consequently, biased estimates. In particular, the estimated trade impact will be upward biased if the omitted variables and the variable of interest (in our case *PTA*) are positively correlated.

This can be resolved by the inclusion of a dummy for country effects (which is equal to 1 for all trade flows involving a particular country, for all countries) and a dummy for pair effects (which is equal to 1 for all observations of trade occurring between a given pair of countries, for all pairs). Country dummies remove cross-section, but not time-series biases. This latter is a serious shortcoming since omitted factors affecting bilateral trade costs often vary over time. Pair dummies perform better with panel data, but cannot be included in cross-section data, since the number of dummies equals the number of observations. Also their inclusion would provide only a partial answer to gravity model problem (Baldwin and Taglioni 2006). In the MRA, in order to control for these biases, we include a dummy for *No-country effects*, which is equal to 1 if the original study did not use country fixed effects to remove cross-section bias.[4]

Another common mistake ("bronze medal") is related to the (also quite common) practice of deflating nominal trade values by an aggregate price index. Since inflation rates show global trends, the inclusion of this term probably creates spurious correlation (Baldwin and Taglioni 2006). When the bilateral trade flow is divided by the same price index, a time dummy corrects for the deflation procedure and possible spurious correlation. In our analysis the dummy *No-time effects* is equal to 1 if the original study did not use time fixed effects to account for common shocks affecting all trade flows equally across-countries.

In terms of typologies of data, it should be noted that the point estimates in our sample are obtained from both the cross-section and panel datasets. Some authors (Baier and Bergstrand 2007; Baldwin 2006) find that the best method for estimating the effect of PTA on bilateral trade flows is to use panel data, since cross-sectional and pooled regression models may be affected by the exclusion or mismeasurement

[4]The "silver medal" mistake arises from the fact that gravity models usually are estimated in log form: in this case, computing the wrong average trade (the arithmetic average corresponding to the log of the sums, rather than the geometric average corresponding to the sum of the logs) tends to overestimate the trade effects. All the studies in our sample use the correct average so we do not have to control for this bias.

of trading pair-specific variables. For this reason, the most recent gravity model estimations tend to use panel data regression techniques.[5] We introduce a dummy *Cross-section*, which is equal to 1 if the original study used cross-section or pooled data. For the second group of dummies describing different features of the studies considered, we expect PTA and their impact on trade to change over time. Accordingly, we use four dummies for the *1970s*, *1980s*, *1990s* and *2000s*, in order to collect studies using data related only to these specific time periods, and to check whether the most recent estimates differ from earlier ones.[6]

Most of the empirical analyses use gravity models with aggregate data for both products and countries. In terms of product aggregation, it is well-know that it is inconsistent to use aggregate export flows to analyse the effects of trade preferences applied at product level. Indeed, the few works based on disaggregated data confirm that aggregation produces significant estimation bias (Aiello et al. 2006). In order to correct for this, we include a dummy for papers employing *Aggregated data*. Engel (2002) criticizes the use of elasticities of substitution estimated without considering the number of countries involved. We add a dummy *Aggregated EU* in order to take into account differences in the results for the EU as a whole, and those for separate member countries.

In addition, since we expect to find that the size of the effect differs in studies that attempt to assess the various determinants of bilateral trade at sectoral level, and since most of these focus on the agricultural sector, we add the dummy *Agriculture* to distinguish studies explicitly dealing with the PTA impact on this sector. The use of disaggregated data implies the presence of a high percentage of zero trade flows. It creates obvious problems for the log-linear form of the gravity equation. Several methods have been proposed to deal with this issue: many empirical studies simply drop from the dataset the pairs with zero trade, and estimate the log-linear form using the OLS estimator. However, when zero values are excluded, we face the problem of selection bias. In our MRA we include a dummy *No-zero treatment* for OLS estimates that do not account for the presence of zero trade flows. When the dependent variable is zero for a substantial part of the sample, but positive for the rest of the sample, econometric theory suggests the use of a Tobit model. However, this procedure relies on rather restrictive assumptions that are unlikely to hold since the censoring at zero is not a "simple" consequence of the fact that trade cannot be negative (Cipollina and Salvatici 2010a). Zero flows, in fact, do not reflect unobservable trade values, but are the result of economic decision making based on the potential profitability of engaging in bilateral trade at all. A recent debate has emerged about the most appropriate econometric approach to avoid the bias that would be implied by dropping the observations with zero flows. Although there is a majority in favour of the Heckman two-step estimator (Linders and de Groot 2006; Helpman et al. 2008; Martin and Pham

[5]In this literature, most of the studies using panel techniques rely on static panel data models.

[6]Dummies for the 1970s, 1980s and 1990s are not included in the MRA considering studies adopting preference margins since most of the estimates relate only to the 2000s (see Table 5.6).

2008), some claim that presence of heteroschedasticity means that estimates of the log-linear form of the gravity equation will be biased and inconsistent. These authors recommend that gravity type and other constant-elasticity models should be estimated in multiplicative form. They suggest a simple quasi-maximum likelihood estimation technique based on Poisson regression (Santos-Silva and Tenreyro 2006; Proenca et al. 2008; Siliverstovs and Schumacher 2009). However, the standard Poisson model is vulnerable to the problems of overdispersion and an excessive number of zero flows. A way to overcome both heteroschedasticity (in the case of an assumption of log-normality) and overdispersion (in the case of the standard Poisson specification) is to use the Zero-Inflated Poisson (ZIP) or Negative Binomial model proposed by Burger et al. (2009). In our multivariate MRA, we include different methodological dummies (*GMM*, *Hausman-Taylor*, *Heckman*, *Poisson*, *Tobit*, *Zip/Negative Binomial*) to deal with selection bias and the presence of zero trade flows.

For (possible) "publication impact," we distinguish between published and unpublished work. Since we believe that published and very specific studies tend to include more accurate econometric analyses, we introduce a dummy *Unpublished* that is equal to 1 for unpublished papers. In order to detect the existence of extreme values, we consider the descriptive statistics for the sample of estimates obtained using dummy variables and preference margins for PTA and find 23 extreme values corresponding to the first and the last percentiles of the distribution. Since removing these extreme values could bias the meta-results (Cipollina and Salvatici 2010b), we prefer to deal with them by including a dummy variable "Outlier" (equal to 1 for outliers) in the MRA.

Finally, since some studies do not specify the type of PTA and others have different dummies for each type of agreement, we add the dummy *PTA*, which takes the value 1 if the original paper did not use a specific variable for each type of agreement. We also include five dummy variables controlling for specific agreement: *ACP*, *EBA*, *Euro-Med*, *GSP* and *GSP-Plus*.

5.3 Results

The Fisher test suggests that the null hypothesis of no effect of PTA on trade should be rejected at any standard level of significance (χ^2 is equal to 6,509 and to 7,536, respectively for estimates from studies using dummies and preference margins for trade policy).[7] The fixed and random effects models provide a synthetic measure of this impact.

---

[7]Under the null hypothesis of no effect ($\gamma = 0$), no publication selection and independence, the statistic minus twice the sum of the logarithms of the p-values is distributed approximately as a χ^2 with $2n$ degrees of freedom (Fisher 1932).

Table 5.3 Meta-Analysis of estimates of Preferential Trade Agreements effect on trade

Sample	Effects	Pooled estimate	Lower bound of 95% CI	Upper bound of 95% CI	p-value for H_0: no effect	Q-test (p-value)
Dummy for PTA	Fixed effects	0.02	−0.01	0.02	0.00	0.00
	Random effects	0.20	0.17	0.23	0.00	0.00
Preference margin	Fixed effects	0.06	0.06	0.06	0.00	0.00
	Random effects	0.07	0.06	0.07	0.00	0.00

Table 5.3 presents the combined meta-estimates of $\hat{\gamma}_{ji}$ and the p-values associated with the tests for lack of an effect. The null hypothesis is easily rejected, confirming the existence of an impact of a PTA on EU bilateral trade. In the case of the fixed effects estimates for papers with a dummy variable proxying for trade policy the coefficients show that PTA increase trade by around 2% ($e^{0.02} - 1 = 0.02$), while in the case of estimates for papers that use quantitative variables to measure preferences, the results show that an increase of 10% in preference margins implies a trade increase of around 0.6%. However, considering the high heterogeneity in our sample estimates, we need to look at the more appropriate random effects results.[8] The random effects estimate indicates an increase of up to 22% ($e^{0.20} - 1 = 0.22$) when the dummy variable for trade is included in the analysis and, when an explicit measure for the preferential policy is used, an increase in trade of 0.7% when the preference margin increases by 10%.

The results from the studies that use dummies tend to be higher in absolute terms than the results from studies using some measure of margin. However, these analyses are not comparable: the estimated coefficient of the dummy for PTA refers to total effects, while the estimated size of the effect of the preference margin is an elasticity.

Table 5.4 presents the combined meta-estimates of $\hat{\gamma}_{ji}$ distinguishing among PTA. Most PTA have a statistically significant effect on trade with the exception of GSP-Plus and Euro-Med. In all cases, except EBA, the coefficient is positive when the dummy variable is used as a proxy for this policy. The sample of estimates obtained using the PTA dummy shows the smallest random effect in the case of EBA, which indicates that this scheme decreases trade by 28%, while the largest effect is for the Cotonou agreement for ACP countries and indicates an increase in trade of more than 90%. If we consider the sample of estimates obtained using an explicit measure for margin of preference, the null hypothesis is rejected for three out five PTA, confirming the existence of an impact of GSP,

[8]The last column in Table 5.3 presents the p-values for the Q statistic, providing a test of homogeneity (for a detailed description, see Higgins and Thompson 2002). As expected, in all cases, the null hypothesis of estimates homogeneity is strongly rejected.

Table 5.4 Meta-Analysis of estimates of different Preferential Trade Agreements effect on trade

Sample	Random effects				
	ACP	EBA	Euro-Med	GSP	GSP-Plus
Dummy for PTA	0.66***	−0.33**	0.05	0.14***	1.32
Preference margin	0.03***	0.02**	0.01	0.02***	−0.01

Note: (**) significant at 5% level; (***) significant at 1% level

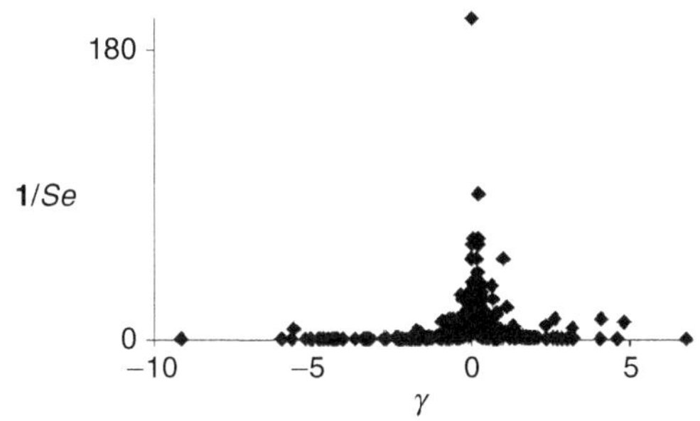

Fig. 5.1 Funnel graph of individual estimates obtained by paper using dummies for Preferential Trade Agreements

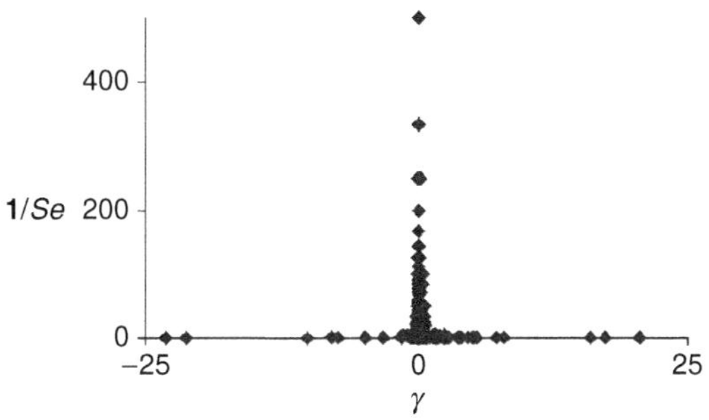

Fig. 5.2 Funnel graph of individual estimates obtained by papers using preference margins for Preferential Trade Agreements

ACP and EBA on bilateral trade with an elasticity coefficient ranging between 0.02 and 0.03, implying that a 10% increase in the preference margin increases trade by 2–3%.

The funnel graphs for detecting the presence of a publication impact are represented in Figs. 5.1 and 5.2. When trade policy is proxied by a dummy variable, the mean PTA effect is 0.02 and the median is 0.18. Although, the graph in Fig. 5.1 can be said to be funnel-like, it does not present the symmetry required to exclude the existence of potential bias. Fig. 5.2 depicts the funnel-graph of the individual estimates obtained using preference margins for PTA. It shows clearly that the plot is overweighted on the right side, with a mean equal to 0.08 and a median equal to 0.4. According to the graphical tests, publication selection is similar for the estimates obtained using dummy variables and preference margins. Although funnel graphs are useful as instruments to detect publication impact, they provide graphical representations only of this effect, but no indication of its magnitude.

In order to filter out publication impact and other biases, and to control for the different features of the studies surveyed, we estimate a multivariate meta-regression (5.5) using OLS. However, the presence of more than one estimate per study is problematic, because the OLS estimator may be consistent, but inefficient unless the dependence among the estimates obtained in the same study is accounted for. In order to estimate correct standard errors, we adopt a "robust with-cluster" procedure, adjusting standard errors for intra-study correlation (Cipollina and Salvatici 2010b). Each cluster identifies to which study the estimate belongs: this changes the variance-covariance matrix and the standard errors of the estimators, but not the actual estimated coefficients.

Tables 5.5 and 5.6, respectively present the results for the sample of estimates based on dummy variables and those based on preference margins. Table 5.6 drops some of the variables in Table 5.5, because of multicollinearity. Studies that estimate the effect of PTA through an explicit measure of preference margin are based on very recent and disaggregated food manufacturing data and always address the issue of zero flows. These studies are also more recent and tend to include the most advanced choices from a methodological point of view. For this reason Table 5.6 does not include the dummies *1970s*, *1980s*, *1990s*, *Aggregated data*, *Agriculture* and *No-zero treatment*.

In Tables 5.5 and 5.6, models 2 and 1 present the estimated coefficients with and without the introduction of a dummy for each type of agreement. If we compare these models we see that the results are largely robust. We now comment on the coefficients in Table 5.5 and then compare with Table 5.6, highlighting the differences.

In Table 5.5, the statistically significant estimates of β_0 confirm the apparent asymmetry of the funnel graph, since the reported effect is not independent of its standard error, whereas the β_1 estimate provides evidence of a significant general PTA effect on trade of 0.17 (model 1) and 0.53 (model 2), indicating a positive impact of preferences on trade, of around 20 and 70%, respectively.

The dummy *No-country effects* is used to correct for the "gold medal" mistake pointed out by Baldwin and Taglioni (2006). Its statistically insignificant coefficient suggests that the omitted variable bias does not seriously affect the estimation of the impact on trade of a PTA. The dummy *No-time effects* is introduced to offset the "bronze medal" error implied by the mistaken deflation procedure. The negative sign associated with this variable shows that uncorrected studies tend to underestimate the impact of a PTA on trade.

The statistical insignificance of the *Cross-section* dummy suggests that the results from cross-section models are not affected by the exclusion or mismeasurement of trading pair-specific variables.

For the variables related to the characteristics of each study, we find significant and negative coefficients associated with the *2000s* dummy: the size effect tends to be smaller in the studies focusing on more recent preferential schemes.

Table 5.5 Meta-Regression Analysis of Preferential Trade Agreements effects for papers using dummies for Preferential Trade Agreements

	Model 1	Model 2
β_0: Intercept	0.53*	0.51
	(0.28)	(0.38)
β_1: 1/Se	0.17*	0.53***
	(0.09)	(0.09)
No-country effects	−0.04	0.13
	(0.22)	(0.21)
No-time effects	−0.28**	−0.41***
	(0.13)	(0.08)
Cross-section	0.06	−0.01
	(0.13)	(0.12)
1970s	0.19	0.21
	(0.20)	(0.21)
1980s	0.27	0.20
	(0.20)	(0.19)
1990s	0.28	0.20
	(0.20)	(0.19)
2000s	−0.39**	0.11
	(0.15)	(0.32)
Aggregated data	−0.55***	−0.67***
	(0.12)	(0.13)
Aggregated EU	0.31*	0.25
	(0.16)	(0.21)
Agriculture	−0.49***	−0.43***
	(0.15)	(0.14)
No-zero treatment	0.37***	0.35***
	(0.10)	(0.08)
GMM	−0.08*	−0.06
	(0.04)	(0.04)
Hausman-Taylor	0.16	0.29*
	(0.15)	(0.16)
Heckman	−0.01	−0.02
	(0.09)	(0.09)
Poisson	0.69*	0.98
	(0.40)	(0.58)
Tobit	−1.67***	−1.97***
	(0.20)	(0.19)
ZIP/Negative Binomial	0.61	6.35**
	(0.39)	(2.97)
Unpublished	0.02	−0.07
	(0.07)	(0.07)
Outliers	3.67***	4.87***
	(0.10)	(0.44)
PTA	0.23***	
	(0.08)	
ACP	–	0.05
	(–)	(0.18)
EBA	–	−0.90***
	(–)	(0.30)
Euro-Med	–	−0.24***
	(–)	(0.05)
GSP	–	−0.12*
	(–)	(0.07)

(*continued*)

Table 5.5 (continued)

	Model 1	Model 2
GSP-Plus	–	−7.01**
	(–)	(3.13)
Adjusted R^2	0.46	0.61

Note: No. of obs. (no. of clusters) = 638 (26); (*) significant at 10% level; (**) significant at 5% level; (***) significant at 1% level. Standard errors adjusted for studies/clusters are reported in parentheses

Table 5.6 Meta-Regression Analysis of Preferential Trade Agreements effects for papers using preference margins for Preferential Trade Agreements

	Model 1	Model 2
β_0: *Intercept*	−0.24	−0.24
	(0.73)	(0.75)
β_1: *1/Se*	0.42*	0.41*
	(0.18)	(0.19)
No-country effects	0.03	0.03
	(0.03)	(0.03)
No-time effects	−3.48***	−3.47***
	(0.58)	(0.60)
Cross-section	4.25***	4.23***
	(0.76)	(0.78)
2000s	−0.47**	−0.46**
	(0.18)	(0.19)
Aggregated EU	−0.44**	−0.44**
	(0.18)	(0.18)
Heckman	−0.25***	−0.25***
	(0.03)	(0.03)
Poisson	−0.01	−0.01
	(0.01)	(0.01)
ZIP/Negative Binomial	−0.01	−0.01
	(0.02)	(0.02)
Unpublished	0.07***	0.06***
	(0.00)	(0.00)
Outliers	16.16***	16.16***
	(3.69)	(3.75)
PTA	−0.01***	–
	(0.00)	(–)
ACP	–	−0.00
	(–)	(0.00)
EBA	–	0.01**
	(–)	(0.01)
Euro-Med	–	0.00
	(–)	(0.00)
GSP	–	0.02***
	(–)	(0.00)
GSP-Plus	–	−0.03***
		(0.00)
Adjusted R^2	0.68	0.69

Note: No. of obs. (no. of clusters) = 338 (10); (*) significant at 10% level; (**) significant at 5% level; (***) significant at 1% level. Standard errors adjusted for studies/clusters are reported in parentheses

Regarding the typologies of data used, the negative coefficient of the dummy *Aggregated data* suggests that the product aggregation bias leads to a serious underestimation of the impact on trade of a PTA. Recall that all the papers using aggregated data employ a dummy variable for the presence of preferences.

Comparing the results for the EU as a whole with the results taking account of the differences in import structure of individual EU members we get positive and statistically significant coefficients of *Aggregated EU*. This result confirms the overestimation consequences of the geographical aggregation bias. Estimation problems apparently increase this overestimation bias when all EU importers are lumped together. Also, estimates that refer to the impact on trade of EU preferences in the agricultural sector tend to be lower. This is not surprising since the agricultural sector plays a very important role, accounts for a large share of developing countries and is heavily protected in the European market (Cipollina and Salvatici 2010a).

In terms of estimation methods, the treatment of zero trade flows seems to be a problem. Studies that do not deal with the problem of zeros in the trade matrix show higher coefficients for the PTA effect; papers that address the issue of zero flows by adopting Tobit and Generalized Method of Moment (GMM) estimators find lower effects; and Hausman-Taylor, Poisson and ZIP/Negative Binomial estimators provide higher coefficients.

The coefficient of the dummy *Unpublished* is statistically insignificant implying that the peer-review process does not affect the magnitude of the estimated effect in estimations that include dummies for preferential policies.

As already mentioned, we manage extreme values in the sample by adding a dummy *Outliers*. The estimated coefficient of this variable is clearly positive since most outliers indicate a positive and very high effect on the size of coefficient of PTA. Excluding this dummy does not significantly affect the results.

Finally, the coefficient of the *PTA* dummy is positive and highly significant: this dummy takes the value 1 if the original estimates do not focus on a specific type of preferential scheme, implying a general effect on trade of 0.40 (i.e., 0.23 + 0.17), that is, trade preferences increase trade by 50%. In studies focusing on specific PTA the impacts on trade tend to be much lower. In particular, the dummies for the *EBA* regime imply a negative overall impact on trade. In contrast, studies focusing on *Euro-Med* and the *GSP* agreements show lower, but still positive impacts on trade.

Table 5.6 presents the estimates obtained using preference margins, showing the intercept β_0 is not significant, means there is no evidence of asymmetry in the distribution of econometric results. Coefficient β_1 suggests that an increase in preferences of 10% increases trade by about 4%. Compared to Table 5.5, the coefficients of the control variables used for the MRA in Table 5.6 are fairly consistent. In what follows, we highlight some of the results that are different.

The positive and statistically significant estimate of *Cross-section* confirms that, in contrast to estimates that use dummy variables, the results from the cross-section and pooled models in studies adopting preference margins, may be affected by the exclusion or mismeasurement of trading pair-specific variables (Baldwin 2006).

Concerning the dummy for the 2000s, the underestimation result is more evident in the case of estimations that explicit variables for the preference margins where the effect size has a tendency to become negative.

If we consider aggregation, the results of studies that use an explicit measure of the preference margin suggest the existence of a "geographical aggregation bias," which can lead to underestimation of the preference impact, since the coefficient of the dummy *Aggregated EU* is negative and statistically significant.

Among the possible approaches used to deal with zero values, the Heckman two-step procedure tends to reduce the estimated impact of PTA by 50%. The Poisson and ZIP/Negative Binomial procedures, on the other hand, do not affect the impact of PTA on trade. The positive coefficient for the dummy *Unpublished* in Table 5.6 may be a good sign, and may suggest that editors are fairly thorough about excluding the highest (and possibly less realistic) results from estimates using preference margins. It should be remembered that this variable is not statistically significant in Table 5.5, which indicates that the magnitude of the effect of a PTA does not differ between published and unpublished studies that include a dummy for PTA. Usually, papers that compute a measure for the preference margin, in order to estimate its potential impact on trade flows, are particularly interested at this issue. However, the negative coefficient of the *PTA* dummy implies that if the original estimates did not focus on a specific type of preferential scheme, then the coefficient is lower. On the other hand, the estimated impact of EBA and GSP is higher, while the impact of the GSP-Plus is lower but still positive. This result hints at the existence of a sort of "psychological bias," since authors interested in estimating the effect of preferential trade policy tend to report larger results.

5.4 Conclusions

There is a body of empirical work on the impact of EU PTA on trade flows, estimated in a gravity framework. The interest of this literature is likely to increase due to the deeper involvement of the EU in a web of preferential trade relations with other countries or regional groupings. One way to carry out a comparative study of the empirical results in this field is simply to tabulate authors, countries, methodologies and results. However, from a policy perspective it is useful to complement qualitative analyses with more precise quantitative research. This chapter uses MA to summarize the trade effects highlighted in the literature.

We need to take account of the different methods of measuring PTA effects. In the MA presented in this chapter we distinguish between estimates from studies that use dummy variables and estimates based on quantitative measures. Using MA techniques, we summarize 638 point estimates based on dummy variables and 388 based on preference margins, collected from a set of 36 studies.

The pooled fixed and random effects estimates reveal an impact ranging between 2 and 22%, respectively, for studies using dummy variables for trade policies, and an elasticity ranging from 0.06 to 0.07 for studies using explicit preference margins.

However, considering the heterogeneity of the estimates in the sample in terms of econometric methodologies and specific features, random effects MA method is the most appropriate and confirms a robust, positive effect of PTA on trade which remains significant and economically relevant even if we consider specific agreements between EU and other countries.

In terms of publication selection, the results suggest a specific path since the magnitude of the reported estimates obtained using dummy variables depend on its standard error, while the elasticity coefficients of the preference margins seem to be unaffected by publication impact. However, even after correcting for this impact, the magnitude of the trade effect remains economically and statistically significant for the coefficients of the dummy variables, which is equivalent to an increase in trade of around 88%.

In terms of the methodological choices, and compared to the general effect of preferences on trade, the MRA provides evidence that the bias due to the omitted variables problem ("gold medal" mistake) does not apply to our sample of estimates, but the problem deriving from inappropriate deflation of nominal trade values ("bronze medal" mistakes) confirms a downward bias for the estimates that do not take account of time effects. Concerning the typology of data used, the MRA highlights that cross-sectional models are affected by the exclusion or mismeasurement of trading pair-specific variables in estimates that use preference margins. For the specific features of each study, the results reveal a decreasing magnitude effect for the most recent years and for product aggregated data. Conversely, extreme values, and the unpublished studies in the sample produce an upward bias in the estimated impact of preferences, respectively through dummy variables and preference margins.

We conclude that the combined estimates of PTA imply a substantial increase in trade, but that the effect varies a lot depending on the estimation method. It should be emphasized that MA is a methodology for reviewing the literature, not an alternative approach to studying the trade effects of PTA. The goal is not to discover the "true" value of the parameter under investigation, but rather to explain the wide variation in the empirical results reported in the economic studies, which purport to investigate the same phenomenon. Our results shed some light on the role played by research characteristics in explaining the variation in reported estimates. They also set the context for the empirical analyses in the second part of this book.

Acknowledgments We acknowledge financial support from the "New Issues in Agricultural, Food and Bio-energy Trade (AGFOODTRADE)" (Small and Medium-scale Focused Research Project, Grant Agreement no. 212036) research project funded by the European Commission, and the "European Union policies, economic and trade integration processes and WTO negotiations" research project funded by the Italian Ministry of Education, University and Research (Scientific Research Programs of National Relevance 2007). We thank Paola Cardamone, Luca De Benedictis and Luca Salvatici for their useful comments on an earlier draft of the chapter. We also thank all participants in the fourth annual international MAER-Net Colloquium, organized by the Meta-Analysis of Economic Research Network and the Hendrix College. The views expressed in this paper are the sole responsibility of the authors and do not necessarily reflect those of the European Commission.

Chapter 6
Trade Impact of European Union Preferences

Maria Cipollina and Luca Salvatici

Abstract This chapter assesses the impact on trade of European Union (EU) trade policies, using a gravity model based on disaggregated trade flows from 169 Developing Countries (DC) to 25 EU member countries. It uses a sample selection framework to account for potential selection bias in positive trade flows and provides an explicit measure for relative preference margins. The results serve to debunk some of the most widespread criticisms of preferential policies: EU preferences matter, and have a positive impact on developing countries' exports at the intensive margin, and an ambiguous impact at the extensive margin with significant differences across sectors.

6.1 Introduction

This chapter analyses the impact of European Union (EU) preferences on trade flows, including traditional non-reciprocal agreements and preferential access granted to Developing Countries (DC) under bilateral reciprocal arrangements. Following Anderson and van Wincoop (2003, 2004), we derive a theoretically grounded gravity equation in which the trade cost factor depends on bilateral distances, tariffs and preferential margins. From a policy perspective, we provide an assessment of the effectiveness of EU preferential trade policies in generating trade from DC.

M. Cipollina
Department of Economics, Management and Social Sciences, University of Molise, Via Francesco de Sanctis, 86100 Campobasso, Italy
e-mail: cipollina@unimol.it

L. Salvatici
Department of Economics, University Roma Tre, Via Silvio D'Amico, 77-00145 Roma, Italy
e-mail: lsalvatici@uniroma3.it

L. De Benedictis and L. Salvatici (eds.), *The Trade Impact of European Union Preferential Policies*, DOI 10.1007/978-3-642-16564-1_6,

Our analysis provides a micro-level assessment of the impact of trade preferences on the intensive and extensive margins of trade. We estimate this impact by modelling bilateral EU imports at the 6 digit level Harmonised System (HS), allowing for heterogeneous trade costs and substitution elasticities across industries. Using disaggregated data raises two problems: (1) the impossibility in relation to some variables to obtain information at the level of detail at which tariff lines are specified; (2) a large percentage of "zero trade flows," which introduces obvious problems in the log-linear form of the gravity equation. In terms of (*i*), in order to control for unobservable country and product heterogeneity, we introduce exporter, importer, and product-specific fixed effects. We address the issue of zero flows by adopting the Heckman (1979) sample selection model. This approach allows us to assess the impact of preferences on number of bilateral trade flows (*extensive margin*) and volumes traded (*intensive margin*).

We estimate cross-sectional models for data on imports at the 6-digit level to the EU (25 countries) for year 2004, and run separate regressions for several commodity groups (Table 6.1) defined according to the World Trade Organization (WTO) Multilateral Trade Negotiations categories, focusing on the network of preferential trade relations between the EU and other countries or regional groupings, in the period under analysis.

We are not interested in the impact on trade of specific preferential schemes, dealt with in other chapters in this book; accordingly, the computed preference margin does not refer to a specific treatment, and we ignore the issue of overlapping preferences. Although we do not know the utilization rates of different schemes, the available information on actual preferential trade flows allows us to provide improved estimates of the impact of trade preferences on EU imports from DC by accounting for the share of preferential flows on total imports.

We are interested in the impact on trade of preferences. We use an explicit measure of the intensity of preference margins at the 6-digit tariff line level. Preference margins are measured in relative terms and our definitions focus on actual preferences with respect to possible competitors, rather than theoretical margins with respect to bound Most Favored Nation (MFN) tariffs – i.e. the ceiling set by WTO commitments.

This avoids possible overestimation of the competitive advantages enjoyed by exporting countries, although the impact of prohibitive tariffs is underestimated since we consider only actual not potential exporters (Cipollina and Salvatici 2010). Our findings point to a significant, but heterogeneous impact of EU trade policy on DC exports. The preferential regimes have a positive impact on both the extensive and intensive margins, although the increased probability of trade is modest, and increases in the intensity of trade vary widely across sectors. The impact on the probability of trade (i.e. the extensive margin) is positive in only one sector, which confirms that preferential policies lead exporting countries to specialize in a smaller set of products.

Table 6.1 Commodity classification

Sectors according to the harmonized commodity description and coding system
Section I: Live Animals; Animal Products (Chaps. 1–5)
Section II: Vegetable Products (Chaps. 6–14)
Section III: Animal or Vegetable Fats and Oils and Their Cleavage Products; Prepared Edible Fats; Animal or Vegetable Waxes (Chap. 15)
Section IV: Prepared Foodstuffs; Beverages, Spirits, and Vinegar; Tobacco and Manufactured Tobacco Substitutes (Chaps. 16–24)
Section V: Mineral Products (Chaps. 25–27)
Section VI: Products of the Chemical or Allied Industries (Chaps. 28–38)
Section VII: Plastics and Articles Thereof; Rubber and Articles Thereof (Chaps. 39–40)
Section VIII: Raw Hides and Skins, Leather, Furskins and Articles Thereof; Saddlery and Harness; Travel Goods, Handbags, and Similar Containers; Articles of Animal Gut (Other Than Silkworm Gut) (Chaps. 41–43)
Section IX: Wood and Articles of Wood; Wood Charcoal; Cork and Articles of Cork; Manufactures of Straw, of Esparto or of Other Plaiting Materials; Basketware and Wickerwork (Chaps. 44–46)
Section X: Pulp of Wood or of other Fibrous Cellulosic Material; Waste and Scrap of Paper or Paperboard; Paper and Paperboard and Articles Thereof (Chaps. 47–49)
Section XI: Textiles and Textile Articles (Chaps. 50–63)
Section XII: Footwear, Headgear, Umbrellas, Sun Umbrellas, Walking-Sticks, Seat-Sticks, Whips, Riding-Crops and Parts Thereof; Prepared Feathers and Articles Made Therewith; Artificial Flowers; Articles of Human Hair (Chaps. 64–67)
Section XIII: Articles of Stone, Plaster, Cement, Asbestos, Mica or Similar Materials; Ceramic Products; Glass and Glassware (Chaps. 68–70)
Section XIV: Natural or Cultured Pearls, Precious or Semiprecious Stones, Precious Metals, Metals Clad with Precious Metal, and Articles Thereof; Imitation Jewellery; Coin (Chap. 71)
Section XV: Base Metals and Articles of Base Metal (Chaps. 72–83)
Section XVI: Machinery and Mechanical Appliances; Electrical Equipment; Parts Thereof; Sound Recorders and Reproducers, Television Image and Sound Recorders and Reproducers, and Parts and Accessories of Such Articles (Chaps. 84–85)
Section XVII: Vehicles, Aircraft, Vessels and Associated Transport Equipment (Chaps. 86–89)
Section XVIII: Optical, Photographic, Cinematographic, Measuring, Checking, Precision, Medical or Surgical Instruments and Apparatus; Clocks and Watches; Musical Instruments; Parts and Accessories Thereof (Chaps. 90–92)
Section XIX: Arms and Ammunition; Parts and Accessories Thereof (Chap. 93)
Section XX: Miscellaneous Manufactured Articles (Chaps. 94–96)
Section XXI: Works of Art, Collectors' Pieces and Antiques (Chap. 97)

6.2 The Gravity Model

6.2.1 Specification

We start from a standard Constant Elasticity of Substitution (CES), monopolistic competition model following Lai and Trefler (2002) and Lai and Zhu (2004). A trade separable model, where allocation of the value of production and expenditure in country j for product class k, is separable from the bilateral allocation of trade across countries (Armington assumption), allows us to determine bilateral trade in a conditional general equilibrium setting, where the product markets for each good produced in each country are conditional on the observed output structure and expenditure allocations.

Following Anderson and van Wincoop (2003, 2004) we derive our gravity equation including many commodity classes of goods (denoted by k where $k = 1, 2 \ldots . K$) flowing between each country i and j:

$$m_{ijk} = \frac{Y_{ik}E_{jk}}{Y_{wk}}\left(\frac{T_{ijk}}{P_{ik}P_{jk}}\right)^{1-\sigma_k} \tag{6.1}$$

where m_{ijk} is the nominal demand for commodity k from country i by country j; Y_{ik} is the production of commodity k for country i; E_{jk} is country j's expenditure on product k; Y_{wk} is world production of product k; T_{ijk} is the trade cost; P_{ik} and P_{jk} are multilateral price indexes, and $\sigma_k > 1$ is the elasticity of substitution among all varieties from different exporters.

The trade cost, T_{ijk}, reflects the impact of transport costs, proxied by distance (d_{ij}), common language (L_{ij}) and colonial links (C_{ij}), and trade policies, proxied by the *ad valorem* equivalent tariff factor imposed by country j on imports of commodity k from country i ($t_{ijk} = 1 + \tau_{ijk}$):

$$T_{ijk} = t_{ijk} d_{ij}^{\rho} e^{\delta_1 L_{ij} - \sigma_k + \delta_2 C_{ij}} \tag{6.2}$$

where $L_{ij} = 1$ if countries i and j share a common language; and $C_{ij} = 1$ if countries i and j were linked in the past by colonial ties.

Trade preferences reduce border costs as a consequence of tariff reduction. In the case of preferential imports, then, the trade cost is a function of the preference factor: higher preferences decrease trade cost and, thus, reduce the negative trade impact of the bilateral tariffs.

Using (6.2) and rewriting (6.1) in logarithmic form, we get:

$$\begin{aligned} \ln m_{ijk} = {} & \alpha - \ln Y_{wk} + \ln Y_{ik} + \ln E_{jk} + \rho(1-\sigma_k)\ln d_{ij} + \delta_1(1-\sigma_k)L_{ij} + \delta_2(1-\sigma_k)C_{ij} + \\ & + (\sigma_k - 1)\underbrace{[\ln(1+\tau_{jk}^{\max}) - \ln(1+\tau_{ijk})]}_{pref_{ijk}} + (\sigma_k - 1)\ln P_{ik} + (\sigma_k - 1)\ln P_{jk} + \varepsilon_{ijk} \end{aligned} \tag{6.3}$$

where $pref_{ijk}$ is the preferential factor defined in relative terms as the ratio of the power of the maximum tariff levied by the EU across all actual exporters ($1 + \tau_{jk}{}^{\max}$) of product k, and the power of bilateral tariff ($1 + \tau_{ijk}$) incurred by a specific exporter i. Apparently, the margin intensity is conditional on the choice of the benchmark tariff; in this chapter we focus on the actual preferences with respect to possible competitors:

$$pref_{ijk} = \frac{(1 + \tau_{jk}^{\max})}{(1 + \tau_{ijk})} \tag{6.4}$$

Accordingly, the preference factor can increase, either because the exporter *i* benefits from a lower tariff, or because a higher duty is imposed on other exporters. It should be emphasized that in the case of overlapping preference schemes, the applied preferential rate considered is the lowest available to each exporter: this may lead to overestimation of the preferential margins, since Bureau et al. (2007) show that some preferential regimes are systematically preferred to others.

In order to distinguish imports by tariff regimes in our estimation the preference factor variable $pref_{ijk}$ is associated with the dummy *PRE,* which is equal to 1 in the case of preferential trade flows, and to zero if imports enter without claiming any preferences. All variables that do not vary across exporters, importers and products are proxied by fixed effects. Fixed effects are applied since they are widely used in the literature to account for the multilateral resistance term in cross-section analysis.

6.2.2 Estimation

The large percentage of zero trade flows associated with the use of highly disaggregated data creates obvious problems in the log-linear form of the gravity equation. We address the issue of zero flows by adopting the Heckman (1979) two-step procedure.

The Heckman two-step approach not only corrects for possible biases, it also allows us to distinguish the impact of preferences on both the extensive and the intensive margins. An increased probability of registering a positive trade flow, signals the existence of a larger set of bilateral trade flows (extensive margin), and can reflect either a larger variety of goods traded or a larger number of exporters of the same good. On the other hand, in the second stage a positive coefficient associated with the preference margin implies larger trade flows than would have been the case without the preference (intensive margin).

In practice, in the first stage we estimate the following probit model:

$$\rho_{ijk} = \Pr\left(m_{ijk}^{*} > 0 \middle| d_{ij}, pref_{ijk}, L_{ij}, C_{ij}, \text{product and country - specific FE}\right) \tag{6.5}$$

The existence of positive trade flows should be affected by fixed rather than variable trade costs: Helpman et al. (2008), for instance, include the variable *common religion* in the first-stage regression, although they acknowledge that a *common language* would be just as useful. Indeed, cultural factors, and especially a common language, are well-known determinants of trade. We posit that the additional complexity inherent in an intermediated relationship, the potential for costly errors, and the increased cost may be large enough to prevent some transactions. Accordingly, the dummy L_{ij} for common language, provides the required identifying restriction: in the second stage we estimate a modified version of (6.3) dropping the language dummy and adding the inverse Mills ratio estimated in the first stage.

Finally, we compute the percentage change due to the hypothetical elimination of existing preferences as follows (Lai and Zhu 2004):

$$\text{Preference effect} = \frac{\sum_{ijk} \left(E[m_{ijk}\,|\,pref_{ijk} > 0\,] - E[m_{ijk}|\,pref_{ijk} = 0]\right)}{\sum_{ijk} E[m_{ijk}|\,pref_{ijk} > 0]} \tag{6.6}$$

In calculating these results, we estimate the counterfactual change in the dependent variable, total EU imports, which would follow from the removal of the preferential advantage. This could be considered a "trade creation" effect, since the trade flow would not take place in the absence of preferences. However, such an effect cannot be interpreted in welfare terms, since additional trade flows may be the result of the diversion of previously previously existing export flows from exports from other countries (Borchert 2009). Moreover, this calculation may overestimate the total sum of the foregone exports, since indirect effects are not captured via changes in world prices.

6.3 Data

Data on trade at the HS6 level of detail are taken from the Eurostat Comext database (http://fd.comext.eurostat.cec.eu.int/xtweb/); data on tariffs are from the MAcMapHS6-V2 database (http://www.cepii.fr/). MAcMap provides a consistent worldwide assessment of protection, including *ad valorem* equivalent rates of specific duties and Tariff Rate Quotas (TRQ), including those introduced at the end of the Uruguay Round for 2004, at the HS6 level (Boumelassa et al. 2009). Data for the remaining explanatory variables are from the Cepii dataset, which includes distances between countries and two sets of dummies for common language and former colonial links.

The choice of a single, specific year (2004) is strictly dictated by the data provided by the MAcMap database. Compared to other tariff databases, MAcMap allows a consistent picture of border protection, while accounting exhaustively for preferential trade agreements and the presence of TRQ (Bouët et al. 2004).

From the data on imports presented in Table 6.2, we observe that half of imports to the EU market enter duty-free under MFN arrangements, and that among the imports that incur MFN duty, only 16% enter using under a preferential scheme. The large share of MFN duty-free imports is not surprising in the case of raw

Table 6.2 Share of imports by type of tariff regime (period 2004)

Sections	% of MFN duty-free	% of MFN duty (no preference)	% of Preferential duty	Total trade (million Euros)	Preferential trade (million Euros)
Overall	50.7	33.4	15.8	450,179	71,300
I	9.5	35.6	55.0	6,950	3,820
II	55.1	20.3	24.6	15,100	3,720
III	0.5	77.4	22.1	3,130	693
IV	43.7	28.0	28.3	16,000	4,530
V	97.4	1.6	1.0	116,000	1,180
VI	31.3	45.1	23.6	15,900	3,750
VII	16.2	59.6	24.2	10,300	2,490
VIII	2.3	88.1	9.6	5,710	549
IX	44.1	43.7	12.2	7,780	953
X	100.0	0	0	3,490	0
XI	1.7	56.0	42.3	52,300	22,100
XII	0.2	64.6	35.3	9,730	3,430
XIII	7.2	56.5	36.3	4,080	1,480
XIV	83.3	9.2	7.5	15,000	1,120
XV	56.5	32.0	11.4	33,800	3,870
XVI	49.1	40.7	10.2	89,400	9,080
XVII	0.4	67.3	32.3	19,300	6,230
XVIII	22.1	68.4	9.5	7,640	723
XIX	0	0	24.4	49	12
XX	38.4	53.0	8.5	18,400	1,570
XXI	100.0	0	0	120	0

materials, such as the Mineral products under Section V, and the lack of protection leaves little room for preferential trade. In the case of the second largest share imports, the Machinery sector (Section XVI), the share of preferential imports is only 10%, but in the case of the third largest sector, Textiles (Section XI), more than 40% of trade is preferential. In the remaining sectors, the shares of preferential imports range from around 10% for Instruments (Section XVIII) and Miscellaneous manufactures (Section XX), to around 55% in the case of the animal products under Section I.

We estimate cross-sectional models, covering imports of 4,941 commodities from 169 DC to 25 EU member countries. The number of observations used (2,190,239) is much lower than the number of potential bilateral trade flows (25 importers*169 exporters*4,941 products), for two reasons.

First, we exclude binding TRQ from our dataset since they may introduce a limited dependent variable estimation problem. We also exclude from the sample a few sectors where there are no preferences (Sections X and XXI), or only trivial preferential trade flows in either absolute (Section XIX) or relative terms (Section V).

More importantly, countries do not produce all possible goods, neither do they all have an effective demand for all available goods. Accordingly, we distinguish between two different kinds of zero-valued trade flows: products that are never traded and products that are not traded, but (potentially, at least) could be traded.

Hence, we can distinguish between flows with exactly zero probability of positive trade, flows with a non-zero probability of trade that still happen to be zero, and positive flows. Since preferential policies cannot influence the first group, in our sample for each exporter we retain only products that present at least one bilateral export flow at the HS6 level, assuming that the excluded commodities are not produced. Similarly, we exclude products that are not imported at all in the EU. This avoids the inclusion of irrelevant information that could bias the estimates, and also reduces the dimensions of the dataset.

The Comext database provides no information on take up of the preference schemes. However, it distinguishes between preferential and non-preferential (MFN) trade. Using the information on preferential trade flows, the level of duty (τ_{ijk}) used to compute the preference margins is equal to the MFN (applied) tariff if the preference is not used, and to the preferential (bilateral) tariff otherwise. Accordingly, our estimation takes account of the volume of trade benefiting from the preferences, and avoids overestimation of the preference impact that can arise from an association between a positive preference and a trade flow that does not exploit it.

Table 6.3 presents the share of preferential tariff lines, the bilateral applied tariff and the preference factor: in the last two cases, we report simple averages implying the same weight for each tariff line regardless of the importance of the product for which preference and protection is granted, and standard deviations in order to provide some information about tariff structure dispersion. The relative preferential factors (Table 6.3) show that the overall simple average is 1.05 with large differences across sectors. In addition to agricultural products (Sections I and IV), with

Table 6.3 Value and preference margins for commodity groups with preferential trade flows

Sections	Bilateral applied tariff (%): τ_{ijk}		Share of preferential tariff lines		Relative preference factor $(1 + pref_{ijk})$		Value of preference (million Euros)
	Mean	(Std. dev.)	Potential	Used	Mean	(Std. dev.)	
Overall	1.93	(0.04)	76	37	1.05	(0.07)	4,580
I	2.48	(0.07)	69	59	1.07	(0.06)	321
II	2.61	(0.07)	60	48	1.06	(0.21)	199
III	4.19	(0.11)	71	50	1.06	(0.10)	22
IV	7.54	(0.10)	73	54	1.09	(0.11)	602
VI	0.65	(0.03)	62	34	1.04	(0.02)	157
VII	0.28	(0.01)	84	36	1.05	(0.02)	108
VIII	0.38	(0.01)	74	43	1.04	(0.02)	21
IX	0.54	(0.01)	65	31	1.03	(0.01)	33
XI	3.27	(0.04)	85	47	1.06	(0.05)	1,870
XII	2.25	(0.04)	74	46	1.06	(0.05)	167
XIII	1.24	(0.03)	80	45	1.04	(0.03)	66
XIV	0.00	(0.00)	64	38	1.03	(0.01)	32
XV	0.30	(0.01)	64	40	1.03	(0.01)	147
XVI	0.14	(0.01)	79	22	1.02	(0.02)	330
XVII	0.92	(0.02)	96	31	1.04	(0.02)	421
XVIII	0.25	(0.01)	78	18	1.02	(0.01)	16
XX	0.08	(0.00)	65	40	1.03	(0.01)	50

respective relative preferential factors equal to 1.16 and 1.08, the next most preferred sectors are textiles and footwear (Sections XI and XII). However, it appears that despite the preferences these are the most protected EU sectors. On the other hand, they are also the sectors showing the largest shares of actually used preferential tariff lines.

The share of "potential" preferential tariff lines is computed as the percentage of observations with a positive preference margin, whereas the share of "used" preferential tariff lines gives some information about the degree of utilization of preferences and is calculated as the percentage of preferential tariff lines that enter the EU under a preferential scheme. The low level of utilization of preferences, only 38% of preferential tariff lines, is likely due to the costs associated with preference utilization and the presence of non-tariff barriers (such as quotas or sanitary and phytosanitary regulations).

Table 6.3 provides evidence on preference values, based on Candau and Jean (2005). Under simplifying assumptions, such as constant world prices, the value of the preference rent for any sectors can be computed as follows:

$$V_s = \sum_k (\tau_{jk}^{\max} - \tau_{ijk})\mathrm{PI}_{ik} \tag{6.7}$$

where PI_{ik} refers to EU preferential imports of product k from partner i. The calculation of (6.7) is likely to provide an upper bound estimate, since the assumption is that none of the rent is included in the export price. The value of EU preferences is more than 4 billion Euros. This is a crude approximation (Candau and Jean 2005). First, the (implicit) assumption that there are no supply constraints is rather simplistic since a change in the EU trade policy regime would likely exert upward pressure on world prices, which would tend, to some extent, to counterbalance the decrease in prices due to preference margins. Moreover, the extent of rent extraction by an exporter is likely to depend on the exporter's bargaining power vis-à-vis the importer. The rent for Textiles (Section XI) alone amounts to roughly half of the overall value, which is not surprising given the importance of this sector in trade terms.

6.4 Results

Tables 6.4 and 6.5 report the estimates related to preferences. In the first stage we estimate the impact of preferential policies on the extensive margin, i.e. the share of positive trade flows over total number of possible bilateral trade flows (Table 6.4); in the second stage we quantify the extent to which trade preferences increase the volume of trade (Table 6.5).

Table 6.4 presents the results of the impact of preferences on the extensive margin of trade, by commodity groups. In the first stage, all control variable estimates have the expected signs. Overall, the results show that the preference

Table 6.4 Results for commodity groups – extensive margin

Probit regression, marginal effects	Independent variables				No. of obs.
	ln d_{ij}	ln(1 + $pref_{ijk}$)	C_{ijk}	L_{ijk}	Pseudo R^2
Overall	−0.22***	0.08***	0.14***	0.07***	2,175,611
	(0.01)	(0.01)	(0.00)	(0.00)	0.25
I	−0.32***	0.14**	0.16***	0.06***	30,488
	(0.01)	(0.06)	(0.02)	(0.01)	0.26
II	−0.21***	0.09***	0.15***	0.11***	99,079
	(0.00)	(0.02)	(0.01)	(0.01)	0.25
III	−0.27***	0.25***	0.13***	0.10***	7,647
	(0.02)	(0.09)	(0.03)	(0.03)	0.22
IV	−0.19***	0.11***	0.18***	0.11***	82,829
	(0.00)	(0.02)	(0.01)	(0.01)	0.23
VI	−0.26***	−0.03	0.14***	0.04**	135,480
	(0.00)	(0.07)	(0.01)	(0.01)	0.23
VII	−0.29***	0.40***	0.15***	0.05***	84,269
	(0.01)	(0.13)	(0.01)	(0.01)	0.33
VIII	−0.24***	−0.09	0.14***	0.09***	31,961
	(0.01)	(0.21)	(0.02)	(0.02)	0.39
IX	−0.24***	−0.09	0.14***	0.09***	51,004
	(0.01)	(0.20)	(0.01)	(0.01)	0.31
XI	−0.22***	−0.04	0.11***	0.09***	430,277
	(0.00)	(0.04)	(0.00)	(0.00)	0.32
XII	−0.27***	−0.94***	0.15***	0.08***	40,814
	(0.01)	(0.09)	(0.02)	(0.01)	0.40
XIII	−0.28***	−0.82***	0.17***	0.04	69,026
	(0.01)	(0.11)	(0.01)	(0.01)	0.36
XIV	−0.15***	−1.24**	0.15***	0.10***	22,867
	(0.01)	(0.54)	(0.02)	(0.02)	0.37
XV	−0.25***	−0.95***	0.15***	0.05***	196,034
	(0.01)	(0.11)	(0.01)	(0.01)	0.31
XVI	−0.18***	−0.83***	0.14***	0.06***	491,423
	(0.00)	(0.07)	(0.00)	(0.00)	0.37
XVII	−0.21***	0.55***	0.18***	0.10***	61,443
	(0.00)	(0.09)	(0.01)	(0.01)	0.34
XVIII	−0.13***	−0.27**	0.12***	0.06***	144,421
	(0.00)	(0.12)	(0.01)	(0.01)	0.36
XX	−0.24***	−0.24**	0.16***	0.09***	104,426
	(0.01)	(0.10)	(0.01)	(0.01)	0.38

Note: dependent variable: Pr(m_{ijk} > 0); Product, Importer and Exporter Fixed Effects (not reported); Intercept (not reported); Standard errors in parentheses; (*) significant at 10% level; (**) significant at 5% level; (***) significant at 1% level

margin has a slightly positive, and statistically significant, impact on the probability of registering a positive trade flow. The estimated coefficient of 0.08 reflects the average impact among sectors of preferential policies on the extensive margin.

In terms of results by commodity group, estimates for the preference margin are statistically significant for 12 out of 16 cases. Sectors where the preference impact on the extensive margin is not significant – Sections VI, VIII, IX and XI – are characterized by very low numbers of preferential tariff lines with positive trade

Table 6.5 Results for commodity groups – intensive margin

Heckman regression	Independent variables				N. of non-zero obs.	Elasticity of substitution, σ_{EU}
	$\ln d_{ij}$	$\ln(1 + pref_{ijk})$ *PRE	C_{ijk}	Mills ratio		
Overall	−2.25***	9.42***	1.16***	2.71***	476,433	10.42
	(0.04)	(0.13)	(0.03)	(0.06)		
I	−2.47***	9.05***	0.96***	2.15***	6,891	10.05
	(0.42)	(0.75)	(0.21)	(0.43)		
II	−1.62***	1.97***	0.93***	1.59***	20,681	2.97
	(0.17)	(0.33)	(0.13)	(0.23)		
III	−2.36***	4.25***	0.29	1.64*	1.586	5.25
	(0.78)	(1.40)	(0.44)	(0.87)		
IV	−1.64***	6.63***	1.16***	1.84***	17,143	7.73
	(0.16)	(0.33)	(0.15)	(0.25)		
VI	−2.94***	18.08***	1.30***	3.26***	29,497	19.08
	(0.23)	(0.84)	(0.13)	(0.28)		
VII	−3.65***	23.22***	1.48***	3.81***	20,614	24.22
	(0.19)	(0.81)	(0.12)	(0.23)		
VIII	−2.14***	15.86***	1.16***	2.18***	8,065	16.86
	(0.15)	(1.38)	(0.12)	(0.18)		
IX	−3.03***	14.50***	1.56***	2.99***	11,452	15.50
	(0.22)	(1.89)	(0.16)	(0.28)		
XI	−1.78***	10.10***	0.83***	2.14***	107,862	11.10
	(0.05)	(0.22)	(0.04)	(0.07)		
XII	−2.27***	10.62***	1.15***	2.08***	10,920	11.62
	(0.13)	(0.65)	(0.11)	(0.13)		
XIII	−2.76***	18.59***	1.20***	2.76***	16,614	19.59
	(0.13)	(0.84)	(0.10)	(0.15)		
XIV	−1.59***	21.75***	1.46***	2.81***	5,266	22.75
	(0.22)	(2.69)	(0.20)	(0.29)		
XV	−3.15***	27.27***	1.53***	3.46***	41,816	28.27
	(0.12)	(0.86)	(0.08)	(0.14)		
XVI	−2.59***	25.06***	1.66***	2.91***	94,614	26.06
	(0.05)	(0.81)	(0.05)	(0.07)		
XVII	−1.78***	24.03***	1.11***	1.75***	12,774	25.03
	(0.16)	(1.10)	(0.15)	(0.22)		
XVIII	−1.44***	10.67***	0.91***	1.70***	26,061	11.67
	(0.07)	(1.49)	(0.07)	(0.09)		
XX	−2.24***	25.75***	1.24***	2.52***	25,522	26.75
	(0.09)	(1.06)	(0.08)	(0.10)		

Note: dependent variable: $\ln(m_{ijk})$; Product, Importer and Exporter Fixed Effects (not reported); Intercept (not reported); Standard errors in parentheses; (*) significant at 10% level; (**) significant at 5% level; (***) significant at 1% level

(Sections VIII and IX), a high level of preference concentration (Section VI) or very high applied tariffs (Section XI). Preferential access leads to an expansion in the number of traded products in the case of agricultural products, namely Animals, Vegetables and Foodstuffs, Fats and oils, Beverages, spirits and tobacco (Sections I, II, III and IV): the highest estimated coefficient (0.25), for Fats and oils, implies that a 10% increase in the relative preference factor – roughly corresponding to an average reduction of 10 percentage points in the bilateral applied tariffs at the estimation point – increases the probability of registering a positive trade flow (i.e. the extensive margin) by 25%. Indeed, the standard deviations of the preference factors (Table 6.3), show that Section III is where preferences are least concentrated. Even if the coefficients of two non-agricultural sectors, Sections VII (Plastics) and XVII (Vehicles), present the largest positive impact on the extensive margin, in the remaining sectors, the estimated coefficients are negative, implying that preferential policies mean that DC specialize in a smaller number of exported products than would otherwise be the case. The negative impact ranges between 0.24 in the case of Manufactured Articles (Section XX) and 1.24 in the case of Precious stones. By and large, then, preferences discourage export diversification of industrial goods, but promote it in the case of agriculture. This issue is of relevance, but we cannot draw conclusions about the eventual welfare impact: it will be positive if the number of exported goods increases as a result of trade creation. However, the reverse will be true if preferences favour products with no comparative advantages – and, also, discouraging export diversification might raise concerns.

In the second stage (Table 6.5), the positive and significant coefficient of the Mills ratio confirms that correcting for sample selection bias is justified. The coefficients of bilateral distance and colonial links show the expected signs. There are large differences for the negative impact of distance, our proxy for transport costs: these results support our decision to run separate rather than a pooled regression, since the latter would have implied unwarranted restrictions on the trade cost coefficients.

Concerning our variable of interest, Table 6.5 shows the impact of preferences on the intensive trade margin. The estimated coefficients are related to the elasticity of substitution across sections and countries by the identity $\hat{\sigma}_S = \hat{\beta}_S + 1$. The estimate of average elasticity of substitution across sections is statistically significant and equal to 10.4, but note that this is likely to underestimate the preference impact.

In order to benefit from preferences, most exporters will incur some additional costs (e.g. due to rules of origin compliance as detailed in Chapter 10). This implies that the “true” (i.e. net of compliance costs) preference margin generating the observed trade flows is lower than the margin associated with our estimates.

The sectoral results show that the estimates for elasticity of substitution are always significant. Therefore, the choice to run separate regressions, which is fairly common in the literature (Baldwin et al. 2005; Lai and Trefler 2002), seems appropriate, since we find evidence of significant differences in elasticity of substitution across industries. The estimated coefficients range between 3 (Vegetables Section II) and 28 (Metal products Section XV), and are largely consistent with those obtained in other studies (Baier and Bergstrand 2001; Eaton and Kortum 2002; Lai and Trefler 2004; Olper and Raimondi 2008). Some values are quite high, but such a degree of substitutability is not inconceivable given the level of disaggregation of our data (Cipollina and Salvatici 2010). What is more surprising perhaps, is the lower substitutability of the primary sectors compared to the secondary ones. In this respect, our results suggest that DC agricultural exports to the EU are more heterogeneous than their industrial exports. The effectiveness of the preferences appears to be inversely related to the height of the applied duties: large impacts are associated to sections with low duties (e.g. Sections VII, XV, XVI, XVII and XX) and large margins are less effective in the presence of high bilateral duties, as in the case of agricultural products (Sections I to IV) and Textiles (Sections XI).

Table 6.6 presents the results for the percentage change in total imports due to the hypothetical elimination of all existing preferences according to (6.6). The average preference impact is around 1%, which means that the absence of preferences would reduce bilateral trade volumes between DC and the 25 EU member countries by 4,315 million Euros. The impact of EU preferences is negligible in the case of Vegetables and Fats and oils (Sections II and III), and this may be explained by the large number of TRQ. The effect for Precious stones (Section XIV), Wood and wood articles (Section IX), is small, which would be expected since the set of goods to be exported is heavily influenced by the endowments of natural resources, and in the case of the Instruments sector (Section XVIII) is characterized by the lowest elasticity value. The largest impacts, at least in relative terms, are for Animal products and Foodstuffs, and Vehicles (Sections I and XVII), both of which have large shares of preferential imports (Table 6.2).

Table 6.6 shows that most of the preference value is represented by the rent earned on exports, which would exist anyway since only 6% of preferential trade would be affected by preference elimination. However, in some cases (Sections VII, XV, and XX) trade volume reductions would reach double digits: it is in these sectors that the preference erosion would be more damaging.

Table 6.6 The estimated preference effect – results for commodity groups

Sectors	Preference effect (%)	Trade volume (million Euros)	% of Preferential trade
Overall	0.96	4,315	6.1
I	2.40	167	4.4
II	0.11	17	0.5
III	0.25	8	1.1
IV	1.84	294	6.5
VI	0.94	149	4.0
VII	1.96	202	8.1
VIII	1.39	79	14.4
IX	0.60	47	4.9
XI	1.65	863	3.9
XII	1.53	149	4.3
XIII	1.81	74	5.0
XIV	0.30	45	4.0
XV	1.81	612	15.8
XVI	0.89	796	8.8
XVII	2.96	571	9.2
XVIII	0.15	11	1.6
XX	1.50	276	17.5

6.5 Conclusions

In this chapter, we investigated whether EU trade preferences are effective at stimulating additional exports through preferential duties. This is a contentious issue and is widely debated in the literature. We present robust estimates controlling for possible biases in three dimensions: measurement of the intensity of the preference margins; impact on the extensive and intensive margins of trade; and distinction between preferential and MFN trade flows.

Methodologically, our study confirms that there is little support for the use of aggregated data and that estimations should be at sector level. Working at the most detailed level allowed by the data increases the problem of zero trade flows. In line with the recent literature, we deal with this problem by applying a Heckman correction procedure in order to control for selection bias due to the presence of zeros.

We quantify the intensity of the preference margins, rather than relying on a simple dummy. In order to emphasize the advantage granted with respect to other importers, preferential margins are computed for each product, as the difference between the highest tariff applied by the EU and the actual duty paid by each exporter.

From a policy perspective, this paper provides new evidence that preferential schemes do impact on trade, but that there are large differences across sectors. First, preferences influence the extensive margins of trade and, overall, there is a slight increase in the probability of registering a positive trade flow. However, the overall positive impact is due to the agricultural preferences (Sections I, II, III and IV), since in all other cases the only significant impacts are negative. This implies that countries benefiting from preferential schemes export a larger set of agricultural goods, and this contradicts the received wisdom that due to preferential policies, exporting countries specialize in a smaller number of products. On the other hand, countries benefiting from preferential schemes export a smaller set of manufactures and, even when they coincide with their true comparative advantages, this may be bad news since some studies point to the contribution of export variety to growth (Broda and Weinstein 2006).

In terms of the impact on trade volumes, we find that EU imports increased by more than 4 billion Euros as a result of preference margins. This is not a trivial amount, and is larger than the value of the preference rent itself (see Table 6.3). On the other hand, it is only a small share (around 6%) of the value of preferential exports to the EU. This means, hypothetically, that the removal of preferences would not affect the vast majority of current flows.

Although decisions about whether and how much to trade does not depend only on a simple substitution elasticity, our results suggest the following implications. Agricultural sectors, namely Sections I and IV, present the largest share of preferential trade, and preferences have been effective in increasing trade at both margins, although the impact on rents is larger than the impact on trade volumes.

The most important sectors in terms of preferential trade flows are manufactures, namely Textiles (Section XI) and Machinery (Section XVI). In both cases, there is a positive impact of preferences on the intensive margins, while exporters tend to specialize in a smaller set of products. Since a significant share of imports still faces positive MFN duties (Table 6.2), DC may look for an enlargement of preferences in these sectors. The same holds for Vehicles (Section XVII), but in this case DC may be worried also about preference erosion since almost 10% of preferential exports hinges on the existence of a preference margin.

To conclude, DC may be concerned about the consequences of preference erosion, in terms of either the negative impact on trade – as in the case of Vehicles – or loss of rents – as in the case of Textiles. On the other hand, there is certainly room to extend current schemes, given that a significant share of EU imports from DC still incurs positive duties. From this perspective, negotiations to increase preference margins are likely to be most effective in such sectors as Plastics which feature a high elasticity of substitution and a large share of imports subject to positive MFN duties.

Acknowledgments We acknowledge financial support from the "New Issues in Agricultural, Food and Bio-energy Trade (AGFOODTRADE)" (Small and Medium-scale Focused Research Project, Grant Agreement no. 212036) research project funded by the European Commission, and the "European Union policies, economic and trade integration processes and WTO negotiations" research project funded by the Italian Ministry of Education, University and Research (Scientific Research Programs of National Relevance 2007). We are grateful to Luca De Benedictis and David Laborde for the comments and the many conversations on the topic. Any remaining errors are solely our responsibility and the views expressed in this paper are those of the authors and do not necessarily reflect those of the European Commission. The views expressed in this paper are the sole responsibility of the authors and do not necessarily reflect those of the European Commission.

Chapter 7
Analysing the Impact of Everything But Arms Initiative Using a Gravity Model

Francesco Aiello and Paola Cardamone

Abstract This chapter assesses the effectiveness of the Everything But Arms (EBA) initiative launched by the European Union (EU) in 2001. It evaluates whether EBA has been effective in increasing exports from Least Developed Countries (LDC) to the EU, over the period 1995–2006. After arguing that the impact of trade preferences should be estimated by using disaggregated trade flows rather than aggregated trade, the analysis is carried out by considering five products (cloves, coffee, crustaceans, molluscs and vanilla beans) which meet three criteria relating to the export intensity of LDC, the actual preferences of EBA and the intra-year distribution of EU tariffs. The export share of the 5-selected goods with respect to national exports is never marginal and, in many cases, is higher than 60%. From an econometric perspective, we improve the reliability of results by giving great attention to the econometric setting and to measurement of the preferential treatment. The evidence differs from one product to another and this supports the decision to work using disaggregated data because it allows us to gauge the sector specificities which would be hidden when analysing total trade.

7.1 Introduction

As trade is widely recognised to be an engine of growth, developed countries have implemented a patchwork of trade agreements under which preferential treatment is granted to exports from Developing Countries (DC). It is expected that trade preferences determine an increase in exports from preference-receiving countries to the market of preference-donor countries *vis-à-vis* other suppliers. The European Union (EU), with its high number of trade preferential arrangements signed with DC, is firmly committed to the promotion of trade with virtually all DC and, through its trade cooperation policy, aims to make a meaningful contribution to

F. Aiello and P. Cardamone
Department of Economics and Statistics, University of Calabria, Via Pietro Bucci – Cubo 1C, 87036 Rende (CS), Italy
e-mail: f.aiello@unical.it; p.cardamone@unical.it

L. De Benedictis and L. Salvatici (eds.), *The Trade Impact of European Union Preferential Policies*, DOI 10.1007/978-3-642-16564-1_7,

stimulate export-led strategies in DC. One important scheme which has been adopted by the EU in order to offer preferential access to DC is the Generalized System of Preferences (GSP). This dates back to the early 1970s when the United Nations Conference on Trade and Development (UNCTAD) recommended the creation of a "Generalized System of Tariff Preferences" to be implemented by each industrialised country. The EU's GSP was adopted in 1971 for a period of 10 years and has been renewed several times, with revisions involving the number of GSP arrangements and the products and countries covered, as well as the tariff cuts. The current GSP, which was renewed in 2008 for a 3-year period, comprises three arrangements: the ordinary GSP, the GSP-Plus and a special agreement for Least Developed Countries (LDC). While only non-sensitive products enter the EU duty-free under the ordinary GSP and additional benefits are granted under GSP-Plus to countries implementing certain international standards of human and labour rights, environmental protection, good governance and the fight against drugs, the special arrangement in favour of LDC provides tariff free and quota free access to all EU imports from the 49 LDC as defined by the United Nations (UN),[1] except for arms and ammunition. This is the reason why the agreement is known as Everything But Arms (EBA). Besides the comprehensive product-coverage of this new initiative, other differences with respect to ordinary GSP and the GSP-Plus are that it will be maintained for an unlimited period of time and will not be subject to the periodic renewal of the Community's scheme of generalized preferences (Council Regulation EC No 2501/2001).

EBA was launched by EU in 2001[2] and its goal is to boost LDC growth by removing all trade restrictions when they export to the EU market. However, even though EBA provides the best market access for LDC exports, its effectiveness is not assured for several reasons. Some of these reasons, such as the weak supply capacity of LDC or the weak institutional capacity of LDC to effectively manage all the administrative issues in order to apply for a trade preference, are external to EBA, while others, like the strict Rules of Origin (RoO), are internal to the new EU initiative. In addition, granting full market access does not necessarily translate into increased exports from LDC because of trade arrangements which pre-existed EBA. For instance, the 36 LDC which are also part of the Cotonou agreement may prefer to export under the Cotonou agreement rather than under EBA, even

[1]A country is classified as an LDC if it meets three criteria based on low-income (3-year average GNI per capita of less than 905 US Dollars, which must exceed 1,086 Dollars to leave the list), weakness of human resources (based on indicators of nutrition, health, education and adult literacy) and economic vulnerability (based on instability of agricultural production, instability of exports, economic importance of non-traditional activities, export concentration and the percentage of population displaced by natural disasters). Countries may "graduate" out of the LDC classification when indicators exceed these criteria. Two countries which have graduated from the LDC status were Botswana in 1994 and Cape Verde in 2007. The classification currently (as of 29th January 2009) applies to 49 countries.

[2]All tariffs and quotas on LDC exports were eliminated in 2001, except for those on bananas, rice and sugar. The removal of import duties applied by the EU in these three sectors was progressively implemented by 2006 in the case of bananas, and by 2009 for rice and sugar.

though tariffs are zero in both schemes. This is for two reasons. The first is that EBA does not introduce particular improvements regarding entry conditions into the EU market with respect to the Cotonou agreement (tariffs faced by African, Caribbean and Pacific countries (ACP) were already very low or zero for a large number of commodities). In other words, many products exported by ACP did not gain any additional tariff preference from the new initiative. The same reasoning may be made for those LDC which already enjoyed duty-free access to EU under the ordinary GSP. The second reason refers to the evidence that the RoO of the arrangement signed by ACP are far less restrictive than those under EBA. This would make the use of EBA preferences more difficult and costly than the use of other preferential treatments (i.e. Brenton 2003; Gallezot and Bureau 2006; UNCTAD 2003).

All these considerations, however, do not necessarily mean that EBA is uneffective in encouraging LDC exports to the EU. This remains an open question which will be addressed in this chapter. One method of evaluating whether a preferential treatment encourages the exports of preferred countries is the gravity equation. This model, in its basic form, posits the idea that trade is positively affected by the economic mass of the trading countries, which is gauged by their GDP and population, and negatively influenced by the geographical distance between them. The appeal of the gravity equation derives from the opportunity it offers for modelling deviations from the normal pattern of trade, where normal is simply meant to be the trade determined by the variables usually referred to as gravitational variables (GDP, population and distance) in the absence of any other disturbance. Deviations from the normal level of trade are captured by augmenting the model with all the factors that may hinder or promote bilateral trade flows, such as a common border, language, religion, or past colonial ties. Preferential trade policies certainly belong to this kind of factor because they entail unilateral reductions in trade barriers granted by developed to DC. Hence, other things being equal, they are expected to stimulate exports from DC to the preference-giving country, so yielding a higher flow of trade than that which would "normally" be expected.

The literature which aims at explicitly analysing the impact of EBA by using the gravity approach is rather limited in quantity. It is comprised of the papers by Pishbahar and Huchet-Bourdon (2008), and Gradeva and Martinez-Zarzoso (2009). These studies share the use of aggregated data, i.e. total exports from LDC to the EU, and the use of a dummy variable as proxy for the preferential policy (this dummy is 1 if the country benefits from EBA and 0 otherwise). From an econometric point of view, Pishbahar and Huchet-Bourdon (2008) use the Ordinary Least Squares (OLS) estimator, while Gradeva and Martinez-Zarzoso (2009) consider the Heckman (1978) procedure in order to control for selection bias due to many zero trade flows. These two works conclude that EBA is not effective in increasing LDC exports to the EU.

The aim of this chapter is to provide further evidence in this field of research by attempting to improve the reliability of results obtained when evaluating the effectiveness of EBA within the analytical framework of the gravity approach. With this aim, the empirical setting considers three key issues regarding the use of disaggregated data of trade flows, the measurement of trade preferences and the econometric estimators to be employed.

With regards the data aggregation on which the evaluation of EBA effectiveness ought to be based, we argue that, in general, the use of total exports is not adequate for evaluating the impact of a trade policy instrument – the preferential treatment – which is conceived to be applied at the product level (see, among many others, Aiello et al. 2010). Indeed, the main objective of any Preferential Trade Agreement (PTA) such as EBA is to alter the incentives for beneficiaries to export more in specific sectors (those in which preferences are granted). This implies that the correct empirical strategy to follow in evaluating the effectiveness of EBA is to use trade statistics at the level of data disaggregation which is parallel to the level at which trade preferences are defined. This has two advantages. On one hand, it allows us to understand whether and to what extent the preferential treatment granted by the EU to LDC through EBA enhances the exports of tariff-triggered products. In this respect, if EBA treatment induces an increase in exports in the sectors for which it makes a difference to market access, the evaluation of the effectiveness of the scheme will be positive, even though aggregate exports from LDC to EU do not significantly change. In addition, the evidence based on disaggregated data does not suffer from the shortcoming relating to the aggregation of tariffs, which, on the contrary, restricts the reliability of results obtained when the gravity equation is estimated using total trade flows (on the bias due to the aggregation of tariffs see, for instance, Cipollina and Salvatici (2008) and Anderson and Neary (2005)). As a study cannot analyse all products, given that the amount of data to be elaborated would be enormous (in 2009 EBA covered 7,140 products at 10 digit level classification, a selection of products must be made. In this chapter, we focus on a group of products at Harmonized System (HS) 4 digit which have been selected by considering three conditions.[3] The first condition refers to the existence of an export capacity of LDC before 2001. The rationale underlying this hypothesis is that if no radical change in the production and export structure of LDC may occur, then a removal of tariffs determines a short run effect which can only be picked up in the empirical analysis if the preferred countries were able to export before EBA was implemented. Therefore, we ordered all HS4 digit goods by the LDC' exports share of the world market in 2000, that is before EBA was in force, and selected products with a market share higher than 4%. The second condition is that GSP tariffs applied by the EU are positive. This ensures that, for the products selected, EBA introduced a real gain in terms of tariff preferences. The rationale for this criterion is that, obviously, it would be pointless to evaluate EBA by

[3]The decision to select the products at HS4 digit level was taken basically because of the necessity to work, at this stage of the research, with groups of commodities which are homogeneous enough to capture LDC' sectoral specialisation in production and exports. At the same time, the HS4 digit level is aggregated enough to limit the amount of information which needs to be elaborated in the descriptive section of the paper. On the other hand, in order to guarantee that the level of data disaggregation regarding the trade flows is parallel to that of preferential tariffs, the successive econometric analysis will be based on data at 8 digit level.

considering individual products with respect to which the EU already guarantees free access under GSP. Finally, we excluded from the study the products with intra-year variability of tariffs because, in such a case, one has to use monthly data on exports and tariffs, thereby increasing exponentially the size of the data to be analysed. Furthermore, the recourse to monthly data would require addressing the issue of seasonality (Cardamone 2011) which is hard to deal with when monthly time series involve many missing values, as is the case with a number of LDC exports.

The HS4 level products which satisfied the above mentioned three conditions are cloves, vanilla beans, coffee, crustaceans and molluscs. Bearing in mind that we are analysing the most vulnerable countries in the world, it is extremely important to point out that many LDC heavily depend on the exports of these five products. For instance, in 2006, exports of coffee accounted for 40.85% of Ethiopia's total exports, about 35% of Rwanda's and 16% of Burundi's. At the same time, the exports of crustaceans made up 21.2% of Madagascar's total exports and 3.81% of Mozambique's. In 2006, molluscs represented 4.3% of the total exports of Senegal, the exports of cloves were 4.2% of Bangladesh's total exports and the exports of vanilla made up about 5% of Madagascar's total exports. Even though we are limiting the analysis to a very restricted sample of products, these figures allow us to say that the selected commodities are really important for some individual countries. Given that the shares of each of these products are not marginal, any increase in their exports surely has an impact on total exports; if this increase can be attributed to the preferential treatment under EBA, then it will be possible to say that the scheme is pro-development.

Limiting the analysis to the literature which explicitly investigates the role of EBA by using the gravity model, the second innovation of this chapter regards the variable used to measure the trade preferences granted by the EU under different arrangements (EBA, GSP, agreements in favour of ACP, Regional Trade Agreements, henceforth RTA). The proxy for preferential treatment that we consider is the margin of preferences, rather than a dummy variable. Due to data availability, this approach is becoming more popular in this field of research, being followed, for instance, by Cardamone (2011) Emlinger et al. (2008), Cipollina and Salvatici (2010), Aiello and Demaria (2009), Agostino et al. (2010), who, however, are mainly interested in studying trade issues other than the impact of EBA. In this chapter, the margin of preference is measured by the difference between the Most Favored Nation (MFN) tariff and the preferential tariff granted under each specific trade arrangement and, therefore, is an explicit measure of the preferential treatment. This overcomes the caveat that dummies do not measure the level of trade preferences (i.e. if we had considered dummies for the different schemes, we would have implicitly assumed that the level of trade preferences under EBA would be the same as those under the Euro-Mediterranean (Euro-Med) or Cotonou Agreements).

Finally, the third distinguishing feature of the study regards the econometric methods used to estimate the gravity model. The methods employed control for heterogeneity, endogeneity and zero-trade flows. While a heterogeneity bias might be due to the likely correlation between specific country-pair fixed effects and regressors, endogeneity could arise because of the simultaneity between the dependent variable (EU imports) and the regressors. Hence, before using a fixed effect estimator, we first perform the Davidson-Mackinnon (DM) test, the results of which suggest that the hypothesis of endogeneity of PTA variables may be rejected. As a consequence of this, we adopt a negative binomial model which, similarly to the Poisson model, controls for zero-trade and heteroskedasticity biases (Santos-Silva and Tenreyro 2006), but relaxes the heavily restrictive assumption regarding the identical mean and variance of the Poisson distribution.

We find mixed evidence with regards the results. When considering the group of LDC which are also part of the Cotonou agreement, we find that during the years of the application of the new initiative, the exports of vanilla and crustaceans have been positively influenced by the trade preferences granted by the EU to LDC. The same applies for the exports of crustaceans from the LDC which are not part of the Cotonou agreement. Unconclusive outcomes or outcomes opposite to the expected ones were found in the remaining cases.

The chapter is organised as follows. Section 7.2 presents a descriptive analysis of LDC exports, Section 7.3 introduces the gravity model and the estimation methods, while Section 7.4 discusses the estimated results. Finally, Section 7.5 concludes.

7.2 The Exports of Everything But Arms to European Union: A Brief Descriptive Analysis

After the introduction of EBA, LDC were expected to react to the new incentives by increasing, *ceteris paribus*, their EU import market share. This expectation is based on the fact that, under EBA, all products from LDC, except arms and ammunitions, enjoy duty and quota free access to the EU (with the exception of bananas, sugar and rice for which there was a progressive implementation by 2006 for bananas and 2009 for rice and sugar). With respect to other exporters, LDC should have improved their competitive position in EU markets because they now get higher prices in a protected market and this should have a positive impact on LDC' incentive to export to the EU. Moreover, EBA is granted for an unlimited period, without periodical renewals, and this reduces uncertainty which, in turn, helps strengthen trade relationships between LDC and the EU, because, amongst other things, it allows long-term investment strategies to be developed.

Table 7.1 presents LDC' market shares regarding three levels of data aggregation (total exports, total agricultural exports and 29 HS2 digit products) for the EU as a whole, over the period 1998–2007.

With regards LDC' total exports, what clearly emerges is that the market share shows an increasing trend from 1998 to 2005, with a substantial shift in 2002, while, more recently (2005–2007), they were stable around a value of 0.18%. On one hand, this evidence suggests that the market shares of LDC have remained very low, but, on the other hand, we find that the relative importance of LDC as suppliers

Table 7.1 Export market shares of Least Developed Countries in the European Union-27 market (1998–2007)

Groups of products (2 digit)	1998	1999	2000	2001	2002	2003	2004	2005	2006	2007
HS01 live animals	0.01	0.01	0.00	0.12	0.01	0.02	0.04	0.28	0.00	0.02
HS02 meat and edible meat offal	0.00	0.00	0.00	0.03	0.05	0.00	0.00	0.00	0.00	0.00
HS03 fish, crustaceans, molluscs, acquatic invertebrates	0.13	0.40	2.12	2.37	2.70	3.29	3.00	2.44	2.38	2.60
HS04 dairy products, eggs, honey edible animal	0.00	0.00	0.00	0.00	0.00	0.00	0.00	0.00	0.00	0.00
HS05 products of animal origin	0.00	0.03	0.39	0.03	0.01	0.03	0.03	0.02	0.03	0.03
HS06 live trees, plants, bulbs, roots, cut flowers	0.00	0.01	0.01	0.01	0.01	0.03	0.03	0.23	0.44	0.85
HS07 edible vegetables and certain roots and tubers	0.05	0.04	0.05	0.15	0.18	0.17	0.29	0.35	0.31	0.33
HS08 edible fruit, nuts peel of citrus, melons	0.07	0.10	0.11	0.09	0.10	0.09	0.12	0.13	0.13	0.11
HS09 coffee, tea, mate and spices	0.47	0.92	1.09	2.36	3.25	3.54	3.01	3.20	3.26	2.57
HS10 cereals	0.01	0.01	0.01	0.01	0.01	0.01	0.03	0.04	0.03	0.03
HS11 milling products, malt, starches, nulin wheat gluten	0.00	0.01	0.01	0.02	0.02	0.03	0.06	0.02	0.05	0.05
HS12 oil seed, oleagic fruits, grain, seed, fruit, etc	0.30	0.17	0.16	0.15	0.15	0.17	0.28	0.26	0.18	0.13
HS13 lac, gums, resins, vegetable saps and extracts	0.35	0.47	0.41	0.96	0.78	0.67	0.47	0.43	0.53	0.58
HS14 vegetables plaiting materials, vegetable products	0.73	0.51	0.35	1.91	2.55	3.31	3.24	2.80	2.33	2.09
HS15 animal, vegetables fats and oils, cleavage products, etc	0.50	0.26	0.95	0.97	0.57	0.34	0.23	0.17	0.06	0.19
HS16 meat, fish and seafood food preparations	0.25	0.12	0.77	0.79	0.52	0.86	0.66	0.52	0.52	0.45
HS17 sugars and sugar preparations	0.02	0.36	0.46	0.71	0.49	0.90	0.80	0.57	0.82	1.03
HS18 cocoa and cocoa preparations	0.03	0.02	0.06	0.08	0.09	0.07	0.11	0.15	0.13	0.12
HS19 cereal, flour, starch, milk preparations and products	0.00	0.00	0.00	0.00	0.01	0.01	0.01	0.02	0.03	0.04
HS20 vegetable, fruit, nut etc	0.01	0.00	0.02	0.01	0.04	0.01	0.01	0.01	0.01	0.04
HS21 miscellaneous edible preparations	0.00	0.00	0.00	0.00	0.00	0.00	0.00	0.00	0.00	0.00
HS22 beverages, spirits and vinegar	0.00	0.00	0.01	0.01	0.01	0.01	0.01	0.01	0.01	0.01
HS23 residues, wastes of food industry	0.05	0.02	0.09	0.11	0.12	0.06	0.03	0.01	0.02	0.02
HS24 tobacco and manufactured tobacco substitutes	0.01	1.13	1.03	0.91	0.91	0.92	0.78	0.91	1.65	1.82

(*continued*)

Table 7.1 (continued)

Groups of products (2 digit)	1998	1999	2000	2001	2002	2003	2004	2005	2006	2007
HS29 organic chemicals	0.00	0.00	0.00	0.00	0.00	0.00	0.00	0.00	0.00	0.00
HS35 albuminoids, modified starches, glues, enzymes	0.00	0.00	0.00	0.00	0.00	0.00	0.00	0.00	0.00	0.00
HS41 raw hides an skins and leather	0.04	0.06	0.06	0.76	1.23	0.87	1.09	1.14	1.29	1.33
HS50 silk	0.00	1.56	3.43	0.01	0.01	0.01	0.01	0.00	0.01	0.01
HS53 wool, animal hair, horsehair yarn and fabric thereof	0.10	0.22	0.10	0.23	4.07	2.57	2.83	3.22	3.27	4.15
Total agricultural exports (HS01-HS24)	0.09	0.16	0.35	0.42	0.42	0.47	0.42	0.41	0.44	0.44
Total exports	0.04	0.05	0.08	0.11	0.20	0.20	0.23	0.20	0.17	0.18

Source: own computations on data from Comtrade (as it is on July 22, 2009)

to the EU27 market registered, as expected, a substantial increase over the period under scrutiny: the 2007 market share was 0.184%, that is to say fivefold that of 1998 (0.038%). The increase in market share was similar when only agricultural exports are considered. LDC market shares are now higher than those regarding total trade, and this fact indicates the more relevant role of EBA for agricultural exports: agricultural market share was 0.089% in 1998, 0.16% in 1999 and increased by 0.4% per year, on average, over the period 2000–2007 (see Table 7.1).

A look at the 2 digit agricultural trade data reveals that the disaggregated picture is extremely confused, in the sense that only seven products (cereals, cereal-flour-starch-milk preparation and products, cocoa, live trees, edible vegetables, tobacco, edible fruit-nuts-peel of citrus-melons) registered a clear increase in market shares after 2001. Market shares declined for other sectors (animal and vegetables fats, residual-wastes of food industry, animal fodder, vegetables-fruit-nut, meat, meat-fish and seafood preparations, lac-gums-resins-vegetable saps and extracts), while no clear pattern emerges for the remaining sectors (milling products, sugar and sugar preparations, and live animals) (see Table 7.1).

Although this examination may help understand the overall changes which have occurred in the capacity of LDC to enter the EU market, it does not lead to any conclusion regarding the role of EBA. This is basically because changes in LDC competitiveness in the EU market do not depend simply on trade preferences granted by EBA, but are also the consequence of other determinants, such as developments in other exporting countries. In addition, at this stage of the research, nothing may be said regarding EBA effectiveness because the HS2 digit level of data aggregation we consider in Table 7.1 is still too high, in the sense that each group at HS2 digit level is composed of a large number of products, which are, in many ways, very different from each other. The main difference we are interested in regards the extent of trade barriers that LDC face in exporting these commodities to the EU. Since tariffs are established at a very detailed level of data aggregation (trade restrictions are established by the EU at 10 digit level), the 2 digit trade statistics of Table 7.1 may hide product-specific behaviours which we are interested in when evaluating the potential role of EBA. Again, we know that the EBA coverage in terms of preferential treatment is at the maximum level (all goods, except for arms and ammunitions, have unlimited free access to the EU), but there is a great difference within each 2 digit agricultural sector when comparing EBA with GSP and ACP tariffs. Indeed, as already mentioned, a tariff preference associated with EBA only exists if the preferential tariffs applied under other trade agreements are positive, and this can occur to a very different extent from one product to another, even within the HS2 digit groups.

Based on these arguments, we identified five products at the HS4 level of aggregation on which the following empirical analyses is based. The selection was made by imposing three conditions which refer to the export intensity of LDC at the HS4 digit level, the existence of an additional preferential treatment due to EBA and the absence of intra-year variability of EU import tariffs.

As for export intensity, we ordered the products at HS4 digit level in terms of LDC' share of world exports in 2000. This ranking allows us to indentify a list of commodities, for which LDC exhibited a certain degree of market competitiveness before EBA came into force in 2001. From this ranking we choose the products for which LDC' market share was higher than 4%, and apply the second criterion of selection to this sub-sample of products. The second condition is meant to identify the products which received an effective tariff advantage from EBA with respect to the pre-existing trade arrangements. In this sense, we restrict the sample to goods with a positive preferential tariff under the ordinary GSP regime, the most general preferential scheme for DC implemented by the EU.[4] Finally, in order to avoid the empirical issues deriving from the use of monthly data – for instance those due to the (1) large amount of missing values, (2) size of the dataset and (3) seasonality – we ignored all the commodities with a tariff calendar.

These three criteria yield a sample composed of the following five HS4 digit products: cloves, vanilla beans, coffee, crustaceans and molluscs. Table 7.2 presents details regarding the application of the three criteria used for selecting the commodities to be analysed.[5] The data displayed shows that the selected sample of products includes certain goods whose world market is largely dominated by exports from LDC (the market share absorbed by these countries was 72% in the case of cloves and 65% for vanilla beans), while the other three products have a market share of 4–5% (coffee, molluscs and crustaceans) (Table 7.2).

For each selected good, Figs. 7.1 and 7.2 show the absolute values and the market shares of LDC' exports to the EU over the period 1995–2006. The five selected products exhibit very different patterns. For instance, total EU imports of

---

[4]Of course, the second condition may be applied also to ACP. We omit to do that, because the sample to be analyzed would be really small and composed by products extremely marginal in terms of export shares.

[5]Within the group of products with a market share above 4%, the exclusion of other products from the successive analysis was for the following reasons: ground-nut oil, copra, lac and gums, oil seed and live sheep were excluded because they have tariff free access to the EU under GSP, whereas nuts, peel of citrus and leguminous vegetables were excluded because they are subject to tariff seasonality (Table 7.2).

Table 7.2 Selecting criteria of the products at Harmonized System 4 digit level

Commodity	LDC world exports (% of world market)	GSP tariff	Seasonality?
Cloves (whole fruit, cloves and stems)	71.03%	Positive	No
Vanilla beans	65.23%	Positive	No
Ground-nut oil, fractions, not chemically modified	32.16%	Equal to MFN (=0)	No
Copra	12.32%	Equal to MFN (=0)	No
Live sheep and goats	8.77%	Since 2002 GSP tariff was equal to 0	No
Coconuts, Brazil nuts and cashew nuts, fresh or dried	8.64%	Equal to MFN (=0)	Yes
Lac, natural gums, resins, gum-resins and balsams	6.78%	Equal to MFN (=0)	No
Peel of citrus fruit or melons	5.96%	Positive	Yes
Oil seeds and oleaginous fruits nec	5.49%	Equal to MFN (=0)	No
Crustaceans	5.02%	Positive	No
Leguminous vegetables, fresh or chilled	4.71%	Positive	Yes
Coffee, coffee husks and skins and coffee substitutes	4.34%	Positive	No
Molluscs	4.05%	Positive	No

Source: own computations on data from Comtrade and TARIC

cloves and vanilla from LDC increased greatly immediately after 2000, but they suffered a sharp reduction in 2001 and 2003, respectively. However, with respect to total EU clove imports, those from LDC decreased, on average, over the period 1995–2006, while LDC export-shares of vanilla beans alternated between decreasing and increasing annual changes (around an average share of around 0.7%). With regards coffee, the time-series of EU imports from LDC (both in absolute and relative terms) was fairly stable, except for an unusual change between 1999 and 2000. Finally, EU imports of molluscs and crustaceans from LDC increased up until 2000 and decreased after 2002 and 2003. The same applies for their export-shares (Figs. 7.1 and 7.2).

Another important issue to be addressed concerns the level of tariffs that countries face when exporting the selected products to the EU market. Figs 7.3–7.7 display the import tariffs under the four main EU preferential trade agreements, namely the ordinary GSP, the preferential tariffs granted to ACP, the EBA and the average tariffs of RTA signed by the EU.

As shown in Figs. 7.3–7.7, GSP duties are higher than those applied under the other preferential schemes (EBA, Cotonou and RTA), whatever the product; this is the result of the tariff-triggered criterion we used in selecting the products, and provides us a measure of the relative tariff advantage that LDC would have enjoyed if they had exported under the EBA regime instead of reverting to GSP. Other evidence regards the fact that the duties levied on EU imports from ACP are zero for the five products concerned. This fact gives further interest to the analysis because the group of LDC can be split into two sub-samples. The first sub-sample

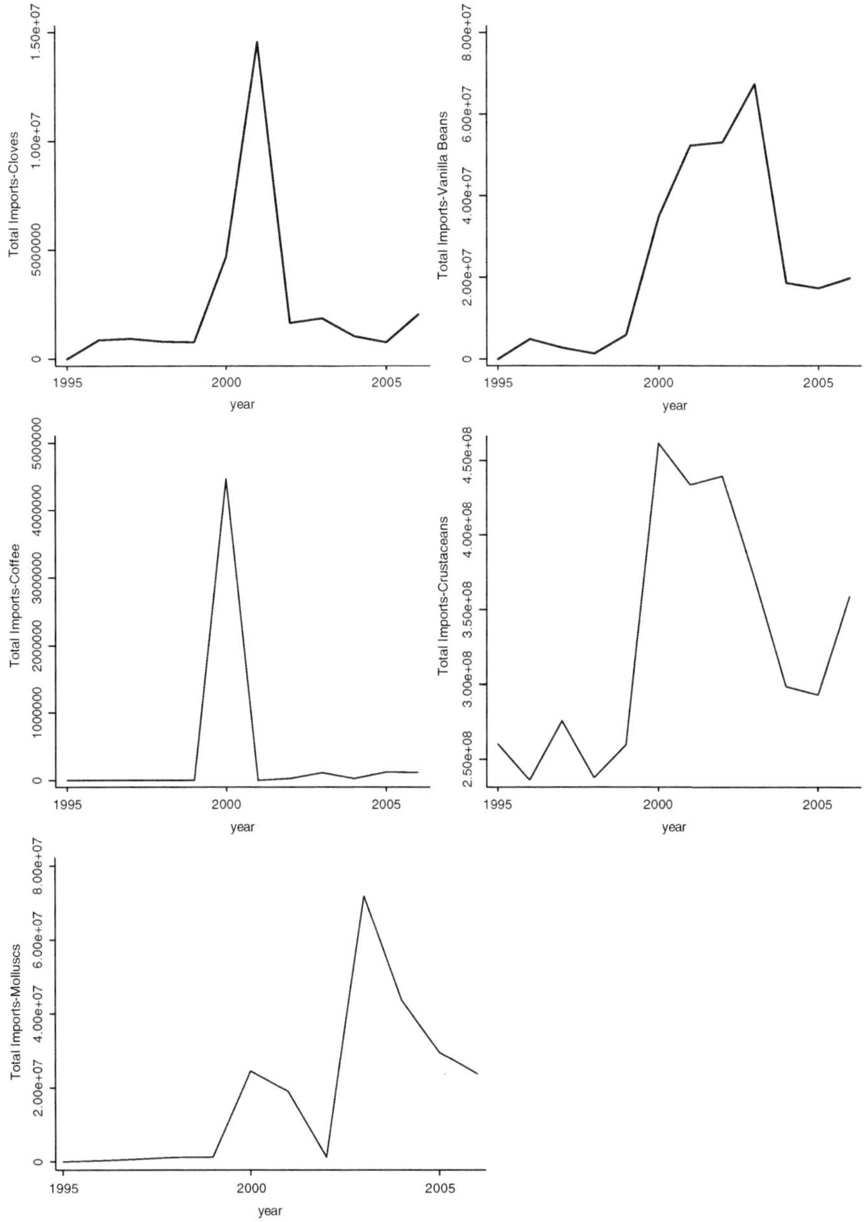

Fig. 7.1 European Union imports from Least Developed Countries of the five selected Harmonized System 4 digit agricultural products analysed (1995–2006). Data (in thousand Euros) are expressed at 2000 constant prices

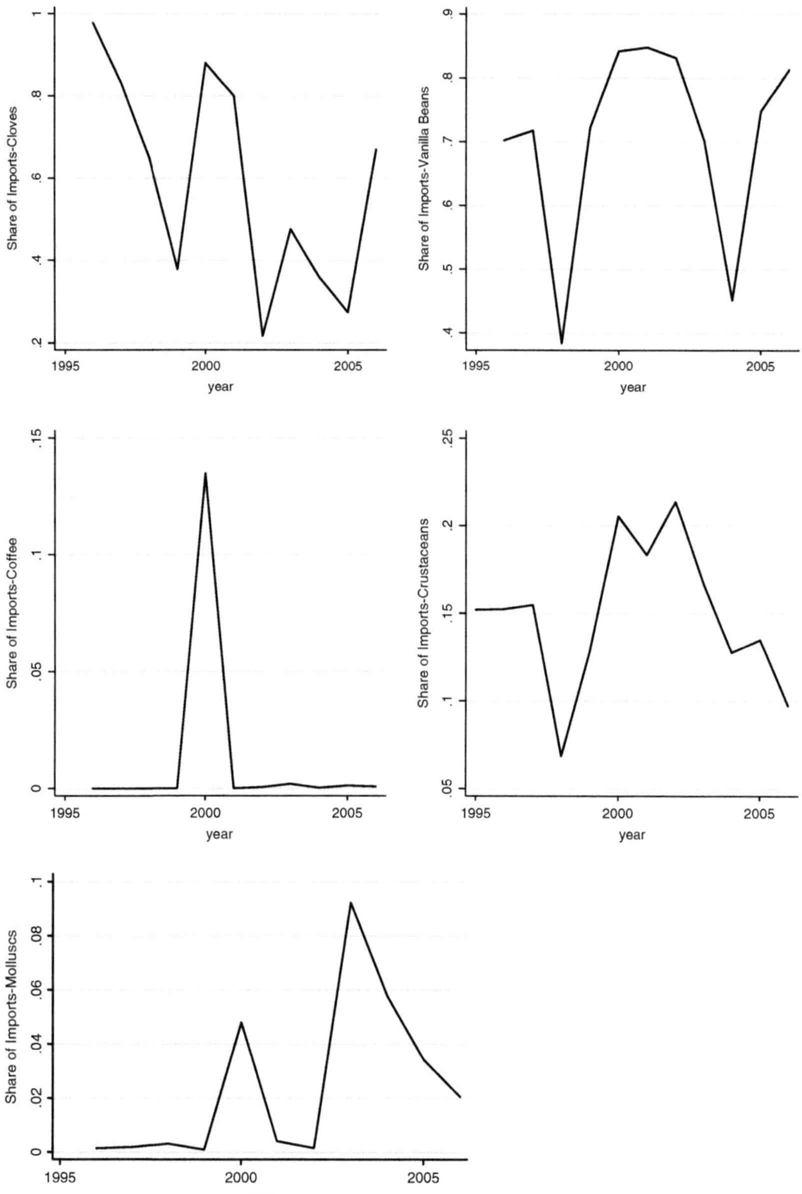

Fig. 7.2 Shares (in percentage) of Least Developed Countries' exports to the European Union market for the five selected Harmonized System 4 digit agricultural products analysed (1995–2006)

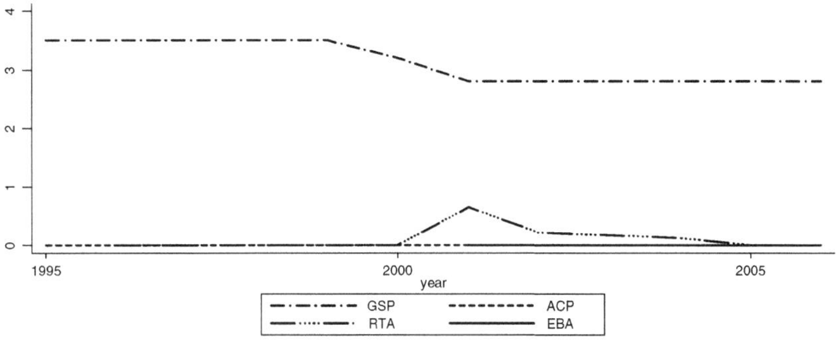

Fig. 7.3 Tariff profile for European Union imports of Cloves by Preferential Trade Agreements, 1995–2006

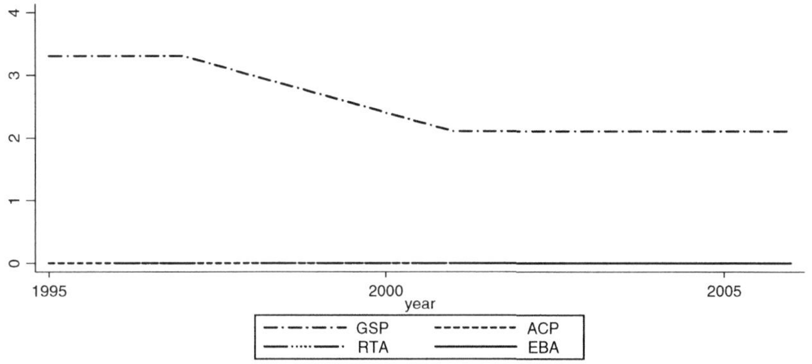

Fig. 7.4 Tariff profile for European Union imports of Vanilla beans by Preferential Trade Agreements, 1995–2006

comprises the 13 LDC which are not part of the Cotonou agreement.[6] Before 2001 the exports from these 13 LDC towards the EU market were levied according to the positive GSP-tariffs and, thus, the free market access they have been given under EBA has increased their competitiveness in the EU (we label these countries as $13LDC_{not\text{-}ACP}$). The second sub-sample is composed of the 36 LDC which were also part of the Cotonou Agreement (henceforth $36LDC_{ACP}$).[7] For the 5 selected products, the $36LDC_{ACP}$ did not obtain any tariff advantage from the new scheme;

[6]Afghanistan, Bangladesh, Bhutan, Cambodia, Djibouti, Kiribati, Lao People's Democratic Republic Maldives, Nepal, Solomon Islands, Yemen, East Timor, Samoa.

[7]Angola, Benin, Burkina Faso, Burundi, Cape-Verde, Central African Republic, Chad, Comoros, Congo Dem. Rep, Equatorial-Guinea, Eritrea, Ethiopia, Gambia, Guinea, Guinea Bissau, Haiti, Liberia, Madagascar, Malawi, Mali, Mauritania, Mozambique, Niger, Rwanda, Sao' Tomé and Principe, Senegal, Sierra Leone, Solomon Islands, Somalia, Sudan, Tanzania, Togo, Tuvalu, Uganda, Vanuatu, Zambia.

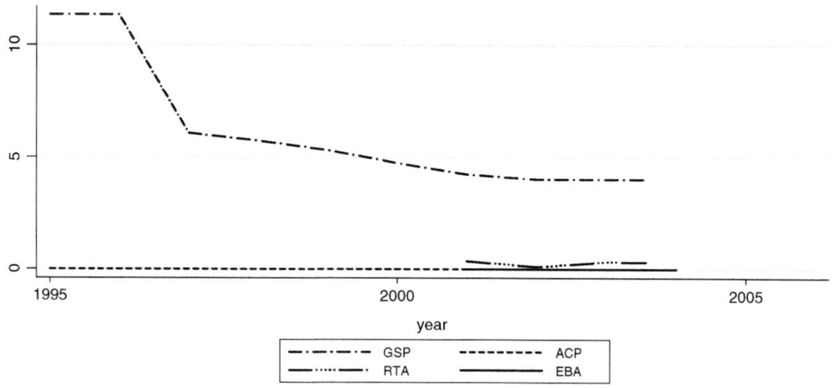

Fig. 7.5 Tariff profile for European Union imports of Coffee by Preferential Trade Agreements, 1995–2006

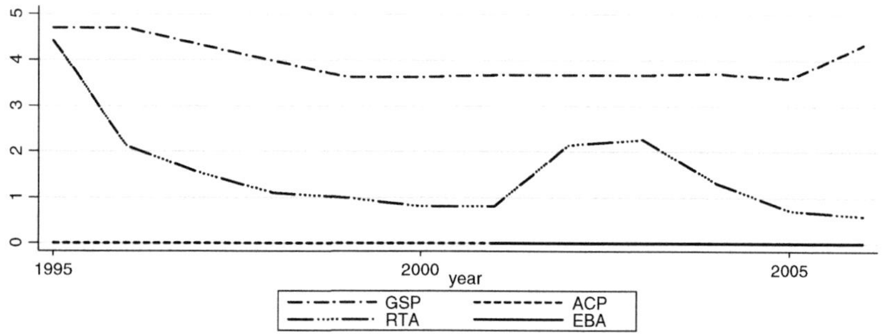

Fig. 7.6 Tariff profile for European Union imports of Crustaceans by Preferential Trade Agreements, 1995–2006

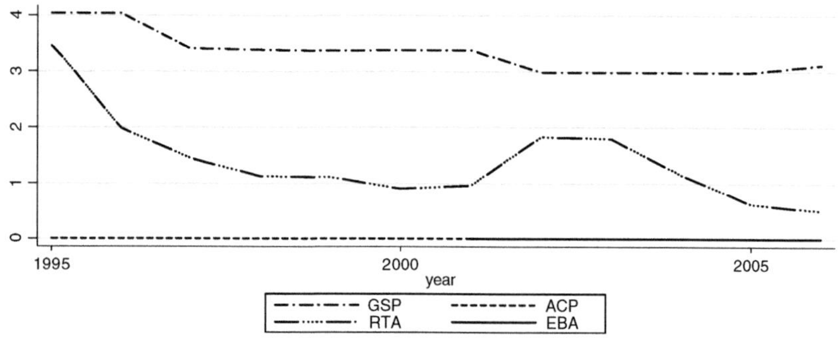

Fig. 7.7 Tariff profile for European Union imports of Molluscs by Preferential Trade Agreements, 1995–2006

the opposite is true for the $13LDC_{not\text{-}ACP}$ which moved from a regime of positive GSP-tariffs to the tariff-free and quota-free access granted by EBA. As far as the five selected sectors are concerned, it is reasonable to argue that the capacity of the $36LDC_{ACP}$ to enter the EU market did not change with the new preferential agreement. At the same time, it is likely that EBA exerts a certain influence in favour of the exports to the EU from the $13LDC_{not\text{-}ACP}$ because the import tariffs they currently face for the five products under scrutiny are zero, while the GSP duties they would have to pay without the EBA initiative would be positive.

As for the other preferential schemes, we find that in the cases of vanilla, coffee and cloves (except for 2000), there was no substantial difference between EBA (or ACP) and RTA tariffs (all of them were around zero). Finally, with regards the exports of molluscs and crustaceans, EBA attributed an effective tariff advantage with respect to those DC which had signed a RTA.

7.3 Empirical Setting: The Gravity Model and The Estimation Methods

In order to assess the effectiveness of the EBA initiative, we estimate the following multiplicative gravity equations over the period 1995–2006:

$$\begin{aligned} X^s_{ijt} = {} & (GDP/POP)_{it}^{\alpha_1} (GDP/POP)_{jt}^{\alpha_2} (POP_{it})^{\alpha_3} (POP_{jt})^{\alpha_4} \\ & \times \exp(\alpha + \alpha_t + \alpha^s_{ij} + u^s_{ijt} + \delta_1 MTR_{it} + \delta_2 MTR_{jt} + \beta_1 GSP^s_{jt} \\ & + \beta_2 ACP^s_{jt} + \beta_3 RTA^s_{jt} + \beta_4\, 13LDC^{s,pre2001}_{NotACP,jt} + \beta_5\, 13LDC^{s,post2001}_{NotACP,jt} \\ & + \beta_6\, 36LDC^{s,pre2001}_{ACP,jt} + \beta_7\, 36LDC^{s,post2001}_{ACP,jt}) \end{aligned} \tag{7.1}$$

where subscript i refers to the individual EU15 importers ($i = 1,\ldots,15$), j to exporters ($j = 1,\ldots 191$), t to the year ($t = 1995,\ldots,2006$), and s indicates the agricultural commodities, at 8 digit level of disaggregation (see footnote 5), which are included in the five groups of aggregate products we selected at HS4 digit level.[8] X is the EU's import flow, GDP is the Gross Domestic Product, POP is the population. $\alpha^s{}_{ij}$ indicates the commodity-country pair fixed effects, while $u^s{}_{ijt}$ is the error term.[9] The acronym MTR stands for Multilateral Trade Resistance and is meant to measure trade barriers that each country faces with respect to all its trading partners. As suggested by Anderson and van Wincoop (2003), bilateral trade should

[8]There is just one commodity at 8 digit level within the HS4 digit of cloves and vanilla beans, while there are seven at 8 digit level within the HS4 digit of coffee, thirty-one in the group of crustaceans and, finally, thirty-two products in the aggregation of molluscs.

[9]The gravity model specification used does not include all the variables, such as distance, common border, common language, the number of landlocked countries in the pair, or past colonial ties that are time invariant and then absorbed by the commodity-country-pair fixed effects.

be higher between trading countries with relatively low trade barriers. We determine a proxy of MTR, following the approach proposed by Carrère et al. (2009), which extends the multilateral resistance approximation used by Baier and Bergstrand (2009) to a panel framework. MTR terms for country i and country j are defined as

$$MTR_{it} = \sum_{k} \frac{GDP_{kt}}{GDP_{Wt}} \ln(DIST_{ik}) \tag{7.2}$$

and

$$MTR_{jt} = \sum_{k} \frac{GDP_{kt}}{GDP_{Wt}} \ln(DIST_{jk}) \tag{7.3}$$

where W is the world, i, j, k indicate the individual countries, t is time, GDP represents the Gross Domestic Product, $DIST_{ik}$ ($DIST_{jk}$) is the distance in km between the capitals of country $i(j)$ and country k.

For each preferential variable (*GSP*, *ACP*, *EBA* and *RTA*) and each tariff-line, we compute the preferential margin as the difference between the applied MFN duty and the preferential duty granted under each specific trade arrangement. We address the overlapping of preferences by assuming that if a country benefits from GSP and ACP agreements, the trade flows enter the EU market under the ACP regime. Similarly, if a country benefits from GSP and RTA, then we assume that the imports enter the EU market under RTA. These choices are based on two arguments. The first refers to the fact that, for the five products considered in this chapter, GSP tariffs are generally higher than the preferential tariffs established in favour of ACP and RTA countries. The second consideration is that RTA and ACP agreements involve RoO which are much less restrictive than those under GSP. Therefore, exporting countries will prefer not to use the GSP scheme even if the preferential margin is equal to that received with the Cotonou agreement or with a RTA. To be more precise, the *GSP* variable is the preferential margin granted by the EU to the imports of the s-*th* product from the developing countries eligible for GSP treatment only. In other words, the *GSP* variable regards a sample of countries net of LDC and ACP. Similarly, the *ACP* variable represents the margin of trade preference in favour of the group of countries net of LDC which signed the Cotonou agreement. The *RTA* variable indicates the margin of preference granted in favour of developing countries which signed bilateral trade agreements with the EU.[10]

[10]The agreements included in the analysis are those with Albania, Algeria, Andorra, Bosnia Herzegovina, Bulgaria, Chile, Croatia, Cyprus, Czech Republic, Egypt, Estonia, Hungary, Iceland, Israel, Jordan, Latvia, Lebanon, Libya, Lithuania, Macedonia, Mexico, Morocco, Norway, Palestinian Authority, Poland, Romania, Serbia and Montenegro, Slovakia, Slovenia, South Africa, Switzerland, Syria, Tunisia, Turkey.

The procedure used to define the variables *GSP*, *ACP* and *RTA* leaves out the LDC, which we split into two sub-samples on the basis of whether they are eligible or not for the Cotonou agreement. Furthermore, for each of these two groups of countries, we consider the preferential treatment received before and after the implementation of EBA, i.e. before and after 2001. Thus, for instance, the variable $13LDC^{pre-2001}_{Not-ACP}$ in (7.1) indicates the margin of preference enjoyed up to 2001 by the group of the 13LDC which did not sign the Cotonou (see footnote 6). By extension, the meanings of $13LDC^{post-2001}_{Not-ACP}$, $36LDC^{pre-2001}_{ACP}$ and $36LDC^{post-2001}_{ACP}$ can be easily inferred.

Data on EU imports are from Comext.[11] Inward processing imports are subtracted from total imports in order to take into account imports entering the EU to be processed and re-exported benefitting from tariff exemption. The set of importing countries is comprised of the individual EU15 member states,[12] while there are 191 exporters, i.e., all the countries for which trade statistics are available. As far as the explanatory variables are concerned, data on GDP and population are from the 2008 World Development Indicators. All data regarding values are in constant 2000 Euros. The preferential variables GSP, ACP, RTA and EBA are determined using the dataset DBTAR (Gallezot 2005) for the period 2001–2004, while for the period 1995–2000 and the years 2005 and 2006, they are calculated by extracting the information needed from TARIC (http://ec.europa.eu/taxation_customs/dds/tarhome_en.htm).

With regards to the methods used to estimate (7.1), it is worth noticing that the results obtained from the estimation of a gravity equation suffers from three main potential sources of bias, which are related to country-pair heterogeneity, endogeneity and the presence of zero trade flows.

Heterogeneity may be due to observable and non-observable factors which are specific to each country-pair. From an econometric perspective, the omission of such factors leads to a mis-specification of the gravity equation, and could produce biased and/or inconsistent estimates. To control for country-pair individual effects, we have included in the gravity equation a set of commodity-country pair fixed effects (α^s_{ij}) derived from the following decomposition of the error term: $\varepsilon^s_{ijt} = \alpha_t + \alpha^s_{ij} + u^s_{ijt}$ (see (7.1)).

[11]The Comext dataset provides data expressed in Cost, Insurance and Freight (CIF) value. Thus, in order to transform data to Free On Board (FOB) values, we compute the CIF/FOB ratio and follow the International Monetary Fund (IMF) Direction of Trade Statistics (DOTS) procedure. For this calculation, data are from Comtrade. This source provides data at HS6 level; hence, we assume that CIF/FOB ratios do not differ if we move from HS6 to 8 digit commodity lines.

[12]In order to work on the same sample of importers over the entire period taken into consideration, we disregard the 2004 EU enlargement to 25 members. However, this fact should not introduce any bias in the estimations because, in the five sectors under scrutiny, LDC exports predominantly go to EU15, while those towards new EU members are extremely limited. Furthermore, this paper covers just 2 years (2005 and 2006) after the new memberships of 2004 and it is highly likely that EBA has had no effect on trade in such a short period of time.

The endogeneity issue is related to the fact that PTA variables could be determined simultaneously with trade flows. In fact, it is not unanimously agreed whether countries trade more because they have a PTA or that they participate in a PTA because they already traded relatively more with each other than with other countries. Thus, we perform the DM endogeneity test, which compares OLS and Instrumental Variable (IV) estimations in a panel framework.[13] As can be seen from Table 7.3, the *p*-values of the DM test allow us to reject the hypothesis of endogeneity of the preferential variables in all estimations.

With regards zero trade flows, we take into account the arguments put forward by Santos-Silva and Tenreyro (2006) according to which a multiplicative gravity specification is more appropriate than a log-linear one. These authors show that the log-linearisation of the gravity equation changes the "properties of the error term in a nontrivial way" (Santos-Silva and Tenreyro 2006, p. 644) because the error terms of the original multiplicative specification are heteroskedastic. This bias violates the statistical independence of the error term and the independent variables and leads to inconsistent estimates (see also Westerlund and Wilhelmsson 2006). Hence, Santos-Silva and Tenreyro (2006) supported the choice of the multiplicative specification of the gravity model and employed a Poisson model. We use the negative binomial model with fixed effects instead, because the Poisson model assumes equal mean and variance of the dependent variable whereas the negative binomial model allows the likely over-dispersion in trade flow observations to be taken into account.

7.4 Estimation Results

Table 7.3 presents the results obtained by estimating (7.1) using the negative binomial estimator. As for the impact of population, it has been argued that larger countries trade more and, thus, the coefficients relating to population are expected to be positive. However, if an exporter is large in terms of population, it may need its production to satisfy domestic demand, so that it may tend to export less (Oguledo and Macphee 1994). On the other hand, it may export more than a small country, as is the case when large firms achieve economies of scale. The same reasoning can be applied to the case of the importing country: if large, it may either import less because it is likely that the domestic sector finds it profitable to develop and make the country self-sufficient, or it may import more because it cannot satisfy all domestic demand with its own production (Pusterla 2007). Even

[13]In performing this test we consider just one preferential variable which includes all preferential schemes. If a country benefits from GSP and ACP or GSP and RTA, then ACP and RTA are the agreements considered in the computation, respectively. The logarithm of aid received by the exporting country is the variable used to instrument the preferential variable. We verify that the endogenous variable is highly correlated with the instrument, even after sifting out the other exogenous variables in the equation, in order to meet the "order conditions" (Wooldridge 2006).

Table 7.3 Estimates of the multiplicative specification of the gravity model

	Cloves			Vanilla beans			Coffee			Crustaceans			Molluscs		
GSP only	−0.28	(0.08)	***	0.12	(0.05)	**	0.05	(0.02)	**	0.05	(0.00)	***	−0.03	(0.01)	***
ACP only	−8.60	(512.82)		−0.03	(0.06)		0.05	(0.03)		0.05	(0.00)	***	−0.06	(0.02)	***
RTA	0.28	(0.06)	***	0.03	(0.03)		0.03	(0.01)	***	0.04	(0.00)	***	0.03	(0.01)	***
LDC_pre2001	–	(–)		–	(–)		–	(–)		0.06	(0.01)	***	−7.84	(605.48)	
EBA	–	(–)		–	(–)		–	(–)		0.04	(0.01)	***	−0.14	(0.07)	*
ACP_LDC_pre2001	−0.09	(0.07)	–	0.25	(0.05)	***	–	(–)		0.05	(0.00)	***	−0.02	(0.02)	
ACP_EBA	−0.20	(0.08)	**	0.41	(0.07)	***	−0.06	(0.06)		0.04	(0.00)	***	−0.00	(0.01)	
log(POP_exporter)	−0.14	(0.06)	**	0.18	(0.05)	***	−0.12	(0.03)	***	0.03	(0.01)	***	0.04	(0.01)	***
log(POP_importer)	0.51	(0.09)	***	0.51	(0.08)	***	0.21	(0.04)	***	0.19	(0.01)	***	0.16	(0.02)	***
log(GDP/POP_exporter)	−0.81	(0.14)	***	0.26	(0.08)	***	0.45	(0.03)	***	0.07	(0.01)	***	−0.04	(0.01)	***
log(GDP/POP_importer)	1.37	(0.31)	***	1.45	(0.3)	***	−0.15	(0.12)		−0.10	(0.03)	***	−0.00	(0.05)	
MTR_importer	−1.22	(0.38)	***	−2.69	(0.45)	***	−0.25	(0.15)	*	0.20	(0.04)	***	0.14	(0.07)	**
MTR_exporter	83.33	(15.62)	***	6.08	(7.33)		7.92	(1.43)	***	8.56	(0.38)	***	8.85	(0.55)	***
Trend	0.19	(0.02)	***	0.18	(0.02)	***	0.16	(0.01)	***	0.01	(0.00)	***	0.16	(0.00)	***
Costant	−410.11	(42.34)	***	−392.52	(41.36)	***	−325.61	(16.87)	***	−24.78	(4.92)	***	−329.34	(7.35)	***
Observations	1,056			1,350			4,877			6,0432			26,322		
Wald Chi-square	297.5			266.44			757.54			1,752.44			2,718.18		
Davidson-MacKinnon test	0.50			0.21			1.50			0.16			2.89		
p-value	0.48			0.65			0.22			0.69			0.09		

Dependent variable: imports in levels, 1995–2006

Note: all regressions include yearly dummies; standard errors in parenthesis (robust to heteroskedasticity). (*) significant at 10% level; (**) significant at 5% level; (***) significant at 1% level though these are very general considerations regarding the expected sign of the standard gravity variables, in our case we expect that the EU population will exert a positive effect on EU imports of the products under scrutiny. This is basically because EU production in these sectors is negligible, and thus domestic demand may be satisfied by imports alone. We find that the population of exporters has a positive impact on EU imports of cloves and while the population of EU importers has a positive and significant effect on imports of coffee, crustaceans and molluscs.[14] The GDP pro capita of exporters has a positive effect on EU imports of coffee, vanilla beans and crustaceans, while the coefficient of importers' GDP per capita is positive in the case of cloves and vanilla beans.

The estimated impact of PTAs on EU imports varies across products. In particular, it is found that the ordinary GSP enhances the exports of vanilla beans, coffee and crustaceans from developing countries to the EU. The trade preferences enjoyed by ACP are only effective in increasing EU imports of crustaceans, while RTA have a positive effect on EU imports in every sector (the coefficient is always significant, with the exception of that estimated in the model explaining EU imports of vanilla beans).

The evidence regarding the effectiveness of EBA is provided by looking at the estimated coefficients of the variables $13LDC^{post-2001}_{Not-ACP}$ and $36LDC^{post-2001}_{ACP}$ and comparing them with those associated with the variables $13LDC^{pre-2001}_{Not-ACP}$ and $36LDC^{pre-2001}_{ACP}$. By referring to the general arguments regarding the positive role of the preferential treatment in enhancing the exports of preferred countries, the sign of the parameters β_5 and β_7 is expected to be positive.

The study reveals that the impact of EBA is mixed. Let's proceed by pointing out that the variables $13LDC^{pre-2001}_{Not-ACP}$ and $36LDC^{post-2001}_{ACP}$ are dropped in three out of five regressions. This is because the $13LDC_{Not\text{-}ACP}$ did not export cloves, vanilla or coffee to the EU over the period analysed. Again, no robust result comes from the regression of molluscs. In this case the coefficient of $13LDC^{pre-2001}_{Not-ACP}$, namely β_4, is negative but not significant, while the parameter β_5 remains negative (-0.13) and smaller than β_4 after 2001. However, the economic interpretation of β_5 should be made with caution because of the 10% level of significance. As regards crustaceans, we find that the exports from the $13LDC_{Not\text{-}ACP}$ to the EU were positively affected by the preferential treatment granted by the EU. This holds both when these countries exported under the ordinary GSP up 2001 (the estimated value of β_4 is 0.06) and when they enjoyed free market access granted unilaterally by the EU through the EBA initiative (the estimated value of β_5 is 0.04). Thus, in the regression of crustaceans, as β_5 is positive we conclude that EBA positively affects the exports from $13LDC_{Not\text{-}ACP}$.

As far as the group of $36LDC_{ACP}$ is concerned, results displayed in Table 7.3 indicate that the estimates obtained when explaining the exports of coffee and

[14]The coefficient associated to population is given by the difference between the estimated parameter of population and that of the ratio GDP/population (see (7.1)).

molluscs are not interpretable because of their low statistical significance, while a negative effect of EBA after 2001 has been found in the case of cloves. Encouraging evidence comes from the regressions of vanilla beans and crustaceans. It has been found that the trade preferences granted by the EU have been effective in increasing these exports, both before and since 2001. When analysing the exports of vanilla beans, it emerges that the estimated impact of ACP preferences is $\beta_6 = 0.25$ before 2001, i.e. when these $36LDC_{ACP}$ countries used the preferences under Cotonou. The effect of trade preferences increases to $\beta_7 = 0.41$ when considering the years (2001–2006) of EBA application. All this suggests that the preferential treatment granted by the EU in favour of the $36LDC_{ACP}$ determines a substantial positive impact in increasing the exports of vanilla beans towards the EU market and that this impact increases with EBA. A similar positive impact of trade preferences emerges when considering the exports of crustaceans from $36LDC_{ACP}$ to the EU. In such a case, exports from the group of $36LDC_{ACP}$ expand, as a result, first for trade preferences during the years of application of Cotonou ($\beta_6 = 0.05$), and secondly when EBA comes into force ($\beta_7 = 0.04$).

The evidence shows how results differ from one sector to another. This, on the one hand, limits the possibility to draw a general conclusion about the role of EBA, but, on the other hand, supports the approach followed in this chapter of conducting a study using data at product level. Indeed, in such a way, we gauge the sector specificities which, otherwise, using aggregated trade flows, would be hidden. In fact, results obtained in this chapter differ from those found by Pishbahar and Huchet-Bourdon (2008) and Gradeva and Martinez-Zarzoso (2009). Pishbahar and Huchet-Bourdon (2008) show that the impact of EBA on EU agricultural imports is always negative when significant. This result is analogous to that provided by Gradeva and Martinez-Zarzoso (2009) when they analyse the effect of EBA on EU total imports from those LDC belonging to the Cotonou agreement. On the other hand, our regressions yield results which, in some cases, do not match expectations but in others do, as in the cases of vanilla beans and crustaceans. Broadly speaking, this is an unexpected outcome given that tariff gains due to EBA were not marginal for the $13LDC_{not\text{-}ACP}$ group (see Table 7.2 and Figs. 7.3–7.7). In a nutshell, EBA did not divert LDC trade from the rest of the world towards the EU, though $13LDC_{Not\text{-}ACP}$ got substantial tariff gains in the markets taken into consideration.

From an econometric perspective, the unexpected evidence obtained for the clove, coffee and mollusc sectors is due to the fact that the array of exports comprises scant observations regarding LDC exports. In other words, the array of exports from LDC is composed of a very limited number of positive values or, equivalently, of a massive number of zeros. This makes the estimation procedures very difficult. In brief, LDC exports to the EU were driven by just few countries which exported to a restricted number of individual EU importers for a limited number of years. By limiting the discussion to the 5-product case studied in this chapter, it emerges that there was no radical change in the structure of trade relationships with the EU over the years of application of EBA.[15] We observe that no LDC country became a new exporter to the EU, a fact that could be interpreted as a result, in these sectors, of the new initiative. In addition, LDC world market share in the five analysed sectors tended to diminish, something which may have been due to the role of emerging actors in the world market or/and to the likely tendency within each LDC country to divert production and exports towards other more remunerative sectors and/or countries. The understanding of these facts lies beyond the scope of this work, but it is likely that they may contribute to explain the weak effectiveness of EBA revealed in some of our estimations.

7.5 Conclusions

This chapter assesses the effectiveness of the EBA initiative on the LDC exports of cloves, vanilla beans, coffee, crustaceans and molluscs over the period 1995–2006. The sample of commodities is derived from a selection process based on three conditions concerning the overall export capacity of LDC, the existence of an effective tariff gain for LDC as a result of EBA and the absence of intra-year seasonality in tariff levels.

With respect to other literature dealing with this issue, the effectiveness of EBA in promoting an increase in LDC exports, and using the same empirical framework, namely the gravity model, we introduce a few innovations. First of all, unlike the rest of the literature using the gravity model to explicitly evaluate the impact of EBA, this chapter proposes a measure of preferential trade policies based on the preferential margin and not on dummies. Secondly, this chapter presents an evaluation obtained by using data disaggregated at 8 digit level in order to avoid aggregation bias in calculating an average measure of tariffs and with the aim of better identifying the key trade flow on which the preferential treatment is expected to have an impact. Thirdly, we control for country heterogeneity, endogeneity and zero-trade flows. Estimations were made using the negative binomial model.

Results, in some ways, contrast with those obtained in previous works which have unanimously found that EBA was not effective in increasing EU imports from LDC. It should be noted that those papers consider total trade and not imports at commodity level. On the contrary, by using trade at a very high level of data

[15]For instance, no country in the $13LDC_{Not\text{-}ACP}$ group exported cloves, coffee and vanilla beans to the EU over the period under scrutiny, only one exported molluscs and, finally, only five exported crustaceans. The same applies when considering the $36LDC_{ACP}$. In this case there were just two exporters of cloves and vanilla beans and seven coffee exporting countries. Furthermore, these products were imported by a very restricted number of individual EU15 countries and the relative trade flows existed, at maximum, for four out of twelve years. As for molluscs, there were just seven $36LDC_{not\text{-}ACP}$ which exported to the EU, while crustaceans were exported to the EU by twenty five $36LDC_{not\text{-}ACP}$. Finally, Tanzania only exported vanilla beans to Belgium and just for 1 year, 2000.

disaggregation, we have shown that the EBA initiative exerts for some products a positive role in enhancing LDC exports to the EU. In particular, the exports of crustaceans and vanilla were positively affected by the preferential treatment provided under EBA while no conclusion can be drawn when considering the exports of coffee, molluscs and cloves.

A limitation of this study is that it is based on a small number of products and, therefore, concerns arise regarding the possibility to generalise about the results. As a partial answer to this criticism, we stress that the main motivation for the work stems from the belief that preferential trade policies have to be evaluated by using disaggregated data and, hence, a selection of products is necessary. Evidently, the possibility of drawing general conclusions about the role of EBA is not to be expected from this study, but our aim is to provide robust sectoral evidence allowing us to argue whether or not EBA has stimulated exports from LDC to the EU of a specific product. Moreover, further research could also be addressed in the estimation of a dynamic model as it also allows us to measure the long-run effect of the EBA treatment.

Many factors contribute to the result regarding the partial effectiveness of the EBA initiative. For instance, we get an indication of the weak trade relationship between LDC, as a group, and the EU by looking at the trade statistics used throughout this work. We find that there are very few LDC actually exporting to the EU and this, from a technical point of view, is a source of the unsatisfactory estimations. This is because, whereas on one hand, EBA may have had a positive effect on an individual country, on the other hand, this effect might not be captured by a gravity equation, because the estimated parameters refer to the average impact of the EU policy in the entire set of LDC. This is, of course, common to all regressions, whatever the specific focus, but in our case it is exacerbated by the massive presence of zeros in the array of exports from LDC. If these arguments convince, then one possible direction for further research could be the addressing of the issues regarding the impact of EBA by carrying out country-case studies with details about the entire export structure in each economy.

From a more general point of view, the fact that only few LDC exported to the EU might be due to the weak supply capacity of LDC, but it is also related to the existence of non-tariff barriers, such as transaction costs associated with RoO, administrative compliance costs and sanitary and phytosanitary standards which might reduce the effectiveness of preferential margins, especially for the smallest or poorest countries. In particular, as Bureau et al. (2007, p. 196) highlighted, the main motivation for the low utilisation of preferences is that DC are unable to "match the technical, sanitary, phytosanitary and traceability requirements imposed by developed countries, and, in particular, the private standards imposed by importers and retailers." This is particularly true for LDC which are often unable to satisfy the standards required by the EU private retail sector. Therefore, one explanation for the partial effectiveness of EBA is that private standards impede LDC exports to the EU market even though they enjoy tariff and quota free access. This means that the advantages relating to the preferential treatment are counterbalanced by the costs to satisfy private standards. Of course, time is a crucial dimension in making compliance with such standards less burdensome than now. Producers in LDC, for instance, might meet standard requirements and gain technological spillovers from participating in large vertical retail supply chains rather than continuing to sell through traditional channels, such as wholesale markets. Another important feature to be considered in order to understand the results of this chapter is that LDC have possibly reacted slowly to the new trade regime introduced by EBA in 2001. For instance they may have taken time to invest in their sectors of specialisation in order to get the advantages to export towards the EU more than before. If these investments have been made, their desired effects will be observable only in the medium term. All this helps to understand why, as this chapter documents for the five products under investigation, LDC still export so little to the EU.

To conclude, our findings support the decision to work on a disaggregated basis and suggest that the right approach for further research is to focus on specific products. In this respect, robust evidence of the impact of EBA on LDC exports is expected to be found when the analyses are made as country-case studies and when the medium and long term effects of adjustments by the LDC, such as compliance to standards and investments in production, are fully revealed. In brief, the analysis suggests that issues which have not been dealt with in this study may help in the understanding the role of EBA and, hence, deserve more attention in the near future.

Acknowledgments The authors thank Giovanni Anania, Luca De Benedictis, Anne-Celia Disdier and Fabrizio De Filippis for their suggestions and comments on an earlier version of the paper. Financial support received from the Italian Ministry of Education, University and Research (Scientific Research Program of National Relevance 2007 on "European Union policies, economic and trade integration processes and WTO negotiations") is gratefully acknowledged.

Chapter 8
Trade Impact of European Union Preferences: An Analysis with Monthly Data

Paola Cardamone

Abstract The goal of this chapter is to assess the impact of Preferential Trade Agreements (PTA) on European imports of fresh grapes, pears, apples, oranges and mandarins over the period 2001–2004. Monthly rather than yearly data are used in order to take into account the fact that both imports and protection vary seasonally. Furthermore, we determine a measure of preferential margins by also considering quotas and the entry price system. Finally, in the econometric estimations we control for heterogeneity, endogeneity and zero-trade flows. The results show that the impact of preferential policies granted by the European Union (EU) varies depending on the specific commodity considered.

8.1 Introduction

This chapter analyses the impact on trade of Preferential Trade Agreements (PTA) granted by the European Union (EU) over the period 2001–2004 for specific Fruit and Vegetable (F&V) products using a gravity model.

We focus on the F&V market since this sector is among the most important ones for the EU in terms of both production and trade.

We analyse five products: fresh grapes, apples, pears, oranges and mandarins (including clementines). There are several reasons for considering only a subgroup of products. First of all, the use of disaggregated data involves a very high number of observations, which tends to make the estimations and empirical tests unwieldy. Secondly, we focus on fresh grapes, apples, pears, oranges and mandarins because EU imports of these commodities are relatively high. Finally, these five fruits are

This chapter is largely based on cardamone (2011). The effect of preferential trade agreements on monthly fruit exports to the European Union. Eur Rev of Agric Economics, doi: 10.1093/erae/jbq052.

P. Cardamone
Department of Economics and Statistics, University of Calabria, Via Pietro Bucci – Cubo 1C, I-87036 Rende (CS), Italy
e-mail: p.cardamone@unical.it

L. De Benedictis and L. Salvatici (eds.), *The Trade Impact of European Union Preferential Policies*, DOI 10.1007/978-3-642-16564-1_8,

subject not only to tariffs and quotas, but also to the "entry price" system (Cioffi and dell' Aquila 2004; Goetz and Grethe 2009; Grethe and Tangermann 1999; Swinbank and Ritson 1995) so that by analysing these products we can take into consideration the main elements of the PTA granted by the EU in the F&V sector.

To the best of our knowledge, in the literature there are few papers assessing the impact of European PTA on F&V imports using a gravity framework (Garcia-Alvarez-Coque and Martì-Selva 2006; Emlinger et al. 2008; Aiello and Demaria 2009; Cipollina and Salvatici 2010). In more detail, Garcia-Alvarez-Coque and Martì-Selva (2006) and Emlinger et al. (2008) discuss the influence of Association Agreements on F&V trade between Mediterranean Countries and the EU only, while Aiello and Demaria (2009) and Cipollina and Salvatici (2010) consider preferences granted to developing countries. As regards estimation methods, Garcia-Alvarez-Coque and Martì-Selva (2006) use Ordinary Least Square (OLS), while Emlinger et al. (2008) and Cipollina and Salvatici (2010) employ the Heckman (1978a) estimator in order to take into account zero-trade flows. Aiello and Demaria (2009) present also estimations based on the multiplicative gravity specification. Results show that Euro-Mediterranean Partnership (Euro-Med) foster F&V trade between members (Garcia-Alvarez-Coque and Martì-Selva 2006). The sensitivity of Israel, Morocco and Tunisia to the preferential tariffs is very high, while Turkish exports to the EU do not seem to be sensitive to tariffs, the estimated coefficients not being significant (Emlinger et al. 2008). As regards EU PTA, Cipollina and Salvatici (2010) find that EU preferences in favour of developing countries have a significant and positive effect on EU imports of F&V. Moreover, Aiello and Demaria (2009) show that only ordinary Generalized System of Preferences (GSP) and the Cotonou agreement positively affect EU imports of fruits while EU imports of vegetables are enhanced by the Cotonou agreement only.

This chapter aims to improve the reliability of the results so far obtained by modifying the empirical and analytical setting in a number of ways, including the use of monthly data disaggregated at 8 digit level classification, the measure of the preferential margins and the econometric estimators.

We employ monthly data on imports and preferences: F&V imports vary according to the harvest time of different exporters, which in turn is subject to climatic conditions. Tariffs, quotas and entry prices vary seasonally according to the EU production of F&V, as a result of domestic protection. We use data disaggregated at 8 digit level. In analysing the impact of preferential treatments most contributions have considered more aggregated trade flows between countries; however, the decision to consider aggregated data on exports is questionable if the goal is to evaluate the impact of a specific policy – the PTA – which is applied at the product level. Furthermore, by using data at the 8 digit level of disaggregation we can overcome the need to determine an aggregate PTA variable, which is often given by a weighted sum of tariffs at commodity level (Cipollina and Salvatici 2008; Anderson and Neary 2005).

As far as preferential margins are concerned, we determine a quantitative preferential variable by taking into account existing quotas and preferential entry prices. Moreover, we account for the overlapping of preferences by including in the model interaction terms between preferential margins; in this way we avoid having to make any restrictive assumptions about the use of one specific preferential scheme when the exporter can choose between two. In addition, we include in the gravity specification an indicator of the export capacity in order to catch the effect of general impediments, such as the difficulties in satisfying quality standards which exporting countries could face when entering the EU market.

Finally, the econometric method which we employ controls for heterogeneity, endogeneity and the presence of zero trade flows. The heterogeneity bias is due to the likely correlation between commodity-country pair specific effects and regressors, while endogeneity could arise because of the simultaneity between the dependent variable (EU imports) and regressors, in particular PTA variables. Hence, we first perform the Davidson-MacKinnon (DM) endogeneity test and we reject the hypothesis of endogeneity of regressors. Then, we estimate a Poisson model with commodity-country pair fixed effect in order to control for the heterogeneity bias, country-pairs not trading and heteroskedasticity of the error term of the multiplicative gravity specification (Santos-Silva and Tenreyro 2006).

Overall, the results show that the GSP scheme is successful in enhancing EU imports of apples and fresh grapes while Regional Trade Agreements (RTA) seem to achieve the goal of increasing EU imports of fresh grapes, pears and mandarins.

The chapter is organized as follows. Section 8.2 presents descriptive statistics of a number of key variables. Section 8.3 introduces the gravity model and variables used. Section 8.4 presents the econometric method used in the empirical analysis and the estimation results. Finally, Section 8.5 concludes.

8.2 The European Market of Fresh Grapes, Apples, Pears, Oranges and Mandarins

In this section we present a number of descriptive features of trade flows and applied tariffs concerning EU imports of fresh grapes, pears, apples, mandarins and oranges.

Table 8.1 presents the monthly simple average of imports and *ad-valorem* duties for each group of exporters. First of all, it can be noted that import flows from countries which benefit from Ordinary GSP and other RTA are relatively high. This is also the case for oranges and mandarin exports to the EU Mediterranean countries (Euro-Med).[1] Furthermore, EU imports of apples are scant from participants

[1]Euro-Med (Barcelona Process) started in 1995. This partnership involved 15 EU members and 12 Mediterranean countries (Algeria, Egypt, Israel, Jordan, Lebanon, Morocco, Palestinian Territories, Syria, Tunisia, Turkey, Malta and Cyprus), with Libya granted observer status in 1999.

Table 8.1 Average European Union imports (in thousand EuroS) and *ad-valorem* duties by country group over the period 2001–2004, based on monthly data and tariff lines at 8 digit level of disaggregation

	Fresh grapes		Pears		Apples		Oranges		Mandarins	
	Average imports	Average *ad-valorem* duty	Average imports	Average *ad-valorem* duty	Average imports	Average *ad-valorem* duty	Average imports	Average *ad-valorem* duty	Average imports	Average *ad-valorem* duty
GSP	1,164.49	10.38	476.52	3.90	370.65	4.30	356.09	–	220.24	12.78
	(3,904.78)	(2.23)	(1,422.26)	(1.55)	(905.57)	(1.04)	(817.43)	(–)	(581.52)	(0.48)
EBA	16.92	0.00	7.47	0.00	18.40	0.00	3.09	0.29	–	0.23
	(21.11)	(–)	(8.95)	(–)	(9.72)	(–)	(1.62)	(1.24)	(–)	(1.12)
DRUGS	516.18	10.30	11.50	3.76	8.55	4.15	17.96	–	125.46	5.75
	(975.85)	(2.23)	(0.00)	(1.48)	(7.49)	(0.94)	(23.32)	(–)	(210.59)	(5.86)
ACP	83.70	0.00	3.85	6.00	21.09	–	36.71	1.58	21.73	1.90
	(145.49)	(–)	(5.15)	(–)	(19.04)	(–)	(68.0)	(1.5)	(24.08)	(1.49)
EUROMED	397.66	0.26	51.64	0.36	10.46	0.54	283.66	2.07	301.59	2.63
	(935.76)	(1.03)	(96.2)	(1.08)	(18.02)	(1.18)	(581.37)	(2.35)	(761.16)	(3.04)
OTHER RTA	1,497.84	5.99	393.44	2.61	369.93	2.14	510.38	–	179.76	–
	(4,134.46)	(5.89)	(874.54)	(2.98)	(1,032.81)	(3.24)	(1,157.83)	(–)	(509.43)	(–)
MFN	986.53	13.64	308.44	7.22	397.29	5.40	298.76	9.82	201.84	16.00
	(3,470.43)	(2.22)	(1,108.95)	(2.13)	(1,246.88)	(3.63)	(727.7)	(5.73)	(535.4)	(0.00)

Source: own computations.
Note: standard deviations are reported in parenthesis

in the "drugs regime"[2] and the Euro-Med, while Everything But Arms (EBA)[3] and African, Caribbean and Pacific (ACP)[4] countries export to the EU only a small amount of fresh grapes, pears and mandarins. As far as tariffs are concerned, excluding the Most Favored Nation (MFN) arrangement, the *ad valorem* duty is higher for Ordinary GSP, except in the case of pears for which tariffs on ACP exporters are relatively high. Moreover, from Table 8.1 it emerges that, except in the case of imports of fresh grapes and mandarins, the differences in EU preferential tariffs applied to the different groups of countries are not substantial. This may imply that exporting countries benefitting from more than one preferential scheme prefer to export under one preferential regime rather than another on the basis of the non tariff barriers involved, rather than the tariffs. Some recent contributions have focused on the importance of rules of origin and sanitary and phytosanitary standards in explaining trade (Bureau et al. 2007; Demaria et al. 2008). On this issue, Bureau et al. (2007) show that countries which benefit from two or more preferential arrangements in general prefer to export under one specific regime (i.e., the Cotonou agreement) rather than others (i.e., EBA). This could be due to the fact that the rules of origin for GSP in general, and EBA in particular, are more restrictive than those requested by the Cotonou agreement. The Cotonou agreement requires fewer administrative constraints and is more flexible on the origin of the inputs used.

In Figs. 8.1–8.5, reported in the Appendix C, the share of imports and the preferential margins, given by the relative differences between the applied MFN and the preferential duties, are plotted for the period 2001–2004.[5] The yearly average preferential margins for each scheme are meant to be the mean values of preferential margins for each year over the months. Analysing preferential margins and import shares by product, we can observe that, in the case of fresh grapes (Fig. 8.1), the preferential margins granted under GSP and RTA increased while those granted under the Cotonou agreement remained constant over the same

[2]The "drugs regime" was a special arrangement signed in 1991with additional benefits for countries affected by the production and trafficking of illegal drugs. In 2005, a more simple and stable GSP regulation was set up. The "drugs regime" was replaced by "GSP-Plus" which is designed for developing countries which meet a number of criteria, such as enforcement of human and labour rights, environmental protection, fight against drugs and good governance.

[3]The EBA initiative was introduced in 2001 and gives tariff free and quota free access to all EU imports from the 49 Least Developed Countries (LDC), except for arms and ammunitions.

[4]EEC and ACP countries signed their first agreements in 1969 at the Yaoundé Convention. In 1975, the Yaoundé agreements were replaced by those signed at the Lomé Convention, followed in 2000 by the Cotonou Partnership Agreements, which have been replaced in 2008 by the Economic Partnership Agreements (EPA). It should be mentioned that South Africa is not considered in the group of ACP countries because its trade relations with the EU are governed by the Trade Development and Co-operation Agreement, which was signed in Pretoria in 1999. Hence, South-Africa is considered as an RTA eligible country.

[5]In Figs. 8.1–8.5 we do not make any assumption about the overlapping of preferences. We report the ratio of EU imports from three groups of countries, i.e., countries eligible for GSP (including EBA and the "drugs regime"), the Cotonou agreements and a RTA, with respect to total EU imports from the same three groups of countries over the period 2001–2004.

period. Export shares from GSP and RTA eligible countries increased over the period analysed while those from ACP countries have a positive trend only over the years 2002–2003. If we consider pear imports (Fig. 8.2) we note that, even though the preferential margins generally increased, except in the case of the Cotonou agreement for which the relative preferential margin remained essentially constant, only import shares from countries benefitting from RTA clearly show an increasing trend over the period 2001–2004. In the case of apple imports (Fig. 8.3), even though the preferential margins did not substantially vary over the years 2001–2004, import shares from GSP and RTA countries clearly increased between 2001–2004.[6] In the case of orange imports (Fig. 8.4), preferential margins and import shares did not increase significantly. As regards mandarin imports (Fig. 8.5), although preferential margins changed only slightly, import shares from countries eligible for GSP and RTA increased over the relevant period. It should be noted that, in the latter figure, percent preferential margins of GSP, ACP and RTA are higher than for the other fruits analysed.

To sum up, it can be observed that EU import shares from the GSP countries of all products but pears increased over the period 2001–2004, even though in the case of oranges and mandarins there was only a slightly increase, while in 2004 import shares from countries belonging to a RTA were all higher than in 2001. Moreover, preferential margins granted under GSP slightly increased over 2001–2004, maybe because EBA came into force. Preferential margins set for ACP countries generally remain constant while those for RTA increased over the years 2001–2004, except in the case of oranges and mandarins. This could be due to both the reduction of tariffs and the entry into force of new agreements such that between EU and Chile. In few cases can be detected a relationship between trade and preferential margins. In the case of RTA both preferential margins and import shares show an increasing trend for fresh grapes, pears and apples. In the case of fresh grapes, apples and mandarins an increasing trend for both preferential margins and import shares is also observed for GSP.

8.3 The Gravity Model and Data Used

As empirical applications of the gravity model have grown, various theoretical bases have been proposed (Anderson 1979; Bergstrand 1989; Deardoff 1995; Anderson and van Wincoop 2003). We adopt the following specification of the gravity model:[7]

[6]The high relative import shares observed in 2002 for pears and apples (Figs. 8.2 and 8.3) from ACP countries is due to the high exports from very few countries eligible for both Ordinary GSP and Cotonou agreements. Thus, the particular trend of the ACP exports could be the result of an overlapping of preferences.

[7]Even though Eurostat Comext distinguishes between total imports and imports which enter into the EU under a preferential scheme (but it is not specified under which specific PTA), we consider total (preferential and non-preferential) trade flows since we posit the question "what is the impact of PTA on total trade?".

$$\begin{aligned} X^s_{ijtm} = {} & (GDP/POP)^{\alpha_1}_{itm}(GDP/POP)^{\alpha_2}_{jtm}(POP)^{\alpha_3}_{itm} \\ & \times (POP)^{\alpha_4}_{jtm}(PROD^s_{itm})^{\alpha_5}(PROD^s_{jtm})^{\alpha_6}(EXP\_CAP^s_{jtm})^{\alpha_7} \\ & \times \exp(\gamma_1 MTR_{it} + \gamma_2 MTR_{jt} + \beta_1 GSP^s_{jtm} + \beta_2 ACP^s_{jtm} + \beta_3 RTA^s_{jtm} \\ & + \beta_4 GSP^s_{jtm} ACP^s_{jtm} + \beta_5 GSP^s_{jtm} RTA^s_{jtm} + \alpha + \alpha^s_{ij} + \alpha_t + \alpha_m + u^s_{ijtm}) \end{aligned} \quad (8.1)$$

which can be easily made linear by taking logarithms:

$$\begin{aligned} \ln(X^s_{ijtm}) = {} & \alpha + \alpha_1 \ln(GDP/POP)_{itm} + \alpha_2 \ln(GDP/POP)_{jtm} \\ & + \alpha_3 \ln(POP_{itm}) + \alpha_4 \ln(POP_{jtm}) + \alpha_5 \ln(PROD^s_{itm}) \\ & + \alpha_6 \ln(PROD^s_{jtm}) + \alpha_7 \ln(EXP\_CAP^s_{jtm}) + \gamma_1 MTR_{it} + \gamma_2 MTR_{jt} \\ & + \beta_1 GSP^s_{jtm} + \beta_2 ACP^s_{jtm} + \beta_3 RTA^s_{jtm} + \beta_4 GSP^s_{jtm} ACP^s_{jtm} \\ & + \beta_5 GSP^s_{jtm} RTA^s_{jtm} + \alpha^s_{ij} + \alpha_t + \alpha_m + u^s_{ijtm} \end{aligned} \quad (8.2)$$

where subscript i refers to the EU importers ($i = 1,\ldots,15$), j to the exporters ($j = 1,\ldots 191$),[8] t to the year ($t = 2001,\ldots,2004$), m to the month ($m = 1,\ldots,12$), and s indicates the agricultural commodity at the 8 digit level ($s = 1,2,\ldots,S$).[9] α^S_{ij} is the commodity-country pair fixed effects and α_t indicates a trend variable, while u^S_{ijtm} is the error term. As fixed effects absorb all effects which are country-pair specific, distance, language and common border (two binary variables equal to one if the trade partners share a common language or border, respectively), colony (a binary variable which is equal to one if country j was a colony of country i) and landlocked (the number of landlocked countries in the pair) are absorbed by fixed effects. This is why in (8.1) these country-pair specific variables do not appear. Moreover, since we use seasonally unadjusted import data we augment the gravity (8.1) with monthly dummies α_m (Wooldridge 2006).

X indicates the dependent variable, i.e., the import flow. Monthly data on imports are from Eurostat Comext. Inward processing imports are subtracted from total imports in order to take into account imports entering the EU for processing which are then re-exported with the benefit of tariff exemption. The Eurostat Comext dataset provides data on imports expressed in Cost, Insurance and Freight (CIF) value. Thus, we transformed data from CIF to Free on Board (FOB) values computing the CIF/FOB ratio using data on trade flows from the Comtrade database, following the International Monetary Fund (IMF) Direction of Trade

[8]The 191 exporters are all the countries for which trade statistics were available. The list of exporting countries by latitude is reported in the Appendix A.

[9]We have two commodities (table grapes, other fresh grapes) at 8 digit level in the fresh grape sector, three commodities in the pear sector (Perry pears, other pears, quince), four commodities (Cider apples, Golden Delicious, Granny Smith, other apples) in the apple sector, five commodities for oranges (blood oranges, sweet oranges, Navels and similar, other sweet oranges, other oranges), and five commodities for mandarins (Clementines, Monreales and Satsumas, Mandarins and Wilkings, Tangerines, other mandarins).

Statistics (DOTS) procedure. As Comtrade provides yearly data at Harmonized System (HS) 6 digit level, we assume that CIF/FOB ratios are constant within each year and do not differ if we move from HS6 to 8 digit commodity lines.

As regards explanatory variables, *GDP* is the Gross Domestic Product and *POP* is the population. Annual data on GDP and population are from the World Development Indicators (WDI) 2005. In order to obtain monthly data, the generation of GDP is assumed constant throughout the year, and hence GDP at year t and month m is given by $GDP_{t,m} = GDP_t/12$. With respect to population, we assume that the growth/reduction of population is constant within each year. Hence, *POP* at year t and month m is given by $POP_{t,m} = POP_{t,m-1} + m^*(POP_t - POP_{t-1})/12$, where $m = 1,2,\ldots,12$ indicates the month, i.e., $m = 1$ stands for January, $m = 2$ for February, and so on.

PROD is the agricultural production and is included in order to adjust the standard specification to represent agricultural trade, that is to capture the impact of agricultural comparative advantage on agricultural trade flows (Garcia-Alvarez-Coque and Martì-Selva 2006). We used data on production from FAO, which are on an annual basis at HS6 level. In order to obtain monthly data, we first determine the monthly share of imports from eight groups of European partners by splitting the sample of exporting countries into eight clusters on the basis of latitude. The monthly production of an exporter is thus given by annual production multiplied by the EU monthly import share from countries belonging to the same latitude group. In other words, the percentage distribution of a country's production of each product by month and commodity-level in a given year is assumed equal to the analogous distribution of the EU imports of the same product from the countries belonging to the same latitude group. In order to move from HS6 to 8 digit level we used the same procedure considered for converting yearly into monthly data. In particular, the percentage distribution of a country's production of each product at 8 digit level with respect to that at HS6 level in a given year is assumed equal to the analogous distribution of EU imports of the same product from the countries belonging to the same latitude group. Similarly, in order to determine monthly production at 8 digit level of importing countries, we assume that the monthly share of production in a given year is equal to the monthly share of intra-European imports at 8 digit level.

EXP_CAP, a proxy of the export capacity, is included in order to take account of competitive capacity of exporting countries on the EU market. The export capacity could be limited by impediments, such as the inability to fully satisfy private quality standards, which each exporting country faces in selling commodity s on the EU market. For example, an exporting country, *ceteris paribus*, could export limited amounts of goods to an EU importer because it is not able to satisfy sanitary and phytosanitary standards required by importing retailers. To the best of our knowledge, this kind of indicator has never been included in the standard specification. The index of the export capacity of each exporter is determined by using export data from Comtrade. For each country this is derived by the share of product k exports with respect to world exports of product k divided by the share of the commodity k production with respect to world production of product k. The monthly distribution of exports is then determined in the same way as for production.

MTR indicate the Multilateral Resistance Terms, that is indicators of barriers to trade that each country faces with respect to all its trading partners. In fact, many authors have put forward that the omission of such terms could imply biased estimators (see, among the others, De Benedictis and Vicarelli 2005; Baldwin and Taglioni 2006). We determine a proxy of *MTR* following the approach proposed by Carrère et al. (2009), which is an extension to a panel framework of the multilateral resistance approximation proposed by Baier and Bergstrand (2009). By indicating with GDP_W the world GDP, GDP_k the GDP of country k and $DIST_{ik}$ ($DIST_{jk}$) the distance in kilometres between the capitals of countries $i(j)$ and k, the *MTR* are given by:

$$MTR_{it} = \sum_k \frac{GDP_{kt}}{GDP_{Wt}} \ln(DIST_{ik}) \tag{8.3}$$

and

$$MTR_{jt} = \sum_k \frac{GDP_{kt}}{GDP_{Wt}} \ln(DIST_{jk}). \tag{8.4}$$

The *GSP* variable is the preferential margin granted by the EU GSP (including the Drugs regime and the EBA). The *ACP* variable represents the margin of preference observed for the Cotonou agreement in favour of ACP countries. The *RTA* variable indicates the margin of preference associated to EU bilateral trade agreements for apples, pears, fresh grapes, oranges and mandarins, such as agreements with Mediterranean Countries, Andorra, Switzerland, Romania, Bulgaria, South Africa, Mexico, Macedonia, Croatia, Chile (from 2003). By using the semi-logarithmic specification for preferential variables we avoid having to drop the observations with zero preferential margins. Indeed, if we put preferential schemes together and consider that when a country does not benefit from a preferential scheme the corresponding preferential margin is zero, then a double-log specification implies working with very few observations. Conversely, the use of a semi-logarithmic specification does not allow immediate assessment of the elasticity of imports with respect to preferential margins. However, tariffs are in *ad valorem* values and this means that, for example, the coefficient β_1 relative to the GSP preferential margin can be easily interpreted in the following way: if the preferential margin of GSP increases by one percentage point than the EU imports increase by $((\exp \beta_1)-1)$ 100%. Finally, with a semi-logarithmic specification the original multiplicative gravity model is the same adopted so far by all contributions using dummy variables to measure preferential schemes (e.g. Aitken 1973; Fidmurc and Fidmurc 2003; Carrère 2006; Ghosh and Yamarik 2004; Baier and Bergstrand 2007; Jayasinghe and Sarker 2008).

The overlapping of preferences is generally considered by assuming that if an exporter could choose between two preferences it systematically chooses one on the basis of lower tariffs. In our analysis, in order to take into account the overlapping of preferences avoiding any restrictive assumption, interaction preferential variables, i.e., *GSP*ACP* and *GSP*RTA*, are included in the standard gravity specification. Indicating with $\overline{GSP}$, $\overline{ACP}$ and $\overline{RTA}$ the mean (or the median) value of preferential margins of GSP, Cotonou and RTA agreements, respectively, the average impact of GSP on EU imports, when a country benefit at the same time of GSP and Cotonou agreements and GSP and RTA agreements are given by $\frac{\partial \ln X}{\partial GSP} = \beta_1 + \beta_4 \overline{ACP}$ and $\frac{\partial \ln X}{\partial GSP} = \beta_1 + \beta_5 \overline{RTA}$, respectively. The effect on EU imports of the Cotonou Agreement and RTA at the mean value of GSP should be computed as $\frac{\partial \ln X}{\partial ACP} = \beta_2 + \beta_4 \overline{GSP}$ and $\frac{\partial \ln X}{\partial RTA} = \beta_3 + \beta_5 \overline{GSP}$, respectively. The expected sign of coefficients of interaction terms is not univocal. Indeed, it could be negative if benefitting from two preferences per se tends to reduce the exports under each of the overlapping preferential schemes. However, if the indirect effect of the overlapping is a further incentive to improve production (in terms of quantity and/or quality), the imports under each of the two preferential schemes could be larger, and the effect on trade of the overlapping of the preferences should be positive. A positive effect of interaction terms on trade could also be due to the presence of quotas in the overlapping preferential scheme which grants lower duties and less restrictive rules of origins (generally, this happens for RTA). In this case, even though exporters should prefer to benefit from the RTA, they could also find it profitable to export under GSP because of binding quotas under RTA.

The preferential variables are determined from data on tariffs provided by the dataset DBTAR (Gallezot 2005a, b), while data on quotas are drawn with reference to the specific EU Regulations.

PTA variables can be measured in different ways. In the literature on the impact of PTA on trade, trade preferences are more often represented by a dummy variable equal to one if the importer grants a preference to the exporter and zero otherwise. This dummy is used to estimate the trade creation effect of a PTA. It is expected that its coefficient is positive because beneficiary countries will be induced to export to the preference-giving country more than they would without the specific trade preference. However, the use of dummy variables to represent PTA in a gravity model is problematic because they capture a range of other country-pair specific effects contemporaneous with PTA implementation. Furthermore, a dummy does not discriminate among the different preferential trade policy *instruments* (preferential tariff margins, preferential quotas, reduced "entry prices") nor does it discern the *level* of trade preferences (i.e., the use of dummies implicitly assumes that the level of preferential margins under GSP is the same as those under the Euro-Med). A more appropriate indicator is the actual preferential margin, that is the difference between the MFN applied and the PTA tariff.[10] Moreover, the entry price system included in EU F&V import regime should be taken into account. European protection for F&V is based on a threshold or "trigger price." When a product enters the European market above this trigger price then the exporter has only to

[10]In the case of specific tariffs, the specific duty divided by the unit value, determined by using data from Eurostat Comext at HS8 digits, are added to the *ad valorem* tariffs.

pay the *ad valorem* duty. If the entry price is below this trigger price, then the exporter will pay a specific duty in addition to the *ad valorem* duty. This specific duty is calculated as the difference between the trigger price and the entry price. However, if the entry price is below 92% of the trigger price, then the specific duty is equal to the "maximum specific duty" fixed by the EU. In formulae, the entry price system works as follows:

$$\text{Applied duty} = \begin{cases} \textit{ad valorem duty only} & \text{if Trigger Price} < \text{Price} \\ \textit{ad valorem}\ \text{duty} + \textit{specific-duty} & \text{if } 92\%\ \text{Trigger Price} < \text{Price} \\ & \quad < \text{Trigger Price} \\ \textit{ad valorem}\ \text{duty} + \max\ \textit{specific-duty} & \text{if } 92\%\ \text{Trigger Price} > \text{Price} \end{cases} \tag{8.5}$$

where *Price* indicates the entry price of EU imports for that specific shipment.

Preferential entry prices are taken into account by including in (8.1) a dummy variable d_EP equal to one if the exporting country benefits from a preferential entry price and zero otherwise. We do not include the entry price explicitly in the computation of the preferential duties because the entry price system is administered per shipment, and we do not have the available shipping data. We could use monthly data; however, the fact that the monthly import price is below the trigger price does not mean that the relevant specific tariff is charged on all shipments. Therefore, with monthly data the effect of the entry price may sometimes be measured incorrectly. The system may also be effective even in the case of no supplementary tariff being charged, as a trader would gain nothing from selling at a lower price (Swinbank and Ritson 1995; Cioffi and dell' Aquila 2004; Goetz and Grethe 2009). It is worth mentioning that no country benefits from preferential entry price for EU imports of fresh grapes, pears and apples. Under the Euro-Med, Morocco, Egypt, Israel and Cyprus could take advantage of reduced entry prices for orange exports to the EU, and Morocco for clementine exports as well.

Another characteristic of the protection system of the EU F&V sector is that tariffs vary within each year. This seasonal protection is related to the EU production calendar; custom duties are higher during the European harvest period in order to protect domestic production from foreign competition. In order to address this issue and assess the effectiveness of PTA more accurately monthly data on preferential policies are used.

The preferential margin could be determined as the difference between the applied MFN duty and the preferential tariffs (absolute difference) or as the difference between the applied MFN duty and the preferential tariffs divided by the applied MFN duty (relative difference). As there is no consensus on which of the two measures (absolute and relative differences) should be preferred, either one could be used to estimate the impact of preferential schemes on trade (see Chapter 3). The absolute difference is preferable as, in our opinion, the interpretation of the coefficient seems more reliable. Indeed, estimates provide us the effect on EU imports of the increase by one percentage point of the preferential margin.

The preferential margin for PTA, $l = GSP, ACP, RTA$, product $s = 1,2, \ldots ,S$, month $m = 1,2, \ldots ,12$ and year $t = 2001, \ldots 2004$, is then determined as follows:

$$\Pr ef\ M\arg_{ltm}^{s} = MFN\ ad\ valorem\ duty_{tm}^{s}\ \Pr eferential\ ad\ valorem_{ltm}^{s}. \quad (8.6)$$

As *ad valorem* duty concessions can either be extended to all imports of the specific product from the partner country or limited in volume by a tariff quota, we checked for all country-pairs and products to find out whether imports were higher or lower than the quota, if any. Quotas are defined over a certain number of months or by calendar year. If, in a given month, cumulative imports exceed the quota, then from that month *out-of-quota* duties are used.[11]

Finally, all variables are valued in constant 2000 Euros.

8.4 Estimation Methods and Results

Before to estimate the effect of EU preferences on European imports, it could be interesting to investigate the probability to export to the EU. Hence, we estimate a probit equation, where the dependent variable is equal to one if country *j* exports to country *i*, and zero otherwise. The results obtained from the probit model are reported in Table 8.2. Results show that the coefficient of the export capacity is positive and highly significant in all estimations, indicating that the capacity to place products on international market is a key factor for the probability to export to the EU from developing countries. Moreover, it can be observed that the probability to export to the EU in positively correlated with the production of exporters. Higher per capita GDP of exporting countries also seems to stimulate exports of fresh grapes and oranges to the EU, while importer per-capita GDP is positively correlated with the probability to export oranges and mandarins to the EU. Importer population has a significant coefficient with a positive sign for the probability of exporting to the EU fresh grapes, pears and apples while exporter population is positively correlated with the probability to export fresh grapes and apples. As far as preferential agreements are concerned, the results tend to show that GSP scheme increases the probability to export fresh grapes from eligible countries to EU market. ACP preferential margins are positively correlated with the decision to export oranges to the EU, even though the coefficient is not significant, while preferential margins granted under RTA seem to significantly enhance the probability to export to the EU all the five fruits analysed in this chapter.

[11]The few cases of exports exceeding the quota over the period 2001–2004 refer to Israel and Chile (2003 and 2004) for fresh grapes, Romania for apples, Tunisia and Egypt for oranges, Morocco and Israel (2001) for mandarins.

Table 8.2 Probit estimates on the decision to export to the European Union (2001–2004)

	FRESH GRAPES		PEARS		APPLES		ORANGES		MANDARINS	
GSP	0.12	(0.02) ***	−0.12	(0.04) ***	−0.03	(0.08)	−0.12	(0.16)	0.01	(0.01)
ACP	–	(–)	–	(–)	–	(–)	0.02	(0.02)	–	(–)
RTA	0.06	(0.01) ***	0.12	(0.02) ***	0.06	(0.02) ***	0.06	(0.02) ***	0.05	(0.01) ***
*GSP*ACP*	0.01	(0.01)	–	(–)	–	(–)	0.00	(0.01)	–	(–)
*GSP*RTA*	0.00	(0.00)	0.00	(0.01)	–	(–)	–	(–)	−0.01	(0.00) **
d_EP	–	(–)	–	(–)	–	(–)	0.07	(0.16)	0.60	(0.35) *
log(*PROD_exporter*)	0.29	(0.02) ***	0.32	(0.02) ***	0.32	(0.02) ***	0.26	(0.02) ***	0.21	(0.03) ***
log(*PROD_importer*)	−0.10	(0.01) ***	0.03	(0.03)	−0.00	(0.02)	−0.03	(0.03)	0.04	(0.03)
log(*POP_exporter*)	0.08	(0.04) **	0.04	(0.04)	0.07	(0.03) ***	−0.06	(0.05)	−0.13	(0.07) *
log(*POP_importer*)	0.41	(0.06) ***	0.20	(0.05) ***	0.32	(0.04) ***	−0.18	(0.33)	−0.07	(0.27)
log(*GDP/POP_exporter*)	0.15	(0.05) ***	−0.06	(0.05)	0.05	(0.04)	0.12	(0.05) **	0.06	(0.07)
log(*GDP/POP_importer*)	−0.06	(0.28)	0.06	(0.30)	0.00	(0.17)	2.33	(1.15) **	1.47	(0.85) *
log(*export capacity*)	0.23	(0.02) ***	0.21	(0.02) ***	0.27	(0.02) ***	0.15	(0.02) ***	0.13	(0.03) ***
MTR_exporter	0.26	(0.04) ***	0.10	(0.03) ***	0.10	(0.01) ***	0.09	(0.02) ***	0.09	(0.01) ***
MTR_importer	0.07	(0.08)	0.07	(0.05)	0.02	(0.02)	−0.09	(0.03) ***	−0.05	(0.03) *
trend	−0.23	(0.05) ***	−0.16	(0.04) ***	−0.03	(0.03)	−0.28	(0.13) **	−0.15	(0.10)
constant	−11.78	(2.48) ***	−7.03	(2.73) **	−10.42	(1.61) ***	−17.07	(3.33) ***	−11.86	(2.94) ***
Observations	24,772		38,181		80,400		37,470		23,370	
Wald-chi squared	510.27		438.2		700.52		381.05		446.09	
Pseudo R-squared	0.50		0.45		0.40		0.37		0.26	

Note: all regressions include monthly dummies; standard errors in parenthesis (robust to heteroskedasticity and adjusted for clustering on commodity-country pair fixed effects). (*) significant at 10% level; (**) significant at 5% level; (***) significant at 1% level. Average marginal effects are available by the author upon request.

We then proceed to assess the effect of preferences granted by the EU to European imports of the five commodity under scrutiny by estimating the gravity specification. The use of a gravity equation for explaining trade flows suffers from three main potential sources of bias: commodity-country pair heterogeneity, endogeneity and the presence of zero trade flows.

Heterogeneity is due to observable and non-observable factors specific for each commodity-country pair. From an econometric perspective, the omission of such factors leads to a mis-specification of the gravity equation, and is bound to produce biased and/or inconsistent estimates. To take account of these individual effects we include in the gravity equation commodity-country pair specific effects α_{ij}^{s}.

As for the endogeneity of regressors, PTA variables could be simultaneously determined with trade flows, since it has not been univocally determined whether countries trade more because they are in a PTA or they belong to a PTA because they already traded relatively more with each other than they did with third countries. Moreover, the relationship between imports of the preference-giving country and the margin of preference granted to preferred countries could also be negative. As Özden and Reinhardt (2005, p. 19) point out "GSP eligibility has been shown to be negatively affected by export volume." In brief, it is likely that trade flows between two countries may affect positively or negatively the probability of signing a PTA and the level of trade protection as well. Thus, we perform the DM endogeneity test, which compares OLS and Instrumental Variable (IV) estimations in a panel framework. The instruments considered are: the logarithm of the relative physical capital of importing and exporting countries, as a proxy of the difference in physical capital endowments, the logarithm of aid received by the exporting country, and a polity indicator, which is drawn from the POLITY IV database (available at http://www.cidcm.umd.edu/inscr/polity/) and goes from -10 (high autocracy) to +10 (high democracy). We checked to see whether the endogenous variables are strongly correlated with the instruments, even after sifting out the other exogenous variables in the equation, to meet the "order conditions" (Wooldridge 2006). As can be seen in Table 8.3, the p-values of the DM test allow us to reject the hypothesis of endogeneity of the preferential variables in all estimations.

In order to take into account the presence of zero trade flows, we estimate the gravity equation by considering the multiplicative specification of the gravity model (see (8.1)). In so doing, we accept the argument put forward by Santos-Silva and Tenreyro (2006) that a multiplicative gravity specification estimated by the Pseudo-Maximum Likelihood is more appropriate. These authors show that, because of the heteroskedasticity of the error term of the originally multiplicative specification, the log-linearization of the gravity equation changes the "properties of the error term in a nontrivial way" (Santos-Silva and Tenreyro 2006, p. 644) and, as a result, the statistical independence between the error term and the independent variables is violated leading to inconsistent estimates.

Finally, in order to compare our results with those obtained without considering monthly observations at the 8 digit level, we report estimates obtained with aggregated data of the five products rather than disaggregated observations. Aggregated preferential margins are based on the simple average of tariffs at the relevant

Table 8.3 Poisson Maximum Likelihood estimates of gravity model

	FRESH GRAPES		PEARS		APPLES		ORANGES		MANDARINS	
GSP	0.05	(0.00) ***	−0.18	(0.00) ***	0.60	(0.05) ***	−0.61	(0.76)	−0.07	(0.01) ***
ACP	–	(–)	–	(–)	–	(–)	0.01	(0.01)	–	(–)
RTA	0.05	(0.00) ***	0.11	(0.00) ***	−0.02	(0.00) ***	−0.01	(0.00) ***	0.06	(0.00) ***
*GSP*ACP*	−0.01	(0.00) ***	–	(–)	–	(–)	0.04	(0.05)	–	(–)
*GSP*RTA*	0.06	(0.00) ***	0.06	(0.00) ***	−1.85	(62.11)	–		0.01	(0.00) **
d_EP	–	(–)	–		–	(–)	2.39	(0.03) ***	17.36	(426.02)
log(*PROD_exporter*)	1.02	(0.00) ***	1.01	(0.00) ***	1.01	(0.00) ***	0.98	(0.00) ***	0.85	(0.01) ***
log(*PROD_importer*)	−0.31	(0.00) ***	−0.01	(0.01)	−0.01	(0.01)	0.67	(0.01) ***	1.40	(0.02) ***
log(*POP_exporter*)	−16.73	(0.22) ***	−29.08	(0.67) ***	24.94	(0.36) ***	−31.84	(0.51) ***	12.28	(0.84) ***
log(*POP_importer*)	−1.38	(0.41) ***	−19.64	(0.61) ***	4.96	(0.25) ***	−6.62	(0.50) ***	−22.85	(1.38) ***
log(*GDP/POP_exporter*)	−0.50	(0.05) ***	0.55	(0.05) ***	3.92	(0.04) ***	2.55	(0.08) ***	−0.35	(0.18) *
log(*GDP/POP_importer*)	0.10	(0.08)	−0.42	(0.13) ***	−7.91	(0.06) ***	9.53	(0.20) ***	−10.92	(0.59) ***
log(*export capacity*)	0.41	(0.00) ***	0.19	(0.00) ***	0.26	(0.00) ***	0.10	(0.00) ***	0.02	(0.00) ***
MTR_exporter	0.16	(0.01) ***	−0.15	(0.01) ***	0.00	(0.00)	−0.80	(0.02) ***	1.39	(0.05) ***
MTR_importer	−0.37	(0.01) ***	−0.26	(0.01) ***	0.01	(0.00) ***	−0.00	(0.01)	−0.02	(0.02)
Trend	0.29	(0.02) ***	0.67	(0.02) ***	0.70	(0.01) ***	−0.29	(0.01) ***	−0.10	(0.03) ***
Observations	4,298		4,704		10,243		4,747		3,637	
Wald Chi-square	741,752		300,270		522,182		140,838		56,125	
Davidson-MacKinnon test	1.40		1.01		0.15		0.78		1.67	
(p-value)	(0.24)		(0.37)		(0.7)		(0.46)		(0.19)	

Dependent variable: imports in levels (2001–2004)

Note: all regressions include monthly dummies; standard errors in parenthesis (robust to heteroskedasticity). (*) significant at 10% level; (**) significant at 5% level; (***) significant at 1% level commodity level. The same procedure is adopted for converting monthly to yearly observations, i.e., we computed the simple average of monthly tariffs.

Estimations results are reported in Table 8.3.

First of all, it should be observed that, while the coefficient of production for the exporters is always significantly positive, other standard gravity variables such as importer production, population and per capita GDP have different impacts depending on the different commodities considered. In more detail, importer production has a positive and significant impact in the case of oranges and mandarins only. Moreover, importer per capita GDP has a significantly positive impact on EU imports of oranges only, while the effect of exporter per capita GDP is always positive except for imports of fresh grapes and mandarins. Furthermore, exporter population has a positive effect only for imports of apples and mandarins, and importer population in the case of apples only. As a matter of fact, it is worth mentioning that the signs expected for populations are ambiguous. Indeed, in most papers the coefficients related to population are expected to be positive because it is believed that larger countries trade more. However, it has been shown (Oguledo and Macphee 1994) that if an exporter is large in terms of population it may either need its production to satisfy domestic demand, thereby exporting less, or it may export more than a small country, as is the case when large firms achieve economies of scale. The same reasoning can be applied to the case of the importing country: if large, it may either import less because it is likely that the domestic sector finds it profitable to develop and make the country self-sufficient, or it may import more because it cannot satisfy all domestic demand with its own production (Pusterla 2007).

The export capacity has always a positive and significant impact on EU imports, suggesting that *ceteris paribus* the ability to market internationally their products matters when considering the volume of exports to the EU.

As far as preferential variables are concerned,[12] we find that GSP has a positive and marked effect in enhancing EU imports of apples and fresh grapes, while the Cotonou agreement has a positive but not significant effect on EU imports of oranges. Furthermore, RTA are very effective in enhancing EU imports of fresh grapes, pears and mandarins and eligibility for both GSP and RTA increases the amount of the exports of these commodities. In particular, considering the interaction variables, if the preferential margin of the RTA increases by one percentage point, the EU imports of fresh grapes, pears and mandarins increase by 14.7, 14.3, and 8.6%, respectively. Moreover, it should be noted that eligibility for both GSP and the Cotonou scheme at the same time has a negative impact on exports of fresh grapes. Hence, results regarding the overlapping of preferential schemes show that, while GSP and RTA are complements in the case of fresh grapes, pears and

[12]In some cases multiplying two preferential margins gives a variable always equal to zero and this is why sometimes the coefficients of interaction variables do not appear in estimations. It should also be mentioned that the ACP preferential margin when positive is often constant and this is why the ACP coefficient does not always appear.

mandarins, GSP and the Cotonou agreement are substitutes in the case of fresh grapes.

The coefficient of the entry price dummy is significant and positive for EU imports of oranges only. This outcome indicates that a reduced entry price could enhance exports of oranges. This result partially contrasts with the results obtained by Cioffi and dell' Aquila (2004) and Goetz and Grethe (2009) and those discussed in the Geie Agrosynergie (2008) that the entry-price is of little relevance for orange and mandarin exports from Mediterranean countries, also because it can be easily circumvented both legally and illegally (Garcia-Alvarez Coque 2002; Goetz and Grethe 2009).

The negative impact of GSP preferential margin on exports of pears and mandarins is somewhat surprising. This result could be due to the bad performance of the EBA exporters, as their exports tend to zero even though they were eligible for duty free access. Moreover, the negative impact of the GSP margin on pear exports is in line with the facts shown in Fig. 8.2, where it emerges that pear imports from GSP eligible countries significantly decreased over the period under scrutiny even though preferential margins increased. It should be mentioned that a negative impact of GSP on trade is found in other contributions, such as Aiello et al. (2010), Rose (2004) and Oguledo and MacPhee (1994) for GSP granted by developed countries, Lederman and Özden (2007)[13] for US GSP, and Aiello and Demaria (2009) for EU GSP. According to Oguledo and MacPhee (1994, p. 116) "other resistance factors (perhaps non-tariff measures) are limiting imports from less developed countries."

Eligibility for both GSP and the Cotonou agreement has a negative effect on EU imports of fresh grapes. This result seems in line with the argument put forward by Bureau et al. (2007, p. 185) that the low rate of preference utilization could be "largely explained by the eligibility of a given product for alternative regimes."

Moreover, no preferential scheme seems to be successful in increasing EU imports of oranges. This outcome could be due to the fact that only a small share of the sizeable orange production is involved in exports, as most of the production goes to domestic consumption and the processing sector for the production of frozen concentrated and fresh orange juice (http://www.unctad.org/infocomm/anglais/orange/market.htm).

Finally, if we consider results obtained using aggregated data (Table 8.4) we note that, if monthly data are considered, all preferential margins have a significant but negative impact on EU imports except for RTA; in addition, results obtained using yearly observations show that the Cotonou agreement and RTA have a significant and positive effect on EU imports. This outcome implies that the use of aggregated data could be misleading also because it does not allow us to identify the effect of preferential trade schemes on EU imports of each specific product.

[13]It is worth mentioning that the GSP effect becomes not significant when correcting for endogeneity of preferential variables (Lederman and Özden 2007). In our case, we cannot correct for endogeneity since the endogeneity test shows that the PTA variables are not endogenous.

Table 8.4 Estimates of gravity model using aggregated data

	Monthly data		Yearly data	
GSP	−0.14	(0.00)***	−0.37	(0.00)***
ACP	−0.11	(0.00)***	0.45	(0.01)***
RTA	0.17	(0.00)***	0.02	(0.00)***
*GSP*ACP*	−0.03	(0.00)***	−0.10	(0.00)***
*GSP*RTA*	−0.05	(0.00)***	0.02	(0.00)***
d_EP	0.11	(0.01)***	1.08	(0.01)***
log(*PROD_exporter*)	0.90	(0.00)***	0.19	(0.00)***
log(*PROD_importer*)	−0.01	(0.00)***	−0.00	(0.00)***
log(*POP_exporter*)	−0.35	(0.00)***	0.19	(0.01)***
log(*POP_importer*)	0.78	(0.00)***	0.71	(0.01)***
log(*GDP/POP_exporter*)	0.20	(0.00)***	0.46	(0.01)***
log(*GDP/POP_importer*)	1.52	(0.01)***	1.14	(0.02)***
log(*export capacity*)	0.59	(0.00)***	0.14	(0.00)***
MTR_exporter	−0.02	(0.00)***	0.12	(0.00)***
MTR_importer	0.03	(0.00)***	0.02	(0.00)***
trend	−0.20	(0.00)***	−0.12	(0.00)***
Observations	9,168		992	
Wald Chi-square	1,650,000		164,808.1	

Note: all regressions include monthly dummies; standard errors in parenthesis (robust to heteroskedasticity). (*) significant at 10% level; (**) significant at 5% level; (***) significant at 1% level

8.5 Concluding Remarks

In this chapter we assess the impact of PTA on EU imports of fresh grapes, apples, pears, oranges and mandarins using a gravity model. With respect to other contributions which use a gravity model to evaluate the effectiveness of PTA on trade, we introduce a number of innovations. First of all, we use monthly data in order to take into account the fact that imports and protection of the product considered vary seasonally, and consider disaggregated data at 8 digit level. Secondly, we address the issue of the overlapping between preferences without making any assumption regarding which one a country is a priori expected to prefer. Similarly to Emlinger et al. (2008), we take into account not only tariffs but also the EU entry price system and quotas. Thirdly, we control for country heterogeneity, endogeneity and non-trading countries as well as heteroskedasticity of the multiplicative gravity specification by employing the Poisson model; we also include monthly dummies for seasonally unadjusted data in the gravity equation (Wooldridge 2006).

The results show that the impact of preferential margins on trade differs depending on the commodity considered. In more detail, beneficiaries of the GSP scheme seem to gain in exporting fresh grapes and apples to the EU, while RTA seem to reach the goal of increasing EU imports from eligible countries of fresh grapes, pears and mandarins. Preferential import regimes granted by the EU for oranges do not seem effective; however, the preferential entry price has a significant and positive impact on imports of oranges only. We also observe a positive impact on European imports of the export capacity indicator introduced in our analysis indicating that, *ceteris paribus*, European imports of the five fruits under scrutiny are significantly affected by the general capacity of exporting countries to market their products internationally.

It is worth mentioning that in this chapter we do not take into account trade diversion effect, since we have considered only the EU as destination market for exporting countries. Further research could investigate if PTA granted by the EU have determined a diversion effect and, eventually, if the diversion effect influences the results of the creation effect obtained in the empirical exercise proposed in this chapter.

Further investigation could also verify whether the results obtained in this chapter are robust to the use of other gravity specifications, such as that proposed by Romalis (2007), where instead of bilateral trade flows, ratios of ratios of bilateral trade flows across partners are considered. This model has the advantage of substantially reducing the number of independent variables used in the empirical analysis. However, it has the disadvantage of needing to identify a control group of importing countries whose trade policy did not change over the period under study with respect to the exporters considered and also requiring trade data between exporters and this control market, which may not be available on a monthly basis.

The limited effectiveness of some PTA granted by the EU in fostering trade found in this study could be due to the fact that developing countries tend to underutilize trade preferences. As Bureau et al. (2007, p. 196) highlighted, the main motivation of the low utilization of some preferences is that developing countries are unable to "match the technical, sanitary, phytosanitary and traceability requirements imposed by developed countries, and in particular the private standards imposed by importers and retailers." The results obtained in the estimations on the significant correlation between EU imports and general export capacity of exporters seem to confirm these considerations. It should be mentioned, however, that Maertens and Swinnen (2008 and 2009) and Minten et al. (2006) claim that demanding standards in agricultural trade could as well stimulate the development of competitive capacity in export markets. Further research could investigate the role of non tariff barriers and quality standards in the medium term on the effectiveness of PTA granted by the EU to developing countries.

In any event, there is no doubt that international institutions should gear their policies in this direction in order to facilitate the attainment of quality standards by developing countries, by stimulating foreign investments and increasing aid to speed up the use of appropriate agricultural technologies. Moreover, a further reduction of tariff levels in favour of developing countries within the GSP scheme might well produce poor results if it is not matched with a revision of the requirements regarding the rules of origin.

Acknowledgments Financial support received from the "Agricultural Trade Agreements (TRADEAG)" (Specific Targeted Research Project, Contract no. 513666) and the "New Issues in Agricultural, Food and Bio-energy Trade (AGFOODTRADE)" (Grant Agreement no. 212036) research projects, funded by the European Commission, and by the Italian Ministry of Education, University and Research (Scientific Research Program of National Relevance 2007 on "European Union policies, economic and trade integration processes and WTO negotiations" – PUE&PIEC) is gratefully acknowledged. The author acknowledges the very valuable contribution made by

Giovanni Anania in identifying the research issues as well as in helping to improve previous versions of the paper. The author is also grateful to Francesco Aiello, Jean-Cristophe Bureau, Alison Burrell, Antonio Cioffi, Maria Cipollina, Luca De Benedictis, Anna-Celia Disdier, Catherine Laroche Dupraz, Alessandro Olper, Priscila Ramos, and Luca Salvatici for their suggestions and comments on earlier versions of the paper.

Appendix A

List of Exporting Countries by Latitude (in Degrees)

Latitude lower than −30: Argentina, Australia, Chile, New Zealand, Uruguay.

Latitude higher than −30 and lower than −15: Bolivia, Botswana, Brazil, Fiji, French Polynesia, Lesotho, Madagascar, Mauritius, Mozambique, Namibia, New Caledonia, Paraguay, South Africa, Swaziland, Tonga, Vanuatu, Zambia, Zimbabwe.

Latitude higher than −15 and lower than 0: Angola, Burundi, Comoros, Congo, Dem. Rep. of the Congo, Ecuador, Indonesia, Kenya, Malawi, Papua New Guinea, Peru, Rwanda, Samoa, Seychelles, Solomon Islands, Tanzania.

Latitude higher than 0 and lower than 15: American Samoa, Aruba, Barbados, Benin, Brunei- Darussalam, Burkina Faso, Cambodia, Cameroon, Cape Verde, Central African Rep., Chad, Colombia, Costa Rica, Côte d'Ivoire, Djibouti, El Salvador, Equatorial Guinea, Ethiopia, FS Micronesia, Gabon, Gambia, Ghana, Grenada, Guam, Guatemala, Guinea, Guinea-Bissau, Guyana, Honduras, Kiribati, Liberia, Malaysia, Maldives, Mali, Marshall Islands, Mayotte, Neth. Antilles, Nicaragua, Niger, Nigeria, Palau, Panama, Philippines, Saint Lucia, Saint Vincent and the Grenadines, Sao Tome and Principe, Senegal, Sierra Leone, Singapore, Somalia, Sri Lanka, Suriname, Thailand, Timor-Leste, Togo, Trinidad and Tobago, Uganda, Venezuela.

Latitude higher than 15 and lower than 30: Antigua and Barbuda, Bahamas, Bahrain, Bangladesh, Belize, Bhutan, Cayman Islands, China Hong Kong SAR, China Macao SAR, Cuba, Dominica, Dominican Rep., Eritrea, Haiti, India, Jamaica, Kuwait, Lao People's Dem. Rep., Mauritania, Mexico, Myanmar, Nepal, Oman, Puerto Rico, Qatar, Saint Kitts and Nevis, Saudi Arabia, Sudan, United Arab Emirates, Viet Nam, Virgin Islands, Yemen.

Latitude higher than 30 and lower than 45: Albania, Algeria, Andorra, Armenia, Azerbaijan, Bermuda, Bosnia Herzegovina, Bulgaria, Canada, China, Cyprus, Egypt, Georgia, Iran, Iraq, Israel, Japan, Jordan, Kazakhstan, Kyrgyzstan, Libya, Lebanon, Malta, Morocco, Pakistan, Rep. of Korea, Romania, San Marino, Serbia and Montenegro, Syria, Tajikistan, TFYR of Macedonia, Tunisia, Turkey, Turkmenistan, USA, West Bank and Gaza, Uzbekistan.

Latitude higher than 45 and lower than 60: Belarus, Channel Islands, Croatia, Czech Rep., Dem. People's Rep. of Korea, Estonia, Hungary, Isle of Man, Latvia, Liechtenstein, Lithuania, Monaco, Mongolia, Norway, Poland, Rep. of Moldova, Russian Federation, Slovakia, Slovenia, Switzerland, Ukraine.

Latitude higher than 60: Faeroe Islands, Greenland, Iceland.

Appendix B

Table 8.5 Most important exporting countries to the European Union by product in descending order of importance, 2001–2004

	Fresh grapes		Pears		Apples		Oranges		Mandarins	
	Exporters	Import value	Exporters	Import value	Exporters	Import value	Exporters	Import value	Exporters	Import value
1	South Africa	442,621.20	Argentina	206,048.80	New Zealand	264,428.00	South Africa	296,524.30	Morocco	140,721.00
2	Chile	347,154.30	South Africa	110,698.40	Chile	250,371.40	Morocco	137,525.00	Turkey	73,801.91
3	Brazil	333,110.30	Chile	82,837.77	South Africa	212,948.20	Argentina	77,433.34	South Africa	71,192.45
4	Argentina	86,696.90	Turkey	17,530.09	Argentina	121,986.30	Uruguay	63,385.81	Uruguay	57,060.47
5	USA	75,896.32	USA	14,830.84	Brazil	95,958.59	Brazil	56,893.03	Argentina	50,363.41
6	Turkey	63,264.84	China	10,947.59	USA	64,655.80	Israel	53,536.20	Israel	25,242.59
7	Egypt	54,564.19	New Zealand	7,639.29	China	47,797.26	Tunisia	33,022.45	Peru	21,037.52
8	India	31,705.27	Rep. of Korea	2,765.64	Australia	13,104.85	Turkey	26,623.62	Chile	14,567.01
9	Israel	25,609.03	Uruguay	1,381.32	Canada	12,590.23	Cuba	18,409.82	Brazil	5,145.14
10	Peru	22,144.87	Australia	1,256.15	Uruguay	7,167.88	USA	3,925.86	Pakistan	1,669.53
11	Morocco	14,245.24	Switzerland	522.44	Switzerland	1,967.12	Australia	3,394.30	Australia	1,381.58
12	Australia	3,914.75	Brazil	502.40	Turkey	654.61	Chile	2,988.10	Jamaica	1,263.53
13	Namibia	3,451.74	Morocco	326.09	Serbia and Montenegro	527.11	Jamaica	2,717.14	USA	980.64
14	Mexico	1,305.60	Canada	97.14	Ukraine	264.82	Zimbabwe	2,087.69	Zimbabwe	539.85
15	Switzerland	495.70	Japan	81.64	Rep. of Korea	221.44	Swaziland	1,990.28	Switzerland	362.73
16	Saudi Arabia	177.08	Serbia and Montenegro	40.57	Romania	187.12	Belize	1,979.12	Croatia	142.15
17	China	145.35	China Hong Kong SAR	34.24	Japan	155.75	Dominica	530.40	Norway	114.22
18	Uruguay	128.78	Norway	32.47	Croatia	153.04	Colombia	502.00	China	28.20
19	Jordan	125.66	Bulgaria	28.13	Iran	144.14	Dominican Rep.	365.31	Paraguay	23.76
20	Norway	98.75	Romania	20.39	Singapore	133.03	Venezuela	329.18	Colombia	0.87

Source: own computations

Appendix C

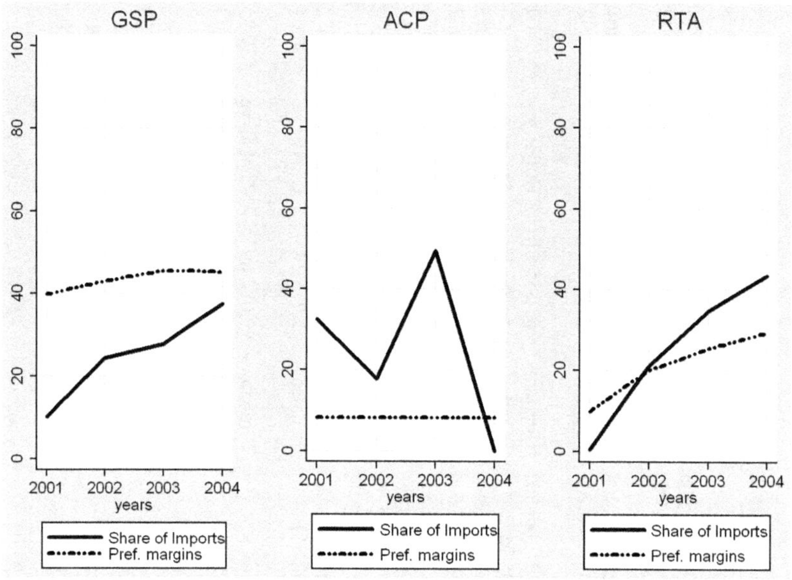

Fig. 8.1 Average share of European Union imports and preferential margins of fresh grapes by country groups, 2001–2004

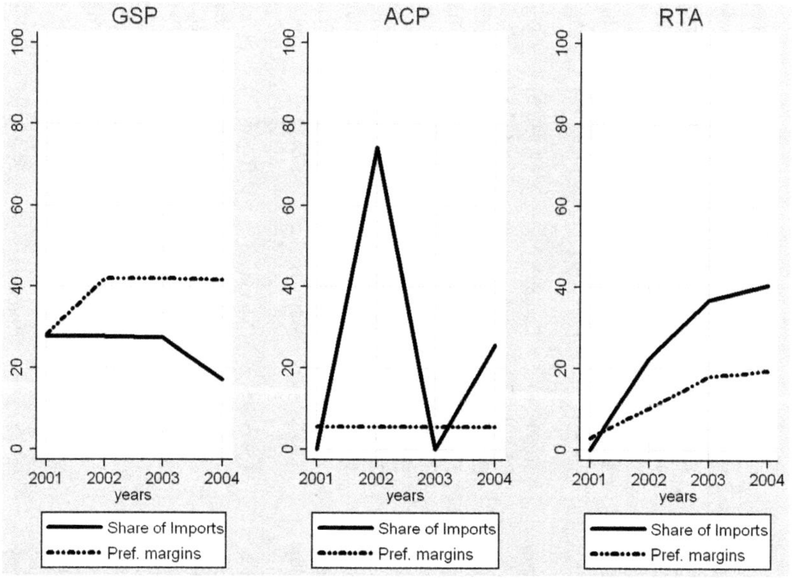

Fig. 8.2 Average share of European Union imports and preferential margins of pears by country groups, 2001–2004

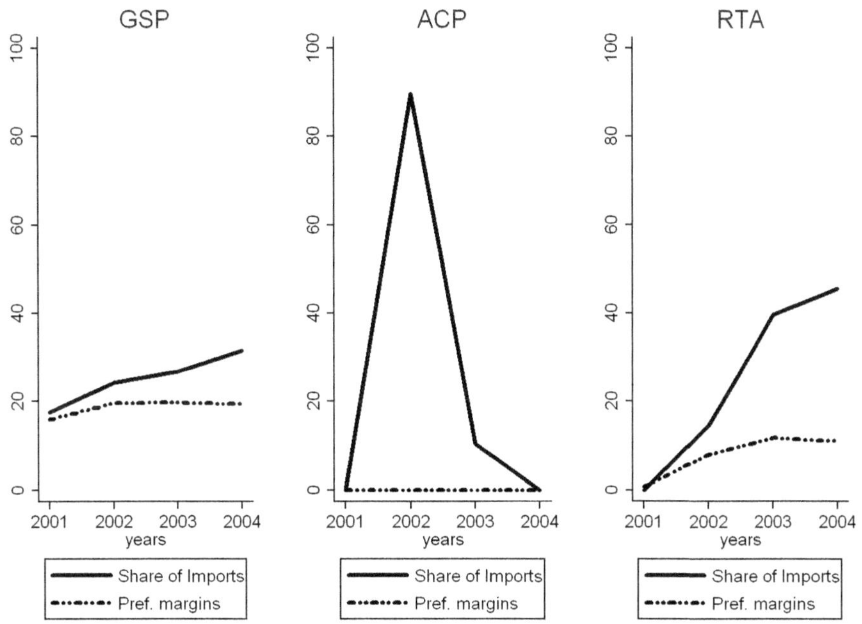

Fig. 8.3 Average share of European Union imports and preferential margins of apples by country groups, 2001–2004

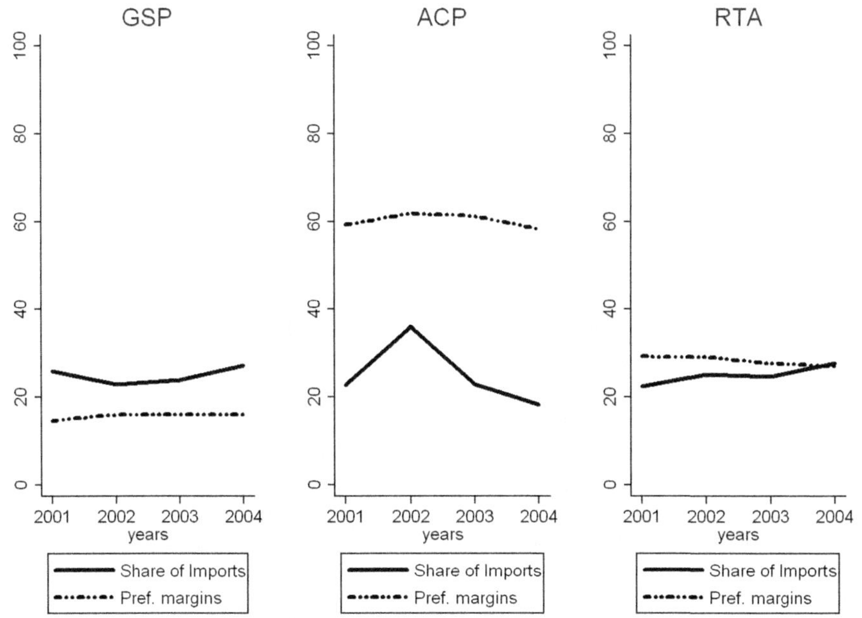

Fig. 8.4 Average share of European Union imports and preferential margins of oranges by country groups, 2001–2004

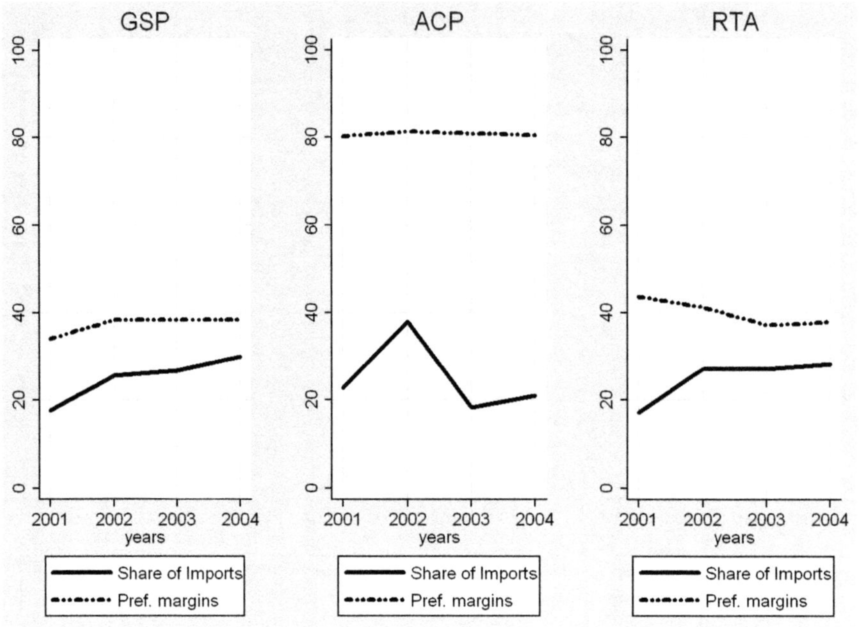

Fig. 8.5 Average share of European Union imports and preferential margins of mandarins by country groups, 2001–2004

Chapter 9
Trade Preference Through Tariff Rate Quotas and the Gravity Equation: Does the Tariff Equivalent Matter?

Valentina Raimondi, Margherita Scoppola, and Alessandro Olper

Abstract The 2003 reform of the Common Agricultural Policy in the rice sector has implied a drastic change of the level and instruments of the border protection. Because the European Union (EU) grants trade preferences to a considerable number of developing countries, the reform of the domestic policy also entailed erosion of preferences. This chapter addresses the impact of preference erosion on the rice exports of the countries which benefit from preferences by the EU, with the aim of contributing to the literature from two points of view: first, by proposing a new empirical approach to compute the preferential margin when tariff rate quotas are in force; second, by estimating the trade elasticities of preferences by means of a panel gravity equation to deal with the issue of endogeneity of the preferential margins. The results show that the way in which preferential margins are calculated matters significantly when assessing the existence and extent of preference erosion and estimating the values of the trade elasticities. Finally, our estimations highlight the fact that preferences still have a market trade impact for almost all countries involved.

9.1 Introduction

The erosion of preferences due to multilateral tariff reductions may result in significant export losses for developing countries. Multilateral liberalization reduces the competitive advantages of developing countries benefiting from trade preferences. Indeed, the reduction of Most Favored Nation (MFN) tariffs lowers the cost

V. Raimondi and A. Olper
Department of Agricultural and Environmental Economics and Politics, University of Milano, Via Celoria 2, 20133 Milano, Italy
e-mail: valentina.raimondi@unimi.it; alessandro.olper@unimi.it

M. Scoppola
Department of Economic Development, University of Macerata, Piazza Oberdan 3, 62100 Macerata, Italy
e-mail: scoppola@unimc.it

L. De Benedictis and L. Salvatici (eds.), *The Trade Impact of European Union Preferential Policies*, DOI 10.1007/978-3-642-16564-1_9,

advantage of preferred developing countries with respect to other competitors. The resulting preference erosion may challenge the already limited ability of developing countries to access markets in developed countries (Manchin 2006). Since the end of the implementation period of the 1994 General Agreement on Tariffs and Trade (GATT) agreement, MFN tariffs have been generally stable. However, there are cases in which significant preference erosion has occurred in the more recent years, as a consequence of domestic policies' reforms. The European Union (EU) rice policy is an interesting example. EU policy in this area has long been a consequence of the domestic policy: both the level and the kind of trade protection were defined to guarantee the effectiveness of the domestic policy. After 2003, the reform of the Common Agricultural Policy for rice has implied a drastic change also in the level and instruments of the border protection. Because the EU grants trade preferences to a considerable number of developing countries, the reform of the domestic policy, by involving a reduction in border protection, has implied preference erosion as well.

The focus of this chapter is the erosion of the preferences granted by the EU in the rice industry. Rice is among the most sensitive products for many developing countries exporting to the EU; for some of them, the EU represents a major export market and rice is among their most important exports. The objective is to assess the impact of the preference erosion over the past decade on exports to the EU from favored developing countries and, more generally, to assess the actual dependence of developing countries on EU preferences in their ability to access the EU rice market. For this purpose we use a gravity model. With respect to the previous literature estimating the trade impact of preferences by means of a gravity equation, this chapter offers contributions in two main directions. The first concerns the way in which the independent variable of interest, that is, the preferential margin, is calculated. As in other recent papers, the independent variable is a continuous – not a dummy – variable (e.g., Cipollina and Salvatici 2010; Cardamone 2011); further, the analysis is here highly disaggregated and there is no bias due to tariff aggregation. Moreover, an innovative approach to calculate the preferential margin is here proposed. Because EU preferences to rice imports are granted by means of tariff rate quotas, to compute the preferential margin one needs to evaluate the tariff equivalent of the tariff rate quota. The literature to date has assessed this tariff equivalent by assuming perfect competition in international agricultural trade. This chapter proposes a new empirical approach to calculate the tariff equivalent of the tariff rate quota, which is shown to be consistent with the assumption of economies of scale and imperfect competition in the international trade. Indeed, fixed costs are often associated with international trading of agricultural products, as traders have to acquire knowledge about the foreign markets and to build the distribution networks; further, there are economies of scale also in shipping and, more generally, in transportation. The chapter compares the preferential margin obtained using this new approach with the one obtained by means of the standard approach, based on the assumption of perfect competition, showing that the latter may lead to an underestimation of the preferential margin. The second methodological contribution is the use of a panel gravity equation. As the literature has shown, the cross-section gravity model is unable to deal with endogeneity arising when estimating the trade preference effects, because of the difficulties in finding the appropriate instrumental variables (Baier and Bergstrand 2007). Theoretically–based gravity models using panel data allow us to make adjustments for endogeneity due to omitted (selection) variable bias.

Overall results show that the way preferential margins are calculated matters significantly when assessing the existence and extent of preference erosion. Under the standard method for computing the tariff rate quota equivalent, no clear-cut evidence of preference erosion emerges, while the opposite is true when the tariff equivalent proposed in this chapter is used. In the latter case, our results suggest that during the examined period there has been considerable preference erosion, though the size of this erosion changes across the groups of preferred countries. The method to calculate the margin also significantly affects the estimated values of the trade elasticities; more specifically, the results show that, by using the preferential margins based on the standard tariff equivalent of tariff rate quotas, the impact of trade preferences is lower than when one assumes economies of scale and imperfect competition. Finally, estimations highlight that the trade impact of preferences is currently still very high for almost all preferred countries.

The chapter is organized as follows. The next section offers an overview of the EU trade policy in the rice industry. The third section explains the new method to calculate the tariff equivalent of tariff rate quotas and compares the preferential margins obtained by using the standard approach with those obtained by using this new approach. The fourth section addresses the issues arising when estimating the trade impact of the preferences by means of the gravity equation, while the fifth illustrates the estimated model and the econometric strategy. The sixth discusses the obtained results, while the final section offers some concluding remarks.

9.2 European Union Trade Policy in the Rice Industry During the Period 2000–2008: An Overview

The international rice market covers a wide range of products, both from the point of view of their characteristics and value added. Two main distinctive types of rice are traded – the Japonica and the Indica – and four different products: paddy, husked, milled and broken rice. Most EU imports are of husked (more than 60%) and milled rice (about 20%), while paddy rice imports are very small (less than 1%). Although the EU accounts for only 5.5% of world imports, it is a very important market for certain developing countries. For example, in 2007 the EU accounted for 95, 65, 47, and 40% (in value) of rice exports of Cambodia, Guyana, Bangladesh and Suriname, respectively.[1]

[1]These figures are drawn from Comtrade database.

The EU trade policy in the rice industry is rather complicated; the policy instruments and the level of the border protection vary significantly across products and among imports regulated by multilateral agreements with respect to those covered by the various preferential schemes. Before 2004, the tariffs applied to the EU imports on a MFN basis were defined by the 1994 GATT Agreement. While for paddy and broken rice specific fixed bound tariffs were applied, for husked and milled rice the applied tariff was established to be set as the smallest one between the bound tariff and the difference between a threshold import price and the international price. This threshold import price for the husked rice was equal to the 180% (for the Indica rice) and 188% (for the Japonica rice) of the intervention price; for milled rice, it was set at equal to the intervention price plus a percentage to be calculated. As a consequence of this import regime, tariffs applied to husked and milled rice fluctuated with the international price: when this was high, the tariff was the difference between the threshold import price and the international price and, hence, smaller than the bound tariff; but when the international price fell to a certain level, then the bound tariff was applied.

With the 2003 reform of the Common Agricultural Policy the EU drastically reduced the value of the intervention price for rice, by 50%. The threshold import prices for husked and milled rice as well as tariffs consequently dropped. The EU and the main rice exporters then agreed to eliminate the threshold import price system and a new set of MFN bound tariffs for husked, milled and broken rice was negotiated, and entered in force in September 2004. While the value of the tariff applied to broken rice imports is fixed, three different values of tariffs may be applied for husked and milled rice depending upon the quantity imported. The values of these new tariffs are significantly lower than the pre-reform values: in August 2004 the tariffs applied to imports were 197 Euro/t and 416 Euro/t for husked and milled rice, respectively, while in September 2004 these fell to 65 Euro/t and 175 Euro/t. In any case, only 55% of EU imports of rice is currently subject to these MFN tariffs (COGEA 2009).

A considerable amount of EU rice imports is currently covered by Tariff Rate Quotas (TRQ), that is, a two-tiered tariff system with the volume imported within the quota charged at a lower tariff than out-of-quota imports. Several agricultural TRQ were introduced by the 1994 GATT Agreement on Agriculture to improve market access where agricultural protection was very high but, as regards EU rice imports, no TRQ were included in that Agreement. However, in accordance with article XXIV of the GATT, after 1998 the EU granted a number of TRQ to the main rice exporters to compensate them for the 1995, 2004, and 2007 enlargements. Country-specific TRQ were granted to the United States, Thailand, Australia, India, Pakistan and Guyana for husked, milled and broken rice; further, there are also non-country specific TRQ. Imports under these GATT TRQ are estimated to account for about 30% of total EU rice imports in 2007 (COGEA 2009).

Additional TRQ are granted by the EU under the preferential agreements. In the rice industry, trade preferences are given exclusively by means of TRQ. Since the early Lomè Conventions a certain volume of rice from the African, Caribbean and Pacific countries (ACP) enters the EU at a lower tariff than the MFN one. More specifically, during the period examined in this chapter, the EU has granted a TRQ of 160,000 tons, 35,000 of which are for rice originating from the Overseas Countries and Territories (OCT). In-quota tariffs have two components: the first part is a percentage of the MFN tariffs, while the second is independent from the value of MFN tariff. Within the Generalized System of Preferences (GSP), Bangladesh benefits from a TRQ of 4,000 tons, with the in-quota tariff made up of two components as well. Under the Euro-Med Agreement, the EU grants a TRQ of 32,000 tons to Egypt, with the in-quota tariff 25% below the MFN tariff. Finally, under the Everything But Arms (EBA) initiative since 2002 a zero-duty TRQ has been in force, with the quota gradually increasing over the period. Almost 15% of total EU rice imports were covered by preferential TRQ in 2007 (COGEA 2009). All the other possible exporters either do not export or do not make use of preferences.

9.3 Preferential Margins with Tariff Rate Quotas

The presence of TRQ raises a number of issues when calculating preferential margins. One is related to the tariff equivalent of a TRQ; the literature on TRQ suggests that the tariff equivalent varies according to which of the three elements of a TRQ regime is binding (Boughner et al. 2000; Skully 2001). When demand and costs are such that the equilibrium quantity is lower than the quota, then the quota is not binding and the in-quota tariff is applied to all imports; in this case, the tariff leaving imports and price unchanged is clearly the tariff applied to the in-quota imports. When the equilibrium quantity is higher than the quota, the binding instrument is the out-of-quota tariff and the tariff which leaves imports and price unchanged is the out-of-quota tariff. Finally, if the binding instrument is the quota itself the tariff equivalent is in between the in-quota and the out-of-quota tariff. The empirical literature relies on this theoretical framework to compute the tariff equivalent of TRQ (e.g., Cardamone 2011; Garcia-Alvarez-Coque et al. 2010). Boumelassa et al. (2009) use the MAcMap-HS6v2 database to determine the tariff equivalent of the TRQ on the basis of a range of fill rates. If the fill rate is lower than 90%, then they assume that the tariff equivalent is the in-quota tariff. When the fill rate is between 90 and 98% the tariff equivalent is computed as the simple average of the in-quota and the out-of-quota tariff. Finally, if the fill rate is higher than 98% the tariff equivalent is equal to the out-of-quota tariff.

The tariff equivalent of a TRQ, however, may be different when one assumes economies of scale. Fixed costs, often associated with international trading, may arise from the expenditure traders sustain in acquiring knowledge about the foreign markets; in addition, evidence exists that there are also economies of scale in shipping and in transportation (Hummels and Skiba 2004). Consider the basic international trade model under economies of scale and monopolistic competition à la Dixit-Stiglitz-Krugman (see Feenstra 2003). In this setting, a number of (symmetric) firms are assumed to produce differentiated products; each firm is a monopolist for the variety it produces and, thus, it maximizes profits by equalizing marginal revenues with marginal costs; variable marginal costs are assumed to be constant. Because of fixed costs, the Average Cost (*AC*) declines with imports and is always higher than the marginal cost; as each firm's profits are positive, if there are no restrictions on entry, new firms enter the market. This reduces the market share of each firm and increases the average cost; in equilibrium, profits are zero and the price equals the average cost. Because of the assumption of symmetry, prices and quantities are identical across all varieties.

The *AC*, of the importing firm under free trade is:

$$AC = \frac{FC}{Q} + c \tag{9.1}$$

where FC are the fixed costs, Q is the imported quantity and c is the constant variable cost.

If $\overline{Q}$, T^{in} and T^{out} are the quotas, the in-quota and the out-of-quota tariffs, respectively, then under the TRQ the average cost is:

$$AC_{T^{in},T^{out}} = \left\{ \begin{array}{ll} \frac{FC}{Q} + c + \frac{T^{in}\bar{Q} + T^{out}(Q - \bar{Q})}{Q} & \text{if } Q > \bar{Q} \\ \frac{FC}{Q} + c + T^{in} & \text{if } Q \leq \bar{Q} \end{array} \right\}. \tag{9.2}$$

In equilibrium, the price is equal to $AC_{T^{in},T^{out}}$.[2] When demand is such that the equilibrium quantity is $Q \leq \overline{Q}$, the tariff that leaves the price and the imported quantity unchanged is the in-quota tariff. However, if demand conditions are such that the equilibrium quantity is higher than the quota, the tariff which would leave price and imports unchanged is the weighted average of the two tariffs.

Hence, within this framework if imports are no greater than the quota, the tariff equivalent is the in-quota tariff while, alternatively, it is the weighted average of the two tariffs. Therefore, the tariff equivalent computed on the basis of the economies of scale-monopolistic competition framework, is always no greater than the one consistent with the perfect competition model.

To compare the Preferential Margins (*PM*) computed under different hypothesis, a database has been built which includes the applied in-quota and out-of-quota tariffs and the quantities imported within the quota and out-of-the quota. The

[2]Under the assumption of symmetric firms, as in the Dixit-Stiglitz-Krugman model, firms are assumed to be identical as they face identical cost and demand curves; thus, within this theoretical framework, firms are assumed to face also the same costs to access the licenses to import within the quota. As a consequence, the quantities each firm imports within and out-of-the quota are here the same across all firms. Obviously, the removal of the symmetry hypothesis, by assuming for instance that firms face different costs to access the licenses, would require a rather different setting and would result in different quantities imported within and out-of-the quota and, therefore, in different average cost curves among firms.

database covers 36 rice products (8 digit level) and 123 producing and/or exporting countries for 9 years (2000–2008). In-quota imports are here drawn directly from the EU Commission, which collects the amount of product actually imported within the quotas, at the 8 digit level of disaggregation. Out-of-quota imports are computed as the difference between total imports of each year from the Comext database, and the in-quota imports data collected by the EU Commission. Tariffs are all drawn from EU Regulations.

If T_{kj}^{PREF} is the *ad valorem* preferential tariff and T_k^{MFN} is the *ad valorem* MFN tariff, with k and j being the product and the exporting country, respectively, the general formula used to calculate the *PM* (the preference discount rate) in a certain year is the following:

$$PM_{kj} = \frac{T_k^{MFN} - T_{kj}^{PREF}}{1 + T_{kj}^{PREF}}. \tag{9.3}$$

Two different *PM* have been computed to take into account the two alternative measures of the tariff equivalent. If Q_{kj} are total imports and $\bar{Q}_{kj}$ is the quota, under the perfect competition hypothesis the *PM* for a given year is the following:

$$PM_{kj}^{P} = \left\{ \begin{array}{ll} \dfrac{T_k^{MFN} - T_{kj}^{in}}{1 + T_{kj}^{in}} & \text{if } Q_{kj} < \bar{Q}_{kj} \\ \dfrac{T_k^{MFN} - T_{kj}^{out}}{1 + T_{kj}^{out}} & \text{if } Q_{kj} > \bar{Q}_{kj} \\ \dfrac{T_k^{MFN} - \frac{(T_{kj}^{out} + T_{kj}^{in})}{2}}{1 + \frac{(T_{kj}^{out} + T_{kj}^{in})}{2}} & \text{if } Q_{kj} = \bar{Q}_{kj} \end{array} \right\}. \tag{9.4}$$

It is worth noting that the tariff T_{kj}^{out} applied to imports exceeding the preferential TRQ may be lower than T_k^{MFN}, because the EU may also grant the (favored) exporting country TRQ within the GATT. For example, Egypt exports broken rice to the EU within preferential TRQ, but there are also additional imports which are charged at the in-quota tariff of the GATT TRQ.

The *PM* under the assumption of economies of scale is:

$$PM_{kj}^{E} = \left\{ \begin{array}{ll} \dfrac{T_k^{MFN} - T_{kj}^{in}}{1 + T_{kj}^{in}} & \text{if } Q_{kj} \le \bar{Q}_{kj} \\ \dfrac{T_k^{MFN} - \frac{(T_{kj}^{out}(Q_{kj} - \bar{Q}_{kj}) + T_{kj}^{in}\bar{Q}_{kj})}{Q_{kj}}}{1 + \frac{(T_{kj}^{out}(Q_{kj} - \bar{Q}_{kj}) + T_{kj}^{in}\bar{Q}_{kj})}{Q_{kj}}} & \text{if } Q_{kj} > \bar{Q}_{kj} \end{array} \right\}. \tag{9.5}$$

The *PM* of (9.4) and (9.5) are in fact marginal and weighted average margins, respectively.

Table 9.1 European Union imports of husked rice from Guyana: preferential margins under different hypotheses

	Over quota Imports (ton)	Relative margin (%)		Absolute margin (%)	
		Weighted PM^E	Standard PM^P	Weighted PM^E	Standard PM^P
2000	0	18.1	18.1	21.7	21.7
2001	96	19.7	9.0	24.4	12.2
2002	0	24.7	24.7	32.1	32.1
2003	23,551	23.3	0.0	31.2	0.0
2004	4,741	25.1	0.0	29.1	0.0
2005	9,733	7.8	0.0	8.1	0.0
2006	0	9.7	9.7	10.0	10.0
2007	2,806	10.2	0.0	10.7	0.0
2008	0	7.1	3.4	7.3	3.6

Source: authors' computations on European Commission and Eurostat data

Table 9.1 reports the different values of the *PM* computed for EU imports of husked rice from Guyana, which is an interesting case study on how the assumptions made on the tariff equivalent of the TRQ may affect the value of the margins. Margins are also reported in absolute terms, that is, by considering only the numerator in (9.4) and (9.5).

The first column shows that in five out of 9 years Guyana exported out-of-the preferential quota. Data confirm, as expected, that $PM^E \geq PM^P$. When out-of-quota imports are zero, the tariff equivalents computed under the two different hypotheses are identical and, thus, $PM^E = PM^P$; however, when there are out-of-quota imports, the tariff equivalent consistent with the assumption of perfect competition is higher and the margin is lower. As the Table 9.1 shows, even a small amount of out-of-quota imports, as in 2001, may sharply reduce PM^P. Overall, PM^E indicates that preferential margins before the 2004 ranged between 18 and 25% while after 2004 they collapse to less than 10%, thus confirming the assumption of clear preference erosion following the policy reform of 2004.[3] This evidence is less clear-cut from the values of PM^P, as in four out of 9 years this is equal to zero because of positive out-of-quota imports.

PM have been also aggregated by country by means of weighted averages of the PM_{kj}, with the weights being the bilateral imported volume in the whole period of a certain country/product.

Figs. 9.1 and 9.2 show the average *PM* by group of preferred countries. The values of PM^E indicate that the margins after 2004 have clearly declined for all groups of countries, with the EBA group showing the sharpest decline. This may be explained by the different ways in which the EU grants preferences to the ACP with respect to the EBA countries. The value of the preferred tariffs granted to the ACP countries is partly linked the value of the MFN tariff; as a consequence, the considerable reduction of the MFN tariffs after 2004 has not been fully transmitted

[3]It is worth noting that since 2003 in-quota tariffs granted to ACP countries have even slightly fallen; the drop in the margin is therefore entirely explained by the fall in the MFN tariffs.

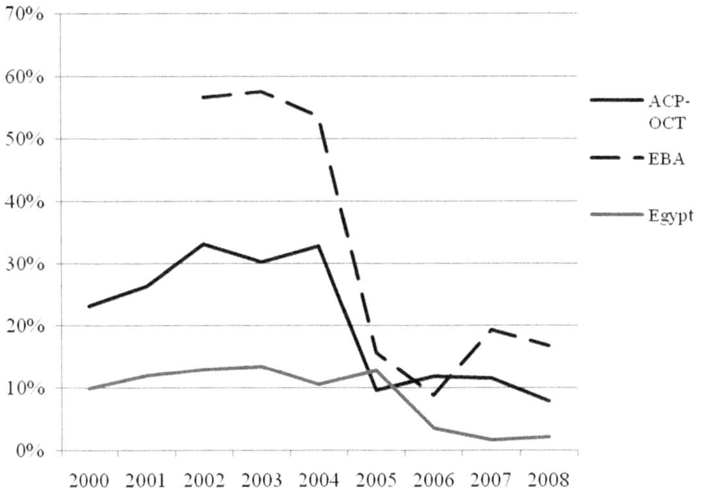

Fig. 9.1 Average preferential margins by countries, under the assumption of economies of scale

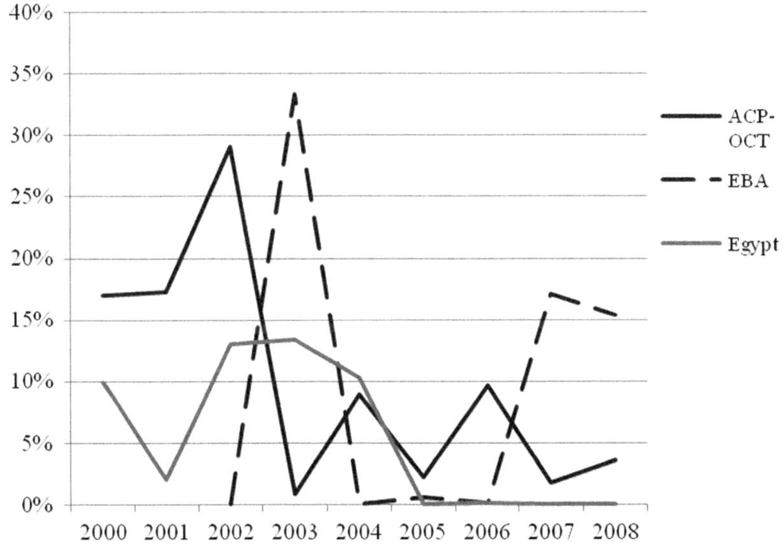

Fig. 9.2 Average preferential margins by countries under the assumption of perfect competition

to the *PM*, also because the preferred tariffs have declined, albeit to a lesser extent. On the contrary, EBA countries during that period benefitted from a zero in-quota tariff; as a consequence, the reduction of the MFN tariffs was wholly translated into a reduction of the *PM*. Egypt has benefitted from lower preferences than EBA and

ACP countries.[4] But in this case the fall in the *PM* is not due to the fall in the MFN tariffs, because the preferential tariff is defined as a percentage of the value of the MFN tariff; thus, the former declines proportionally with the latter. In fact, Egypt's *PM* declined drastically in the final years of the period because Egypt started to export considerable amounts of broken rice out-of-the-quota at the MFN tariffs.

The values of the PM^P (Fig. 9.2) for the three groups of countries again do not clearly indicate any erosion of preferences after 2004. As for EBA countries, for example, there is no clear-cut evidence of preference erosion. The main reason is that in certain years EBA countries imported small quantities out-of-the quota, even if their TRQ were not wholly filled.[5] This occurred, for example, in 2002, 2004, 2005, and 2006. Hence, the PM^P becomes zero in 3 years and almost zero in 2005. It is well known that Least Developed Countries (LDC) often face difficulties in exploiting preferences, because this entails a costly procedure especially when a quota is in place.

The evolution of the PM^P indicates that there has been no preference erosion because the LDC have been able to export anyway (even if in small amounts) out-of-the quota before and after 2004. No clear-cut evidence of preference erosion exists either for the ACP-OCT countries when observing the PM^P; this sharply declined in 2003 because of out-of quota imports despite the TRQ being unfilled, while in 2002 there were no out-of-quota imports and the margin was rather high. Overall, because the ACP and the EBA countries have never filled their TRQ, the fluctuation in the PM^P in these cases reflects the (in)ability of countries to use preferences, which varies from one year to the next, according to the observed different values of the TRQ fill rate over the period. On the basis of the PM^P one should conclude that there has been no erosion of preferences after 2004, even though in principle this is not the case. The PM^P indicates that preferences to Egypt fell to zero after 2004 but, as mentioned above, this is not due to the 2004 reduction of the MFN tariffs, rather to the improved ability of Egypt to export out-of-the quota at the MFN tariffs.

9.4 Estimating the Trade Effect of Preferential Margins with Gravity Equation

The literature studying the average treatment effect of trade preferences using the gravity equation is largely based on the assumption that *PM* is an exogenous variable (e.g., Nilsson and Matsson 2009; Cipollina and Salvatici 2010; Cardamone 2011). This approach consistently identifies the average treatment effect of *PM* if the economic agents' decision to select a programme is unrelated to unobservable

---

[4]The in-quota tariff in this case has been set as equal to the 75% of the MFN tariff, which is much higher than the preferential tariffs granted to the ACP and to EBA countries.

[5]As for EBA countries, over the examined period the fill rate has ranged between 56 and 79%.

factors influencing the outcome. However, as discussed in Baier and Bergstrand (2004; 2007), in the context of Free Trade Agreements (FTA), many trade-policy analysts have noted that trade inhibiting policies, such as non-tariff barriers, may be one of the main reasons why governments select a specific FTA.

In this specific context we face a similar problem. Indeed, the EU choice to engage in a preferential regime could also be, among other things, a function of several unobservable factors: for example, the existence of specific domestic regulations, such as stringent EU food safety and quality standards, or non-trade related political motives. Hence, countries may select a preferential regime for reasons that are difficult to observe and are often correlated with the level of trade. This raises the classical problem of endogeneity in right-hand side variables.

Endogeneity usually arises under three forms: omitted variables, measurement error, and simultaneity bias (Wooldridge 2002). While the use of a continuous instead of a dummy variable to measure preferences can mitigate the *measurement error* bias, Baier and Bergstrand (2007) suggest that *omitted variable* (selection) bias and, to a lesser extent, simultaneity remain the major sources of endogeneity in the estimation of trade preference effects by means of the gravity equation. In this situation, the standard cross-sectional gravity equation is unable to account for such endogeneity, as any potential instrument for trade preferences is also a determinant of bilateral trade (Magee 2003; Baier and Bergstrand 2004).

The recent literature has shown that the most plausible estimate of the average effect of an FTA, that allows adjustment for endogeneity from omitted variable bias, is obtained from (theoretically-based) gravity models using panel data (Baier and Bergstrand 2007; Magee 2008; Martínez-Zarzoso et al. 2009).

Specifically, the panel gravity equation should include time-varying country dummies to account for time-varying multilateral-resistance terms as well as to eliminate the bias stemming from the gold-medal error identified by Baldwin and Taglioni (2006). In this way, variables that are difficult to measure, such as "infrastructure, factor endowments, multilateral trade liberalization, and unobserved time-specific shocks, are captured by the *importer-year* and *exporter-year* fixed effects." (Magee 2008, p. 353). Last but not least, the presence of unobserved time-invariant bilateral factors influencing simultaneously the presence of a preferential treatment and the volume of trade have to be controlled for by *country-pair* fixed effects (Baier and Bergstrand 2007).

We follow this approach to estimate the average effect of the *PM* on rice exports to the EU. Thus, our main contribution is to estimate the trade effect of preferential agreements using a panel data setting and a continuous preference variable, in order to evaluate how this average effect changes with the use of different methods to calculate the *PM*.

As mentioned in Section 9.2, trade flow data come from the External Trade Statistics (Comext), produced by Eurostat which provides the value and the quantity of goods traded by EU member states with third countries. Due to the common nature of the EU trade policy, the EU is here treated as a single entity; hence, we consider the aggregated EU imports from all existing origins, also taking into account of the enlargement processes in 2004 and 2007. As for the dependent variable, we take account of the overall trade, and not just that benefiting from preferences – as was the case in some previous papers (e.g., Nilsson and Matsson 2009). Indeed, there are various reasons that call into question the use of only preferential trade, that are related to both spill-over effects and the reallocation of market shares towards more productive firms. First, when a firm decides to export to the EU because of the introduction of a preferential tariff – for rice, this has been the case, for instance, of the zero-duty quota introduced in 2002 under the EBA initiative – it has to face sunk costs linked to the marketing of the product, such as the new (trade) infrastructures and various transaction costs to meet EU standards and, eventually, the setting-up of a foreign distribution chain (Arkolakis 2008). These may generate spillover effects on total trade, as they are likely to improve overall ability to export to the EU. Second, as suggested by the recent trade theory, firms' exposure to international trade induces only the more productive firms to export while simultaneously forcing the least productive firms to exit. Both the exit of the least productive firms and the additional exports sales gained by the more productive firms reallocate market share towards the latter (Melitz 2003). As a consequence of this selection process, the ability of the average firm to export increases irrespective of the existence of preferences. Finally, the productivity boost of exporting firms is also attributable to the effect of the learning process (Greenaway and Kneller 2007) that clearly will affect overall, and not just preferential trade.

9.5 Empirical Specification and Estimation Strategy

The standard gravity equation commonly estimated using cross-section data is:

$$m_{ijk} = \beta_0 (GDP_i)^{\beta 1} (GDP_j)^{\beta 2} (d_{ij})^{\beta 3} (t_{ijk})^{\beta 4} e^{\beta 5 (Lang_{ij})} e^{\beta 6 (Cont_{ij})} \varepsilon_{ijk} \tag{9.6}$$

where m_{ijk} is the trade flow to country i from country j of good k; GDP_i (GDP_j) is the nominal gross domestic product in the destination (origin) country; d_{ij} reflects the impact of transport costs and is proxied by distance between countries; *Lang* and *Cont* are binary variables assuming the value 1 if i and j share a common language or a common border, and 0 otherwise. Finally, t_{ijk} are the trade policies, proxied by the *ad valorem* equivalent tariff factor imposed by country i on commodity k imports from country j: $t_{ijk} = (1 + T_{ijk})$, with T_{ijk} being the *ad valorem* equivalent tariff. Rewriting (9.6) in logarithmic form and introducing the time dimension, as well as the fixed effects suggested by the theory, the basic empirical model can be expressed as:

$$\ln m_{ijkt} = \beta_0 + \beta_1 \ln(1 + T_{ijkt}) + \alpha_{jt} + \alpha_{it} + \alpha_{ij} + \alpha_{hs6t} + \alpha_t \tag{9.7}$$

where α_{ij} are bilateral fixed effects to control for unobserved time-invariant heterogeneities accounting for the impact on trade of any observed and unobserved characteristics of country pair that are constant over time, such as the existence of common language, common border, colonial relationship as well as other historical, cultural and political ties between trading partners (Magee 2008); $\alpha_{\iota t}$ and $\alpha_{\varphi t}$ are the importer-year and exporter-year fixed effects that account for country variation in real GDP, population as well as other variables that are difficult to measure such as infrastructure, factor endowments or time specific shocks. These country-and-time effects account explicitly for the time-varying multilateral price terms (Baier and Bergstrand 2007). Finally α_t and α_{hs6t} are year and product-time dummies to account for any shocks that affect global trade flows in a particular year or in a particular time-product group, respectively.

Because we consider the EU as the unique importer, the importer-year α_{it} and bilateral fixed effects α_{ij} are dropped in this case because they are perfectly collinear with the time dummies and the exporter-year dummies.

Moreover, our definition of *PM* in (9.3) can be written as

$$\left(1 + PM_{kj}\right) = \frac{\left(1 + T_k^{MFN}\right)}{\left(1 + T_{kj}^{PREF}\right)} \tag{9.8}$$

which, by including the time dimension, can be expressed as

$$\left(1 + T_{kjt}^{PREF}\right) = \frac{\left(1 + T_{kt}^{MFN}\right)}{\left(1 + PM_{kjt}\right)}. \tag{9.9}$$

Plugging (9.9) in (9.7) we have:

$$\ln\, m_{jkt} = \beta_0 + \beta_1\left[\ln\left(1 + T_{kt}^{MFN}\right) - \ln\left(1 + PM_{jkt}\right)\right] + \alpha_{jt} + \alpha_{hs6t} + \alpha_t. \tag{9.10}$$

Since T_{kt}^{MFN} does not vary across exporters, it is captured by time-product fixed effects, thus the final empirical equation becomes

$$\ln\, m_{jkt} = \beta_0 + \beta_2 \ln\left(1 + PM_{jkt}\right) + \alpha_{jt} + \alpha_{hs6t} + \alpha_t. \tag{9.11}$$

To estimate (9.11) consistently we have to address two further (econometric) problems. The first comes from the selection bias, as defined by Heckman (1979). Indeed, a standard feature of bilateral trade flows is the presence of a high number of zeros, an issue which increases with highly disaggregated data. Thus, to account for selection bias, we follow one of the most common methods of dealing with zero trade, the Heckman (1979) two-stage selection correction. In a panel data setting, this means estimating a panel random-effects probit with exporter and importer fixed effects and time effect, as a first step selection equation. From this estimation, the inverse Mills ratio is retrieved and included as regressor in the so-called output equation, namely a Least Square estimator with Dummy Variable (LSDV) with time dummies and exporter-year dummies (see Martínez-Zarzoso et al. 2009).

The second problem related to gravity models, raised in an influential paper by Santos-Silva and Tenreyro (2006), is heteroskedasticity. These authors emphasised that because of Jensen's inequality, the parameters of a log-linearized gravity equation cannot be interpreted as the true elasticities. As an alternative approach, they recommended the Poisson Pseudo Maximum-Likelihood (PPML) estimator, with a log-linear function instead of log–log one. Indeed, the Poisson regression remains consistent in the presence of heteroskedasticity and, due to the multiplicative form, provides a natural way to deal with zero trade flows.

More recently Martin and Pham (2008) through a Monte Carlo experiment have shown that the Heckman method performs well if true identifying restrictions are available. By contrast, the PPML solves the heteroskedasticity problem, but yields biased estimates when zero trade observations are frequent, an issue highlighted also by Burger et al. (2009) and Raimondi and Olper (2010). Thus, given the large fraction of zero trade flows in our sample, our preferred econometric approach to estimate the *PM* effect will be the Heckman procedure. However, in our specific context it is impossible to fully account for the exclusion restriction suggested by the theory,[6] and given the uncertainty about estimators, we also apply the standard LSDV on positive trade flows, and the PPML approach to check for robustness.

9.6 Results

We start by estimating a cross-section gravity equation for each year of the time period covered. Table 9.2 provides the *PM* impact for the year 2001, 2005, and 2008. The two sets of estimates, for both *PM*, present coefficients that are quite unstable from year to year and in some years are even negative for PM^P.[7] With a value of about 14, the only statistically significant elasticity estimate is the one for 2008, and refers to PM^E. Thus, it appears quite difficult to reach any conclusion about the effect of *PM* on trade flows from these cross-section results.

While several reasons can be offered for this instability, the preliminary evidence is in line with the recent literature that criticised the use of cross-section

[6]A close inspection of (9.11) clarifies this point. Indeed, to implement the exclusion restriction suggested by the theory we have to find a (bilateral) variable that affects fixed trade costs but has a minor effect on variable trade costs. This variable should be used in the (first step) selection equation, but excluded in the (second step) outcome equation. However, as we work with only one importer (the EU) and bilateral fixed effects (a_{jt} in 9.11), it is not possible to include in the selection equation an additional variable that affects fixed trade costs (e.g., the language dummy) simply because it will be perfectly collinear with the included fixed effects.

[7]The instability of coefficients of Table 9.2, obtained using only the non-zero trade flows, are generally unaffected by the use of the Heckman procedure to control for sample selection (results not reported).

Table 9.2 The trade effect of preferential margin: Cross-section regressions

	Dep. Var.: ln ($Import_{jkt}$)					
	PM^P – Standard			PM^E – Weighted		
	2001	2005	2008	2001	2005	2008
ln (1 + PM_{jkt})	−0.14	−2.51	4.66	4.38	9.72	14.24**
	(7.15)	(4.73)	(6.59)	(6.38)	(7.74)	(6.07)
No. of obs.	300	363	425	300	363	425
R-Sq	0.43	0.47	0.57	0.43	0.47	0.57

Note: exporter and HS6 digit product fixed effects included in each regression. Robust standard errors in parentheses. *, ** and *** indicate statistically significance at 10, 5, and 1% level, respectively

Table 9.3 The trade effect of preferential margin: Panel regression

	Dep. Var.: ln ($Import_{jkt}$)				Dep.Var.: $Import_{jkt}$	
	LSDV		HECKMAN		PPML	
	Standard PM^P	Weighted PM^E	Standard PM^P	Weighted PM^E	Standard PM^P	Weighted PM^E
	(1)	(2)	(3)	(4)	(5)	(6)
ln (1 + PM_{jkt})	4.20**	10.45***	20.54***	20.75***	10.64***	18.36***
	(2.06)	(1.95)	(4.41)	(5.19)	(1.90)	(1.38)
Mills ratio			3.37***	1.85**		
			(0.74)	(0.82)		
No. of obs.	3,195	3,195	3,195	3,195	17,944	17,944

Note: exporter-year, time and HS6 digit product-time fixed effects included in regressions (1)–(4). Exporter-year, time and HS6 digit product fixed effects included in regressions (5)–(6) (see text). Robust standard errors clustered by exporter country in parentheses. *, ** and *** indicate statistically significance at 10, 5, and 1% level, respectively

regressions to infer the effect of preferential margins (Baier and Bergstrand 2007; Martínez-Zarzoso et al. 2009). Indeed, as discussed above, the simple inclusion of country fixed effects does not correct for the endogeneity bias induced by the country selection in preferential regimes. In a cross-section gravity equation, we should use instrumental variable technique to adjust for this endogeneity bias. However, finding good instruments correlated with *PM* and uncorrelated with bilateral trade is a well known problem in the gravity literature.

Econometric evidence based on panel data is reported in Table 9.3. Due to the panel structure of the dataset, the estimated robust standard errors are now clustered by exporter country, to take into account both heteroscedasticity and autocorrelation of unknown form. Columns 1-2 present the regression results when the gravity model is estimated over the full time period considered (2000–2008), using LSDV with country-time fixed effects. Column 1 includes the "Standard" margin, PM^P, while column 2 considers the "weighted" margin that accounts for economies of scale and imperfect competition, PM^E. Under perfect competition, the trade elasticity of the preferential margin factor (1 + *PM*) in the rice sector, namely the estimated coefficient, has a magnitude near to 4. Interestingly, the estimated preferences effect strongly increases in magnitude when the PM^E is considered. In particular, the coefficient increases by almost 2.5 times, from 4.2 to 10.4.

Columns 3 and 4 estimate the effects of preferences taking account of selection bias problems and thus adding to the second step Heckman equation the inverse Mills ratio, retrieved from the first step (probit) selection equation.[8] The high presence of zero trade in our dataset (about 80%) makes the inverse Mills ratio coefficient significant, providing evidence of selection bias. Both PM^P and PM^E coefficients strongly increase in magnitude, and this is particularly true for PM^P. Indeed, the magnitude of the estimated effect of the two margins is now quite similar. However, as will be shown, despite this apparent similarity between the values of the estimated coefficients, the hypothetical elimination of preferences may result in rather diverse trade impacts depending upon which *PM* is actually used.

As robustness check, Columns 5-6 of Table 9.3 report estimates of the gravity equation using the PPML estimator.[9] The trade elasticities are consistently higher than the LSDV ones, and only slightly lower than those obtained by using the Heckman procedure, confirming the importance of sample selection in the dataset. However, due to the vulnerability of the Poisson model to over-dispersion with an excess of zero flows, only the regression results obtained from the Heckman procedure will be considered.

On the other hand, whatever the estimation method, the message is the same: assuming scale economies and imperfect competition (vis-à-vis perfect competition) to measure the TRQ tariff equivalent significantly increases the sensitivity of trade flows to preferences.

Table 9.4 reports the results when three different preferential groups are considered separately (ACP-OCT, EBA, Egypt).[10] In line with previous results, the impact of preferences estimated using PM^E is higher than that based on PM^P. In particular, the strongest impact of preferences on trade is found for Egypt, with a magnitude of 25.3, followed by ACP-OCT and EBA countries. The positive and statistically significant coefficients indicate that EU imports from these developing country groups increase with the size of the *PM*, suggesting that EU preferences do matter.

A weakness of the preference effects discussed above is that, because they are estimated on the 2000–2008 period, they do not provide any information about the actual impact of the erosion of preferences occurring after 2004. Indeed, the trade elasticity of the *PM* factor may have undergone changes after 2004, as a consequence of variation in the *PM*. Thus, to capture the effect of *PM* reduction in the

---

[8]The probit selection equation (not reported) presents estimated coefficients that are statistically significant and with the expected sign. As expected, the PM increases the probability of registering positive trade flows.

[9]In the Poisson procedure, we used product dummies instead of time-product dummies due to convergence problems from the high number of dummies. Results obtained using smaller sample show tiny variations in the estimated coefficients.

[10]To isolate the preferential margin impact on the three groups we removed the export flows from the two preferential country groups different from the one analysed. We maintained exports from non-preferential countries as the benchmark.

Table 9.4 The trade effect of preferential margin: results across preferential groups

	PM^P – Standard			PM^E – Weighted		
	ACP-OCT	EBA	EGYPT	ACP-OCT	EBA	EGYPT
$\ln(1+PM_{jkt})$	18.63***	15.24***	15.20*	21.20***	20.28***	25.27***
	(4.84)	(3.14)	(5.62)	(6.02)	(2.68)	(6.52)
Mills ratio	2.94***	4.39***	4.14***	1.65**	4.26***	4.25***
	(0.70)	(0.68)	(0.66)	(0.81)	(0.68)	(0.66)
No. of obs.	2,884	2,924	2,825	2,884	2,924	2,825

Note: all regressions correspond to the second stage Heckman procedure. Exporter-year, time and HS6 digit product-time fixed effects included in each regression. Robust standard errors clustered by exporter country in parentheses. *, ** and *** indicate statistically significance at 10, 5, and 1% level, respectively

Table 9.5 The trade effect of preferential margin: results over different time-periods

	PM^P – Standard			PM^E – Weighted		
	ACP-OCT	EBA	EGYPT	ACP-OCT	EBA	EGYPT
Year 2000–2004						
$\ln(1+PM_{jkt})$	17.88**	20.85***	57.71***	14.50*	21.79***	68.65***
	(8.30)	(1.73)	(17.43)	(8.66)	(4.54)	(13.20)
Mills ratio	2.60**	4.87***	5.15***	0.53	4.75***	5.01***
	(1.20)	(1.12)	(1.06)	(1.26)	(1.11)	(1.10)
No. of obs.	1,487	1,471	1,449	1,487	1,471	1,449
Year 2005–2008						
$\ln(1+PM_{jkt})$	16.72***	15.48***	7.39*	24.66***	20.85***	17.04**
	(6.14)	(4.14)	(3.85)	(8.32)	(4.71)	(6.73)
Mills ratio	3.12***	4.02***	3.76***	2.55***	3.84***	3.83***
	(0.89)	(0.95)	(0.93)	(0.96)	(0.95)	(0.92)
No. of obs.	1,397	1,453	1,376	1,397	1,453	1,376

Note: all regressions correspond to the second stage Heckman procedure. Exporter-year, time and HS6 digit product-time fixed effects included in each regression. Robust standard errors clustered by exporter country in parentheses. *, ** and *** indicate statistically significance at 10, 5, and 1% level, respectively

observed period, we have also estimated the trade impact by splitting the overall period into two sub-periods: from 2000 to 2004, and from 2005 to 2008. Table 9.5 reports the results.

In evaluating these additional results, however, one important caveat is that in 2004 EU trade flows were also subject to a considerable trade shock, that is, the enlargement process.[11] Obviously, this shock can represent an additional source of (potential) variation of the differentiated effect in the *PM* before and after 2004. Keeping this in mind, the estimated preferences coefficients, which are all but one statistically significant, are always lower in the second period than before 2004 showing, as expected, a general decrease in the trade effect of preferences. This is particularly true for Egypt, where the trade impact of preferences markedly

[11]In the database the EU is considered of 15 members until 2003, from 2004 to 2006 of 25 members, and since 2007 of 27 members.

diminishes in the second period, from 68.6 to 17.0, when the PM^E is considered.[12] This appears to confirm the reduced importance of preferences for Egyptian rice exports after 2004, also due to the considerable increase in out-of-quota exports of broken rice. Therefore, we could expect that a hypothetical zero setting of the *PM* could have a smaller impact on Egypt's exports to the EU in the final period, than before the 2004.

On the contrary, for EBA countries, whose preferences have drastically decreased after 2004, we detect little reduction in their PM^E factor coefficients in the second period, showing that preferences still have a strong effect on trade flows, irrespective of erosion. Finally, the ACP-OCT group, whose *PM* cut has been partially mitigated by the link between preferential tariffs and MFN tariffs, preserves a high coefficient in the second period; thus, we can also expect *PM* to maintain a strong impact on EU trade flows in more recent years. The estimated coefficients obtained by using the PM^P outline a similar, albeit generally lower, trend.

To sum up, the above results appear to confirm the idea that measuring the *PM* under economies of scale and imperfect competition (vis-à-vis perfect competition) significantly increases the elasticity of trade flows to preferences. At the same time they also show that, whatever the estimation method used, trade elasticities, with an average value of about 20, are significantly higher than those obtained by previous similar empirical exercises. For example, Cipollina and Salvatici (2010) find the trade elasticities to EU preferences ranging from 3.6 (fruit and vegetables) to 16 (tropical products) with an average of 6.7; thus, they obtained values which are all well below the ones obtained in this paper. Several reasons can explain such differences. First, as already mentioned, we use overall trade instead of preferential flows. Second, it is recognised in the gravity literature that a more disaggregate level implies higher trade elasticities, simply because the homogeneity of products increases (Anderson and van Wincoop 2004). Finally, accounting econometrically for the endogeneity of the *PM* variable should increase the *PM* factor trade elasticity as well (Baier and Bergstrand 2007).

To evaluate the impact of a hypothetical elimination of preferences on developing countries' exports, we used a Monte Carlo simulation to convert the raw output of the estimated coefficients of Tables 9.4 and 9.5 in simulation results (King et al. 2000). Basically, by drawing randomly we can obtain the "estimated coefficients" (the result of one simulation) that can be multiplied by the value of its corresponding explanatory variable (i.e. the preference factor). The variability of the simulated coefficients translates into variability in the expected value of trade (the dependent variable), while the effects of the other independent variables are held constant at their means. By repeating this procedure 1,000 times, we generated 1,000 expected values of the status quo, and 1,000 expected value under the hypothesis of the elimination of preferences, setting $MP^i = 0$. Then, we calculated the 1,000 expected trade variations induced by the elimination of preferences, ranking

[12] This reduction is even more severe when using the PM^P, but less statistically significant. Indeed, as previously described, the PM^P indicates that preferences to Egypt fell to zero after 2004.

Table 9.6 The trade effect of an hypothetical elimination of preferences

	PM^P – Standard			PM^E – Weighted		
	ACP-OCT	EBA	EGYPT	ACP-OCT	EBA	EGYPT
2000–08	−69.9%	−10.8%	−9.4%	−89.7%	−34.0%	−23.3%
95% Conf. interval	−84.8%	−15.9%	−15.8%	−97.3%	−42.2%	−32.4%
	−45.3%	−5.2%	−2.5%	−71.8%	−24.3%	−13.8%
2000–04	−72.3%	−10.4%	−46.6%	−80.6%	−39.5%	−52.1%
95% Conf. interval	−91.1%	−18.8%	−60.7%	−97.2%	−53.4%	−67.1%
	−31.7%	−0.4%	−28.7%	−28.2%	−22.1%	−33.2%
2005–08	−54.4%	−12.9%	−0.7%	−67.9%	−22.9%	−9.4%
95% Conf. interval	−77.4%	−20.1%	−1.9%	−89.9%	−32.7%	−17.3%
	−15.8%	−6.0%	0.5%	−20.0%	−12.1%	−1.1%

Note: figures report the average trade effect, and their 95% confidential interval, of a simulation exercise of preferences elimination. The results are obtained starting from the second stage Heckman regressions by using the STATA programme *Clarify*. (See text)

them from the lowest to the highest. The 25th and 976th positions represent, respectively, our lower and upper bounds of a 95-percent confidence interval.

Table 9.6 reports the percentage changes in the exports of the three preferred countries groups, both for the entire period and for the two sub-periods considered, together with the implied confidence intervals. Several interesting patterns emerge.

First, and independently from the country groups or the time period considered, the trade reduction effect is always lower when using PM^P rather than PM^E. Thus, we have clear confirmation of the (potential) underestimation arising from the perfect competition assumption in determining the TRQ equivalent tariff. Second, we observe a drastic change in the PM^E elimination effect on Egyptian exports: the volume traded after 2004 drops by about 10%, while before 2004 the elimination of preferences would have produced a loss in trade of about 52%. Thus, after the reduction of MFN tariffs the ability to export out-of-quota has increased and the dependence of Egyptian rice exports on EU preferences has been reduced. By contrast, for ACP-OCT countries, the cut in PM^E, occurring after 2004 and softened by the reduction of both MFN and preferential tariffs, maintains in the final period the strong impact of *PM* on trade. Indeed, any hypothetical elimination of preferences could dramatically reduce rice exports from these countries by more than 67% in the final period. For the EBA countries group, the trade reduction effect consequent on the loss of preferences changes from 40 to 23%; thus once again we witness a clear reduction of the dependence on preferences when passing from the first to the second period considered.[13] Finally, while the upper and lower bounds of the 95% confidence interval are quite wide in some circumstances, in all considered cases but one they display a negative effect. Thus, our exercise appears quite robust in terms of the direction of the simulated effects.

[13]We are using here two different concepts. On one hand, preference erosion refers to the reduction in the value of the preferential margin, while, the dependency of a country on preferences is the responsiveness of its exports to the variation in the preferential margin, which is measured by the trade elasticity: the higher the elasticity, the greater its dependency on preferences.

A final issue concerns the comparability of our results with previous evidence. Due to the high level of product disaggregation, the country group aggregation as well as the panel dimension of the data set, it is quite difficult to compare our results with previous findings. However, in a recent work, van der Mensbrugghe (2009), using the GTAP dataset in a partial equilibrium model, finds that low-income countries (excluding India) "are poised to lose significant market share as their preference margins are eroded" (p. 364). In particular, he evaluated in 23% the exports reduction in rice exports to EU coming from these countries. Thus, the trend shown in our results are not so different from this evidence, although they are not directly comparable.

9.7 Concluding Remarks

Preference erosion is a key issue in the trade relationships between the EU and developing countries. Beyond progress in multilateral liberalization under the WTO, there are other reasons why the preferences granted by the EU to developing countries are declining; the change in the EU trade policy in the rice industry over the past decade is one good example. Although it is evident to many observers that the EU trade policy changes have implied some erosion of preferences in the rice industry – one of the most sensitive industries for a number of EU favored developing countries – to date there has been no quantitative assessment of the extent of this preference erosion and on its impact on trade. This paper has addressed these issues with the aim of contributing to the existing literature on the trade impact of preferences in two main directions: first, by proposing a new empirical strategy to calculate the preferential margin when tariff rate quotas are in force; second, by assessing the trade impact of the preferential margins by means of a panel gravity model to deal with endogeneity of the preferential margin.

The results show that, when dealing with highly disaggregated data such as in this paper, the use of the "standard" tariff equivalent, i.e. the one consistent with the assumption of perfect competition and increasing marginal costs, may lead to an overestimation of the preferential tariff, and thus to an underestimation of preferences, when there are economies of scale in international trade. Further, on the basis of the value of the "standard" preferential margins one should conclude that no preference erosion has occurred, while this is not the case when using the preferential margins based on the tariff equivalent proposed in this paper. Thus, the main implication of this part of our analysis is that when preferences are granted by means of tariff rate quotas the implicit assumption made about the market structure is very important. Although, to the best of our knowledge, no empirical evidence is available on the market structure and the cost curve of EU rice importers, we do believe that the assumptions of the existence of fixed costs and, thus, of the presence of economies of scale in the international trade of agricultural products are, in general terms, quite plausible. In this case the use of the "standard" tariff equivalent of tariff rate quotas may result in misleading conclusions about the extent of the trade preferences or their erosion.

The second major finding of this paper is that EU preferences matter significantly as regards the ability of developing countries to export rice to the EU. Compared to other papers, our estimates provide quite high values for the elasticities of the preferential margins to trade for all groups of countries, but this appears to be consistent with what the most recent panel gravity literature on FTA has emphasised. In addition, trade elasticities are always lower when using the standard tariff equivalent; thus, the assumption made about market structure matters also when assessing the trade impact of a change in preferences. Further, we have found that, after the EU trade policy change of 2004, elasticities have been increasing for ACP-OCT and EBA countries, while they have diminished for Egypt; this suggests a differentiated effect of preference erosion on the sensitivity of trade flows to the preferences granted. Finally, simulations on the trade impact of preference elimination suggest that the exports of ACP-OCT countries are to date the most dependent upon preferences, while the EBA countries and Egypt would undergo a reduction in their exports from the elimination of preferences, albeit to a lesser extent.

The analysis can be improved in several directions. Given our assumption of fixed (sunk) costs of exporting, the most natural extension would be to specify the model dynamically, through something on the lines of a Generalized Method of Moments panel estimator. This extension, indeed, could properly take into account persistency and hysteresis in bilateral trade, an issue rarely investigated in the gravity literature (see De Benedictis and Vicarelli 2005), and never in the context of asymmetric trade preferences.

Acknowledgments The authors thank Giovanni Anania, Piero Conforti, Luca De Benedictis and Luca Salvatici for their useful comments on an earlier draft of the chapter. Financial support received by the "New Issues in Agricultural, Food and Bio-energy Trade (AGFOODTRADE)" (Small and Medium-scale Focused Research Project, Grant Agreement no. 212036) research projects funded by the European Commission, and by the "European Union policies, economic and trade integration processes and WTO negotiations" research project funded by the Italian Ministry of Education, University and Research (Scientific Research Programs of National Relevance 2007) is gratefully acknowledged.

Chapter 10
Trade Impact of European Union Preferences: The Role of Compliance Costs

Mariarosaria Agostino, Federica Demaria, and Francesco Trivieri

Abstract We explore the effect of European Union (EU) non-reciprocal preferential schemes and the compliance costs they entail on the agricultural import flows from beneficiary countries. Since such costs are heterogeneous and mostly unobservable, we gauge their influence by some estimated proxies, and specify a gravity model that allows for a different preferential margin impact according to the costs level. For a large sample of developing countries in 2002, we find that the costs of compliance seem to play a role in making the schemes work: the lower the costs, the greater the impact of the preferential margins. Moreover, the margin effect seems different across different regimes.

10.1 Introduction

Non-Reciprocal Preferential Trade Agreements (NRPTA) are unilateral tariff reductions conceded by developed countries to developing and least developed countries, with the aim to promote their exports. In this work, we empirically assess whether and to what extent agricultural imports that enter the European Union (EU) market under a preferential scheme are affected by both the benefits and costs entailed by the scheme itself. In particular, we consider the most relevant non-reciprocal agreements granted by the EU in 2002: the Cotonou Agreement, the Generalized System of Preferences (GSP) and the GSP-Drugs, and we focus on the agricultural sector as developed countries have always shown a certain reluctance in granting deep and effective tariff reductions to agricultural imports. In addition, many Most Favored Nation (MFN) duties on agricultural commodities are still very

This chapter is largely based on: Agostino, M., Demaria, F., and Trivieri, F., (2010). Non-reciprocal trade preferences and the role of compliance costs in the agricultural sector: exports to the EU. J Agric Econ 61(3), 652–679.

M. Agostino, F. Demaria, and F. Trivieri
Department of Economics and Statistics, University of Calabria, Via Pietro Bucci – Cubo 1C, I-87036 Rende (CS), Italy
e-mail: m.agostino@unical.it; demariaf@unical.it; francesco.trivieri@unical.it

L. De Benedictis and L. Salvatici (eds.), *The Trade Impact of European Union Preferential Policies*, DOI 10.1007/978-3-642-16564-1_10,

high, which makes the benefit from any preferential agreement potentially relevant.[1]

With the present contribution we seek to provide evidence that any study aiming at investigating the impact of preferential regimes on the export flows of beneficiary countries should account not only for the benefits, but also for the costs which may deter recipients from actually using available preferential schemes.

We gauge the aforementioned benefits by the tariff cuts that beneficiary countries can profit from accessing the EU market. In other words, given the different degree of protection characterizing different product lines, we model preferential benefits by means of preferential margins instead of dummy variables (on this point see also Cardamone 2007, 2011; Cipollina and Salvatici 2010).

As far as the costs of compliance are concerned, these arise from factors related to the scheme requirements, such as rules of origin, technical, sanitary and traceability requirements.[2] A recent debate on the use of trade preferences has suggested the potential relevance of impediments to utilize the schemes. On one hand, some contributions document an underutilization of preferences: exports of a product which could benefit from preferential access usually occur both at the preferential and the MFN rate (Brenton 2003; Brenton and Manchin 2003; Inama 2003; Gallezot 2003). For instance, Brenton (2003) and Gallezot (2003) suggest that many Sub-Saharan African countries underutilize the Everything But Arms (EBA regime – despite the higher preferential margins it offers – and tend instead to make use of the less generous Cotonou regime. On the other hand, some studies (Bureau et al. 2007a; Gallezot and Bureau 2005) point out that – since many countries are entitled to use several preferential schemes – preferential regimes considered as a whole are, in fact, largely utilised. Nevertheless, some regimes (such as the Cotonou agreement) tend to be preferred to others (GSP and EBA). Bureau et al. (2007a) investigate the determinants of the choice of a particular regime by estimating probit models where the underlying latent variable is the compliance cost of a given preference. According to their findings, in the EU case, the Cotonou scheme tends to be preferred by exporters to the GSP or the EBA, and "higher preferential margins (e.g., the Cotonou compared with the EU GSP regime) are only part of the explanation. The rules of origin requirements contribute to explaining why the Cotonou is preferred to the EU GSP, including the EBA, because Cotonou is less restrictive in terms of geographical cumulation"(Bureau et al. 2007a, p. 195).

---

[1]Since we focus on 2002 and learning effects are likely to affect the utilisation of any schemes, even more so when beneficiary countries are Least Developed Countries (LDC), we do not consider the EBA initiative, which has been in force only from 2001. For a detailed description of the EU non-reciprocal preferences see Chapter 2 as well as Bureau et al. (2007a); OECD (2005); Persson and Wilhelmsson (2007).

[2]It is worth mentioning that other obstacles, not directly connected to the scheme requirements, may also hinder the capability of exporting developing countries to access the EU market (e.g., high qualitative standards imposed by private importers, weak infrastructures and institutions, corruption, etc). In estimating our measure of compliance costs, we try to control for them.

As put forward by the above contributions, the costs of complying with the rules of a preferential scheme (costs of compliance) may potentially outweigh the benefits of a trade preference, thus diluting the competitive advantages for the exporters (on this point see also Bureau et al. 2007b; Candau and Jean 2009). If this scenario were to occur, then a larger preference margin would not necessarily provide a greater incentive to export.

In this chapter, after retrieving some estimated measures of the costs of satisfying the regime rules, we investigate the impact of the preferential margin making it conditional on our indicators of compliance costs. Failing to account for such costs would translate into estimating the same (average) influence of a certain preferential regime for all country-product lines we consider.

Using data on 669 lines of agricultural exports for a cross section of 136 developing countries observed in 2002, we estimate a gravity equation by using nonlinear models, which are heteroskedasticity consistent, and allow us to deal more appropriately with the existence of many zero trade flow values. By and large, according to our findings the costs of compliance seem to play a role in making the schemes work: the marginal impact of the preferential margins changes within a particular scheme according to the costs level, the higher the compliance costs, the lower the impact of the preferential margins. Further, the marginal effect of the preferential margins seems different across regimes. Indeed, the Cotonou margin granted by the EU to ACP countries seems to exert a high and always significant influence on the export volumes of beneficiaries – influence that is considerably affected by the costs of compliance. On the other hand, the GSP margin appears to have a much lower impact on trade flows, which is also affected by the same sort of costs. Finally, the GSP-Drugs preferential margin influence, although potentially higher than that of the GSP scheme, seems to have significantly affected a smaller share of recipients.

The rest of the chapter is organized as follows. In the next section we describe the empirical question and the models adopted. Section 10.3 presents the data used, while Section 10.4 comments on the results obtained. Finally, Section 10.5 concludes.

10.2 The Empirical Strategy

The above considerations suggest that the key variables of our analysis are represented by the preferential margin and the costs of compliance. In this section, after retrieving these two variables, we estimate a gravity equation for each preferential scheme, where the influence of the preferential margin is made conditional on the costs of compliance, specifying an interaction term. By doing so, the marginal impact of the preferential margin changes within a particular scheme according to the costs values. The following sections describe in more detail the steps we follow.

10.2.1 Preferential Margins and Estimated Costs of Compliance

Recent studies, which investigate the impact of NRPTA adopting a gravity framework, capture the potential effects of preferences on trade flows by means of preferential margins, rather than using dummy variables (for instance: Cardamone 2011; Cipollina and Salvatici 2010).[3] We compute the preferential margin as the difference between the EU (*ad valorem* equivalent) MFN tariff and the (*ad valorem* equivalent) tariff granted by the scheme, divided by the MFN tariff. That is, preferential margins are equal to $(MFN_{ik} - PREF_{ik})/MFN_{ik}$, where i refers to exporters, and k to the tariff line; MFN and PREF are the Most Favoured Nation and the preferential tariffs, respectively. Computing the preferential margin as the absolute difference between the MFN tariff and the preferential tariff would not take into account the relative size of the preference granted for the particular product with respect to the MFN tariff. In fact, if the maximum level of protection (MFN tariff) across product lines is different, the value of the same absolute preferential margin varies.

As far as compliance costs are concerned, to better illustrate how we estimate them, it is worth underlining two important points. First, the decision of utilizing a preference scheme is taken at the firm level, and different producers may face different compliance costs.[4] However, we have no firm-level data to control for firms heterogeneity. Therefore, as Carrère and de Melo (2004), we suppose that the aggregation from firms to tariff line does not imply systematic biases. In particular, we assume that the higher the costs of satisfying the rules, the fewer the producers that find convenient to satisfy the requirements. Second, quantifying total compliance costs (stemming from many factors, such as rules of origin and fixed administrative costs) is problematic, as they are largely unobservable. Consequently, we retrieve some measures of compliance costs by estimating alternative models of the preferences utilisation determinants.[5] More precisely, supposing that the costs of compliance are mostly unobservable determinants of the utilisation ratio, our measures of costs are estimated residuals retrieved from independent regressions, explaining the utilisation ratio of each specific preferential regime. As the dependent

---

[3]Such an approach would attempt to capture preferential policies by means of a dummy variable coded one if the exporting country is eligible to a preferential scheme and zero otherwise. For a review of the contributions adopting this method, see Cardamone (2007), and Aiello et al. (2010).

[4]As Low et al. (2005, p. 9) claim: "Since producers use different technologies, it may be convenient for some to use the preference and satisfy the requirements, while the origin rules may make it less convenient for others." Furthermore, Manchin (2006, p. 1251) points out that "if the value of the preferences does not exceed those of the costs of getting the preferences a trader should have no incentive to ask for them."

[5]A non-parametric measure of the compliance costs has been proposed by Anson et al. (2005), while Carrère and de Melo (2004) rely on non-parametric as well as parametric estimates. Francois et al. (2006) use a sample splitting method to identify a threshold at which the benefits from the preferential regime are offset by the relative compliance costs. See Bureau et al. (2007a) for a review of the methods used to assess the costs of compliance.

Table 10.1 Main categories of utilization rate determinants, which enter the Tobit models

	Model 1	Model 2	Model 3
Incentives	Preferential margin	Preferential margin	Preferential margin
Capability	Gross Domestic Product (*GDP*), population (*POP*), distance between each exporter and the EU (*DIST*), common language (*LANG*), colonial links (*COL*), Economic Freedom Index (*ECOFREE*)	Gross Domestic Product (*GDP*), population (*POP*), distance between each exporter and the EU (*DIST*) common language (*LANG*), colonial links (*COL*), Economic Freedom Index (*ECOFREE*), education (*EDU*), Foreign Direct Investments (*FDI*), total exports (*EXP*)	Exporter Fixed effects
Costs	Unobservable	Unobservable	Unobservable

For the definition of the variables see also Table 10.3

variable is a regime's utilisation ratio, ranging from 0 to 100, we estimate a double-censored Tobit model for each scheme,[6] by using three different specifications of the regressors set (Model 1-2-3) summarized in Table 10.1. Then, we regard the difference between observed and predicted values as an estimated measure of compliance costs: higher residuals expressing lower costs, and vice-versa, lower residuals indicating the presence of higher costs.[7] To facilitate the interpretation of the results, we compute a measure that increases as the costs increase, by considering the difference between the maximum sample residual and each of the residuals. Besides, since the data we use are disaggregated at the Harmonised System (HS) 6 digit level, we obtain costs that, within each regime, are specific to each country-commodity line observation. In our opinion, this feature appears plausible as the costs of compliance depend not only on the fixed costs that the request for eligibility to each regime involves – which, in turn, depend on the regime requirements and on the specific capabilities of each beneficiary country to meet these requirements – but also on the specific characteristics of the commodity for which the preferential tariff is requested, e.g., its degree of processing. Indeed, as recalled in Sect. 10.4.2, proving the origin of more elaborated products is more problematic than for unprocessed commodities, implying higher compliance costs.

As regards the explanatory variables, the first specification that we employ has been suggested by the extant literature (Carrère and de Melo 2004; Manchin 2006),

[6]On the use of this estimator, see Carrère and de Melo (2004).

[7]Since we lack data on exporting firms, the Tobit that we adopt models the decision of a hypothetical representative (aggregate) exporter that makes the collective choice to utilize the preference at the line level. Such a decision depends on an underlying latent variable, which represents the utility of utilisation. Higher residuals, being associated to higher utility of utilisation, mean a higher propensity to utilize the scheme; thus, they express lower compliance costs.

the second one represents an attempt to extend it, including some other utilisation determinants which we think should not be neglected. Broadly speaking, we expect that the utilisation ratio is positively affected by the incentives and capabilities that countries have to use the schemes, while it is negatively affected by the costs of compliance. The influence of the first two categories of determinants (incentives and capabilities) is captured by a set of observable variables, while the costs of compliance, mostly unobservable, tend to be captured by the model error term (see Table 10.1 for the categorization of the variables).

In Model 1 most of the variables used to account for the capability of using the schemes are the same country characteristics that may affect trade flows and that are frequently considered in the gravity approach (Manchin 2006, p. 1252, expects: "utilization rates to map the same variables that determine trade itself"). *GDP* proxies for the economic size of the exporting country, while *POP* is the relative population;[8] *DIST* is the distance, in kilometers, between each exporter and the EU; *LANG* is a dummy variable coded 1 if the exporting country language is spoken in at least one of the EU member states, and zero otherwise; *COL* is a dummy that takes value 1 if colonial links existed between the exporter and at least one of the EU countries, and zero otherwise. Further, the Economic Freedom Index (*ECO-FREE*) is a composite score, which combines ten different freedoms, from property rights to entrepreneurship, which are all likely to affect the utilisation ratio of preferences. Among the others, trade freedom and freedom from corruption may be particularly relevant, the latter being likely associated with a more efficient provision of customs services.

In Model 2, we include some extra explanatory variables, such as incoming Foreign Direct Investment (*FDI*), total exports (*EXP*) – both as share of GDP – and a proxy of human capital (secondary education pupils to population, *EDU*). All of these regressors are expected to positively affect the capability of using the schemes. Higher level of *FDI* may strengthen the viability and competitiveness of domestic exporters; higher export volumes may indicate higher export capacity and a lower anti-export bias of domestic policies; finally, better educated private exporters and customs agents may better understand and deal with the requirements, being also better prepared to share inspection procedures and computerized services with EU customs.

Finally, in Model 3 we replace all exporting country specific variables by exporter fixed effects.

[8]Since we use very disaggregated data on agricultural lines, the source country GDP might be an unreliable measure of the comparative advantage in the specific sector. When we have tried, though, to retrieve figures on the national production (source FAOSTAT database), we could not obtain data at the HS6 digit level for many lines. As mentioned in the results section, we have also used the agricultural GDP obtaining the same qualitative results as those based on the total GDP, but in smaller samples.

10.2.2 Gravity Equation

For each scheme, we estimate the following (log-linear) equation:

$$IMP_{ik} = \beta_0 + \beta_1 MARGIN_{ik} + \beta_2 COSTS_{ik} + \beta_3 (MARGIN_{ik} * COSTS_{ik}) + u_{ik} \quad (10.1)$$

where *IMP* measures the total imports of EU from the eligible country *i* for the *k* product line.[9] We use disaggregated agricultural data at the HS 6 digit level, considering imports of the EU15 as a whole. *MARGIN* is the preferential margin of the regime considered; *COSTS* is our measure of costs of compliance;[10] *MARGIN** *COSTS* is an interaction term between the latter two variables. Finally, u_{ik} is a composite error term, equal to $v_i + e_{ik}$, where v_i is the exporter fixed effect, included to proxy for "multilateral resistance" *à la* Anderson and van Wincoop (2003), and e_{ik} is the idiosyncratic error term.[11] Since the import region is unique, each dummy (v_i) also captures the influence of unobservable political, historical and cultural factors characterizing the trade relations between the EU and each partner.

Equation (10.1) is estimated adopting a Poisson model (Santos-Silva and Tenreyro 2006) to address the problem of heteroskedastic and non-normal residuals in gravity regressions.[12] In addition of being heteroskedasticity consistent, this method allows us to cope with the existence of many zero trade values.[13]

---

[9]We do not employ preferential imports as dependent variable of our gravity equation (as Nilsson and Matsson 2009, do) to allow the possibility of comparing our findings with those obtained by several other empirical studies which investigate the impact of NRPTA on total imports, using only preferential margins within a gravity framework (for instance, Aiello and Demaria 2009; Aiello and Cardamone Chapter 7 of this book ; Cardamone 2011).

[10]Incidentally, one could argue that frequent and large values of *IMP* could influence the *COSTS* values if scale and learning economies were relevant. To shed light on the latter issue, yet, we would need information (that we lack) on the number and average size of the shipments towards the EU, as large flows could reach the EU through several shipments and vice versa, limited export volumes could enter the EU market through few deliveries.

[11]According to these authors, trade flows between two countries depend not just on the barriers between them, but also on the barriers between them and the rest of the world. Therefore the exporter specific effects are intended to capture the policy attitude of a country towards all its trading partners.

[12]We have also estimated (10.1) by Ordinary Least Square (OLS), accounting for trading partners' fixed effects via the inclusion of exporter dummies (v_i's). This estimator has been traditionally employed in the literature that uses the gravity model to evaluate the impact of non-reciprocal preferential trade policies. In order to account for the existence of zero trade flows, we have added one to our dependent variable to ensure that the logarithm is well-defined. The OLS results confirm those obtained when adopting non-linear estimators.

[13]Indeed, as illustrated in the data section, we do not limit our sample to those countries for which positive flows are recorded, because preferences may influence not only the existing trade volume between two countries, but may also open new trade flow routes. Disregarding zero trade observations would translate into disregarding emerging new trade relationships, and this could

Since, in (10.1), the impact of the preferential margin is made conditional on the level of the compliance costs – through the interaction term – we compute the marginal effect of each preferential margin as follows:

$$\frac{\partial IMP}{\partial MARGIN} = \hat{\beta}_1 + \hat{\beta}_3 * COSTS \tag{10.2}$$

Where $\hat{\beta}_3$ is the estimated coefficient of the interaction term, and $\hat{\beta}_1$ is the estimated coefficient of *MARGIN* – which would indicate the marginal effect of the scheme if the costs were zero. We test the significance of (10.2) by calculating the relative standard errors:

$$\hat{\sigma} = \sqrt{var(\hat{\beta}_1) + (COSTS)^2 * var(\hat{\beta}_3) + 2COSTS * cov(\hat{\beta}_1, \hat{\beta}_3)}. \tag{10.3}$$

As both (10.2) and (10.3) depend on the costs level, the marginal impact of *MARGIN* may change and gain or lose significance depending on the value of the *COSTS* variable.[14]

10.3 Data

Our data are drawn from several sources. Figures on total imports and imports under each EU preferential regime are from the TRADEPREF database, developed by Gallezot (2005b). In this dataset, which provides information at the CN (Combined Nomenclature) 8 digit level for the year 2002, the import flow under each scheme is retrieved from the SAD (Single Administrative Documents), that are requested by the EU customs for each importation. The TARIC database has been consulted to establish whether the preferential tariff declared in the SAD is indeed applicable to the commodities that have been imported from the country requiring the benefit. In fact, some declarations may be erroneous: it occurs that there is no correspondence between the required preferential regime and that actually applicable. Given the high reliability of the TRADEPREF data, we consider all the observations that are missing as zero trade flows. In other words, we expand the original data by adding observations equal to zero where the product lines are missing. Non-recorded data are also treated as zeros in Coe et al. (2002), Santos-Silva and Tenreyro (2006), Felbermayr and Kohler (2006), Cardamone (2011), and Aiello et al. (2010).

lead to underestimate the effect of preferences on developing countries exports (on this issue see: Aiello et al. 2010; Helpman et al. 2008; Piermartini and The 2005).

[14]At the same time, since multiplicative interaction models are symmetric, our model allows for the possibility that the effects of *COSTS* vary according to the values of the *MARGIN* measure. Further, it worth underlying that, as the Poisson model is linear in the log of the expected value, we apply (10.2) and (10.3) to the *ln*[*E(IMP)*]. If we wanted to compute the marginal effect of our regressors on *E(IMP)*, we should account for the fact that the Poisson model is not linear in the expected value of the dependent variable (see Norton et al. 2004).

The variable *DIST* and the dummies *LANG* and *COL* are drawn from the dataset provided by the *Centre d'Etudes Prospectives et d'Informations Internationales (CEPII).*[15] Information on tariffs come from *DBTAR*, a dataset focusing on the EU's applied tariffs at the 10 digit level (Gallezot 2005a). Further, *GDP*, *POP*, *FDI*, *EXP* and *EDU* are from the World Bank's World Development Indicators (WDI 2008). The Economic Freedom Index is provided by the Heritage Foundation and Wall Street Journal. Finally, we exclude from our analysis bananas, sugar and rice: the product lines that, in 2002, were subject to tariff quotas.

Table 10.2 reports some relevant statistical information on our variables, described in Table 10.3, while Table 10.4 shows the average preferential margins

Table 10.2 Summary statistics

Variable	Mean	Std. dev.	Min	Max	Obs.
UTIL COTONOU[a]	48.59	47.46	0	100	2,605
UTIL GSP[a]	14.35	32.24	0	100	10,091
UTIL GSP-Drugs[a]	50.67	47.23	0	100	1,056
MARGIN COTONOU[a]	35.70	45.76	0	100	65,416
MARGIN GSP[a]	43.60	29.68	0	100	49,368
MARGIN GSP-Drugs[a]	88.67	29.47	0	100	72,624
COSTS COTONOU[b] (MOD1)	414.44	148.93	0	808.60	22,126
COSTS GSP[b] (MOD1)	251.14	103.36	0	548.84	36,663
COSTS GSP-Drugs[b] (MOD1)	320.09	121.17	0	535.27	5,874
COSTS COTONOU[b] (MOD2)	649.62	208.93	0	1,076.63	16,835
COSTS GSP[b] (MOD2)	263.93	110.39	0	525.38	30,855
COSTS GSP-Drugs[b] (MOD2)	371.29	137.29	0	582.96	5,340
IMP[c]	417.0	12,400	0	1,890,000	90,984
GDP[d]	48,000	155,000	50	1,450,000	85,632
POP[e]	36,600	145,000	47	1,280,000	88,308
DIST[f]	6,617	3,431	813	16,848	90,984
LANG	0.68	0.46	0	1	90,984
COL	0.78	0.41	0	1	90,984
ECOFREE	56.77	9.79	8.90	87.40	73,633
EDU[a]	8.12	3.31	0.89	16.11	77,604
FDI[a]	3.84	6.02	−10.14	522.22	81,659
EXP[a]	39.08	23.21	7.63	193.20	84,336
POLITY	1.99	6.38	−10	10	69,617
TELE[g]	127.97	147.83	1.28	870.92	88,357

[a]In percentage terms
[b]See Sect. 10.2.1 of the text
[c]In thousands of US Dollars
[d]In millions of US Dollars
[e]In thousands
[f]In kilometres
[g]In units
The other variables are dummies or indexes (ECO FREE, POLITY). For the description of the variables see Table 10.3. Summary statistics for the utilisation rates are obtained without expanding the original data (TRADEPREF) by adding observations equal to zero where the product lines are missing.

[15]Available at: www.cepii.fr/anglaisgraph/bdd/distances.htm.

Table 10.3 Description of variables used in the estimations

Variable	Description
UTIL	Ratio of EU actual imports under a given NRPTA (Cotonou, GSP, GSP-Drugs) to the value of total imports, computed at the country-HS6 product line level (i.e., both numerator and denominator of the ratio are country-HS6 product line specific)
MARGIN	Preferential margin (Cotonou, GSP and GSP-Drugs schemes), computed as $(MFN_{ik} - PREF_{ik})/MFN_{ik}$, where i refers to exporters, and k to the tariff line; MFN and PREF are the Most Favoured Nation and the preferential tariffs, respectively
COSTS	Estimated measure of the costs of compliance, retrieved by estimating three models (MOD1-2-3) of the preferences utilisation determinants (see Sect. 10.2.1)
IMP	EU import flows from NRPTA eligible countries, at the HS6 digit level, computed aggregating 8 digit level figures from the TRADEPREF dataset (Gallezot 2005b)
GDP	GDP of exporting country
POP	Population of exporting country
DIST	The distance, in kilometers, between each exporter i and the EU
LANG	Dummy variable, coded 1 if the exporting country language is spoken in at least one of the EU member states, 0 otherwise.
COL	Dummy variable, coded 1 if there existed colonial links between the exporter and at least one of the EU member states, and 0 otherwise
ECOFREE	Composite score, which combines ten different freedoms, from property rights to entrepreneurship (Heritage Foundation and Wall Street Journal)
EDU	Secondary education pupils to population
FDI	Foreign direct investment, net inflows, % of GDP
EXP	Exports of goods and services, % of GDP
POLITY	Polity score ranging from −10 (high autocracy) to +10 (high democracy) (available at http://www.cidcm.umd.edu/inscr/polity/)
TELE	Telephone lines per 1,000 people

and compliance costs for each preferential regime and product line, aggregated at the HS2 digit-level. We recall that our measures of costs are estimated as residuals retrieved from independent regressions for each specific preferential scheme (more precisely, the *COSTS* variable is the difference between the maximum sample residual and each other residual). Hence, being measures relative to each sample, they are not comparable across different regimes. Indeed, in the results section, what we compare is not the level of costs of different schemes, rather the impact of costs on the preferential margin influence of the different schemes. Further, within each regime, one cannot assess the absolute relevance of our estimated costs. Looking at Table 10.4, what can be said is that, within each regime, there is little variation around the overall mean of the costs. In the GSP case, each line cost is never greater (or lower) than 2% of the overall mean of the regime costs. In the GSP-Drugs case, each line cost is never greater (or lower) than 4% of the overall mean of the regime costs (with the only exception of the live trees and plants line, whose mean cost is about 10% lower than the overall mean). Finally, only four lines of products (dairies; products of the milling industry; waste from food industry; preparations of cereals) display mean costs that are from 10 to 15% lower than the overall Cotonou mean cost.

Table 10.4 Average preferential margins and compliance costs at the Harmonized System 2 digit level

Product lines	MARGINS			COSTS		
	Cotonou	GSP	GSP-D	Cotonou	GSP	GSP-D
01- Live animals	63.38	35.18	69.57	621.46	269.65	369.96
02- Meat	79.78	66.18	100	632.33	266.62	384.89
03- Fisheries	100	59.44	91.40	688.36	262.30	367.74
04- Dairies	32.62	66.80	96.53	542.80	267.21	381.09
05- Other animal products	–	37.25	100	–	268.42	384.89
06- Live trees and plants	100	56.69	91.68	685.44	260.62	331.80
07- Vegetables	69.67	37.39	97.80	626.85	265.55	370.93
08- Fruits	78.66	62.85	98.55	640.56	261.51	370.88
09- Coffee, tea, spices	100	67.03	100	693.24	261.79	374.48
10- Cereals	67.69	–	91.49	601.61	–	376.91
11- Products of the milling ind.	31.51	32.50	68.54	552.56	266.69	359.15
12- Oilseeds	88.10	85.16	94.74	670.17	262.74	366.91
13- Lac, gums, resins	100	76.86	89.87	697.00	263.23	372.84
14- Other vegetable products	–	–	–	–	–	–
15- Oils and fats	96.19	58.25	98.41	686.49	265.24	376.85
16- Preparations of meat, fish	86.83	55.27	100	667.05	262.79	375.06
18- Cocoa	81.51	28.46	100	653.11	268.56	359.20
19- Preparations of cereals	44.32	14.93	100	577.11	265.45	373.94
20- Preparations of fruits and veg.	91.35	26.70	100	673.45	264.63	371.34
21- Miscellaneous edible preparations	84.75	37.49	100	660.32	263.34	370.62
22- Beverages	90.76	47.17	100	669.88	262.22	371.41
23- Waste from food industry	34.86	84.69	100	562.22	261.48	384.17
24- Tobacco	100	44.23	100	688.16	264.34	369.98

GSP-D is the GSP-Drugs scheme. Within each regime, the average margin is the mean of the margins computed at the country-HS6 product line level. Computations exclude bananas (belonging to line 08), rice (belonging to line 10), and sugar (line 17), which are not considered in our analysis. Compliance costs have been retrieved from the Tobit estimates reported in Table 10.4, Model 2

10.4 Results

10.4.1 Tobit Results

Table 10.5 reports Model 1 and 2 Tobit estimates. According to Model 1 results, the use of the GSP-Drugs and the Cotonou schemes appears positively and significantly related to the preferential margin. The margin estimated coefficient is negative but not statistically significant in the GSP case. As far as the variables capturing country characteristics are concerned, the GDP variable appears to positively and significantly affect the utilisation ratio of all initiatives. By contrast, population and distance are never significant except in the GSP-Drugs case, where the distance is unexpectedly positive and significant. Further, the Economic Freedom Index coefficient appears always negative, and significant in the GSP-Drugs case (an analogous result is in Manchin 2006). Finally, the common language and colony

Table 10.5 Tobit estimations to retrieve our measures of compliance costs included in the Gravity regressions (Table 10.6)

	Model 1			Model 2		
	1 Cotonou	2 GSP	3 GSP-D	4 Cotonou	5 GSP	6 GSP-D
MARGIN	2.07	−0.12	0.44	2.06	−0.13	0.37
	(0.33)	(0.12)	(0.23)	(0.41)	(0.12)	(0.24)
GDP	89.47	48.43	162.20	87.03	24.11	110.10
	(24.83)	(13.37)	(44.59)	(45.59)	(17.53)	(30.52)
POP	23.10	10.06	−78.99	107.80	34.01	147.70
	(23.65)	(13.00)	(55.53)	(39.11)	(19.21)	(37.40)
DIST	−22.78	−9.94	1072.50	−194.00	−9.460	1551.20
	(92.56)	(22.89)	(316.70)	(106.5)	(20.44)	(200.10)
LANG	−238.02	−50.11		−409.40	−15.72	
	(59.63)	(34.49)		(94.03)	(31.81)	
COL	243.20	43.30		291.20	46.71	
	(73.37)	(31.23)		(107.8)	(33.97)	
ECOFREE	−0.98	−0.43	−11.50	2.55	0.17	−4.56
	(3.28)	(1.55)	(3.68)	(3.13)	(1.50)	(2.61)
EDU				24.08	12.20	−80.41
				(17.26)	(4.62)	(8.92)
FDI				−9.61	−2.92	43.12
				(6.51)	(4.09)	(8.01)
EXP				4.71	0.96	9.79
				(1.33)	(0.62)	(1.37)
N. of observations	22,126	36,663	5,874	16,835	30,855	5,340
Model test	11.37	15.92	16.18	8.76	12.53	48.72
	0.000	*0.000*	*0.000*	*0.000*	*0.000*	*0.000*
Log pseudo-likelihood	−8,197.20	−14,565.70	−3,494.90	−5,841.50	−13,773.40	−3,253.40

GSP-D is the GSP-Drugs scheme. In brackets are reported the standard errors, while in italics the p-values of the tests. For the description of the variables see Table 10.3. The *GDP*, *POP* and *DIST* variables are taken in natural logarithmic. In all estimations, observations have been clustered at the country level. In the GSP-Drugs case, the *LANG* and *COL* variables have been automatically dropped due to their low variability in the sample

variables appear to significantly affect the Cotonou utilisation, the former being surprisingly negative.[16]

Turning our attention to Model 2 output, when individually significant, the extra explanatory variables (*EDU*, *FDI*, *EXP*) display always the expected positive sign, except for the secondary education, which is negative in the GSP-Drugs case. More in detail, the total export variable is always positive, being not significant only in the GSP case. The *FDI* regressor is positive and statistically significant in the GSP-Drugs case, and the secondary education indicator is positive and significant in the GSP case, being

[16]The fact that our measures of costs are retrieved from independent regressions for each preferential regime may explain why some variables display a different sign for different schemes. For instance, in the GSP-Drugs case, the positive sign of the distance variable may be due to the small group of countries eligible to this specific regime (Andean and Central American countries, and Pakistan). Indeed, being the recipients a limited number of countries, almost all relatively close to each other, the distance regressor does not vary much in the sample.

negative for the GSP-Drugs initiative. It is also worth mentioning that, although the extra explanatory variables are not always individually significant, the relative F-test (not reported) is always significant.

As the specification of our utilisation models might condition the subsequent findings, further robustness checks are implemented. Our main conclusions are substantially unaltered when we add an indicator of the level of democracy (*POLITY*) and one of telecommunication availability (*TELE*) to Model 1.[17] Further, our findings are not affected when we re-estimate Model 2 omitting the variables *LANG* and *COL*, as it might be argued that – considering the EU as a whole – they are not much informative (for instance, there will often be a coincidence of language with at least one EU country) and this could affect the significance of other parameters.[18]

Finally, Model 3 estimates confirm Model 2 results: the margin estimated coefficient is positive and statistically significant for the Cotonou scheme, positive but not significant for the GSP-Drugs regime, and negative but not statistically significant for the GSP case. To save on space, we do not report these results, making them available on demand.

10.4.2 Gravity Results

The gravity estimation results are reported in Table 10.6. As aforesaid (see Sect. 10.2), we estimate (10.1) by a Poisson model, including exporter fixed effects. Further, the inference is based on robust (heteroskedasticity consistent) standard errors, which also allow for correlation of the idiosyncratic error terms at the product line level. By doing so, we aim at controlling for common shocks to the production of each commodity line, independent from the exporter's identity.

To begin with, columns 1.1 of Table 10.6 reports the results for the Cotonou scheme, when using the measure of costs based on Model 1. Focusing on the variables of interest, the *MARGIN* coefficient is positive, while the interaction coefficient negative, none of them appearing individually significant.[19] The negative sign of

[17]The polity score ranges from -10 (high autocracy) to +10 (high democracy), and is drawn from POLITY IV database (available at www.systemicpeace.org/polity/polity4.htm). The telecommunication availability (WDI 2008) is measured as telephone lines per 1,000 people. We have also tried to control for the availability of physical infrastructures (such as railways and road kilometers, WDI (2008), encountering convergence problems in our estimations, possibly due to the presence of many missing values and/or a high correlation between them and the gross domestic product variable.

[18]Detailed results of these further robustness checks are available from the authors.

[19]Nonetheless, as shown by the F-tests reported, the interaction term is always jointly significant with the *MARGIN* regressor. The divergence between individual and joint significance may be interpreted as a symptom of multicollinearity (see Brambor et al. 2006) induced by the inclusion of the interaction term. As Brambor et al. (2006, p. 70) draw attention to, "even if there really is high multicollinearity and this leads to large standard errors on the model parameters, it is important to remember that these standard errors are never in any sense "too" large – they are always the "correct" standard errors. High multicollinearity simply means that there is not enough information in the data to estimate the model parameters accurately and the standard errors rightfully reflect this."

Table 10.6 Gravity estimations to assess the impact of preferential margin (*MARGIN*) on European Union imports (*IMP*) as compliance costs (*COSTS* from Models 1 or 2) change

	Model 1					
	Cotonou scheme		GSP scheme		GSP-Drugs scheme	
	1.1 POISS	2.1 NEGB	3.1 POISS	4.1 NEGB	5.1 POISS	6.1 NEGB
MARGIN [a]	23.48	10.23	1.275	-0.034	7.341	3.217
	(15.41)	(1.66)	(2.28)	(0.50)	(1.35)	(1.08)
COSTS [b]	−12.22	−13.64	−3.267	−10.85	−5.392	−16.70
	(11.50)	(1.26)	(1.62)	(0.88)	(0.68)	(1.12)
MARGIN*COSTS [c]	−2.506	−1.08	−0.136	0.063	−1.214	−0.483
	(2.55)	(0.28)	(0.40)	(0.09)	(0.20)	(0.18)
No. of observations	21,632	21,632	36,663	36,663	5,874	5,874
Model test	24,604	194,789	51,607	144,219	463.56	1,073.4
	0.000	*0.000*	*0.000*	*0.000*	*0.000*	*0.000*
Test joint sig. ([a], [b], [c])	278.62	265.31	44.06	180.69	137.63	223.61
	0.000	*0.000*	*0.000*	*0.000*	*0.000*	*0.000*
Test joint sig. ([a], [c])	65.64	232.13	11.65	13.92	209.09	10.22
	0.000	*0.000*	*0.003*	*0.001*	*0.000*	*0.006*
Log pseudo-likelihood	−10,212	−28,835	−53,333	−99,521	−5,306	−13,696
	Model 2					
	Cotonou scheme		GSP scheme		GSP-Drugs scheme	
	1.2 POISS	2.2 NEGB	3.2 POISS	4.2 NEGB	5.2 POISS	6.2 NEGB
MARGIN [a]	19.98	45.56	1.320	0.005	8.529	3.252
	(18.37)	(3.88)	(2.73)	(0.63)	(1.29)	(1.29)
COSTS [b]	−29.54	−8.37	−4.329	−10.68	−6.826	−20.63
	(13.37)	(2.29)	(1.98)	(0.99)	(0.90)	(1.52)
MARGIN*COSTS [c]	−1.822	−6.42	−0.142	0.050	−1.384	−0.494
	(2.85)	(0.59)	(0.48)	(0.11)	(0.19)	(0.21)
No. of observations	16,402	16,402	30,855	30,855	5,340	5,340
Model test	3,044.4	98,191.8	18,316	19,364	418.52	1,044.1
	0.000	*0.000*	*0.000*	*0.000*	*0.000*	*0.000*
Test joint sig. ([a], [b], [c])	425.13	445.27	15.35	165.36	147.86	188.51
	0.000	*0.000*	*0.001*	*0.000*	*0.000*	*0.000*
Test joint sig. ([a], [c])	60.50	444.82	40.00	11.34	165.34	6.91
	0.000	*0.000*	*0.000*	*0.004*	*0.000*	*0.032*
Log pseudo-likelihood	−7,242	−21,392	−48,270	−89,530	−5,222	−12,840

In brackets are reported the standard errors, while in italics the *p*-values of the tests. For the description of the variables see Table 10.3. All variables are taken in natural logarithms. Poisson (POISS) and Negative Binomial (NEGB) estimations have been carried out by including exporter country dummies (not reported). In all estimations, observations have been clustered at the HS6 product line level. In columns 1.1-6.1 (1.2-6.2) COSTS has been retrieved from the Tobit estimates reported in Table 10.4, Model 1 (Model 2) the interaction parameter indicates that, as expected, the positive *MARGIN* effect tends to decrease as *COSTS* raises.[20] The individual coefficients, however, do not convey full information on the magnitude, sign and significance of the marginal effect of *MARGIN*. In fact, the *MARGIN* individual coefficient represents its estimated marginal effect only when the *COSTS* variable is equal to zero, a case occurring only once in our analysis (indeed *COSTS* is computed as the difference between the maximum sample residual and each residual, see Sect. 10.2 for details).[21] To test our conditional hypothesis, we need to assess whether the *MARGIN's* effect on *IMP* is different in magnitude and significance according to different levels of *COSTS*. Hence, using formulas (10.2) and (10.3), we compute the marginal effect of the Cotonou margin and its 95% confidence intervals, for the entire range of the values of *COSTS*, and report them in Fig. 10.1. This allows us to see that the positive impact of *MARGIN* on *IMP* (represented by the continuous central line) is always statistically significant (the confidence band never includes the zero line), but it considerably declines in absolute value as the *COSTS* variable increases. In other words, compliance costs seem to exert a detrimental influence on the positive preferential margins impact on trade flows. A similar pattern emerges in Figs. 10.2 and 10.3 – which are based on the estimations reported in columns 3.1 (GSP) and 5.1 (GSP-Drugs), respectively – the GSP *MARGIN* partial effect being statistically significant for about 85%, and the GSP-Drugs *MARGIN* partial effect for about the 43% of the sample observations. These percentages, computed as the ratio of the observations lying in the significance region to the total estimation sample observations, give an idea on the amount of countries/lines for which each scheme has been beneficial. Besides, comparing the slopes of the central lines in the figures so far considered, we can observe that the influence of costs on the preferential margin impact is higher for the Cotonou and GSP-Drugs schemes.

Analogous graphs are obtained using the estimated costs retrieved from Model 2 and 3, therefore we omit them (reporting only the gravity estimates based on

[20]On the other way round, the preferences influence is expected to increase for lower costs of compliance. It is not obvious, however, to find that – as the costs of compliance decrease – the impact of the margins on exports is positive and statistically significant. In other words, as Bureau et al. (2007a) highlight, low utilisation costs are not synonymous of trade creation. A preferential scheme may be used because exporters find it convenient to comply with requirements, but exporters may not significantly increase their export volumes.

[21]Similarly, the *COSTS* individual coefficient represents its estimated marginal effect when the *MARGIN* is zero. Besides, it is worth recalling that the Poisson regression models the log of the expected dependent variable, which is usually a count variable, as a (linear) function of the explanatory variables. Thus, using the approximation properties of the log function, an estimated coefficient may be interpreted as the percentage change in the (expected value of the) dependent variable for a one unit change in the explanatory variable, given that the other predictor variables in the model are held constant. As a consequence, if a regressor is taken in log, the associated parameter may be interpreted as an elasticity.

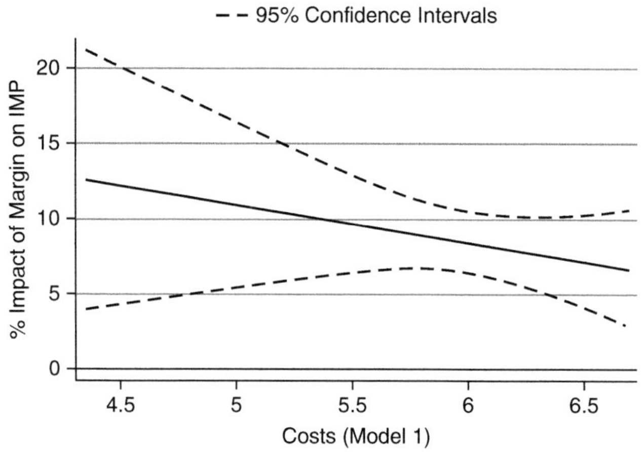

Fig. 10.1 The impact of preferential margin as costs change (Cotonou scheme)

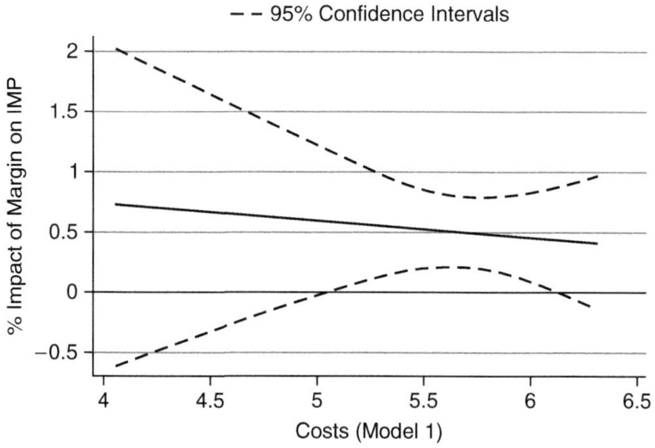

Fig. 10.2 The impact of preferential margin as cost change (Generalised System of Preferences scheme)

Model 2 costs in columns 1.2, 3.2 and 5.2 of Table 10.6), and make them available on request.[22]

Summarizing, our results suggest that the depth of the preferential margin tends to be a statistically significant determinant of import flows from recipient countries – displaying the highest potential influence in the Cotonou case and the lowest in the GSP one – but its relevance decreases at higher level of compliance costs.

[22]The only exception is represented by the GSP case when using Model 3 specification. We do not emphasize this result, yet, as the Tobit model did not converge when including exporter fixed-effects, hence we had to estimate it by including only the margin variable.

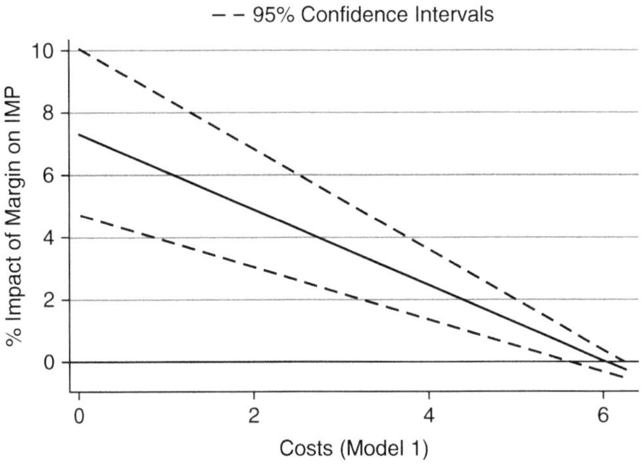

Fig. 10.3 The impact of preferential margin as cost change (Generalised System of Preferences-Drugs scheme)

10.4.3 Robustness Checks

As a preliminary check, since our measure of *COSTS* is a generated regressor and this calls for caution in evaluating the inference, using the costs retrieved from Model 2, we apply the non-parametric bootstrap method that allows to estimate the distribution of the parameters by re-sampling (with replacement) the data. More precisely, we obtain estimated bootstrapped standard errors by re-sampling the observations 200 times. As they confirm the main findings discussed above, we make these results available on demand.

As a second sensitivity test, we replicate the estimations, using costs retrieved from Model 2, by replacing the total with the agricultural GDP in the Tobit model. The results, based on smaller samples, confirm the main findings discussed above. The Cotonou scheme effect is always the highest we observe, its significance region now including the 98% of the sample observations.[23] The GSP and GSP-Drugs significance regions gets a bit larger, including about 80 and 55% of the sample observations, respectively. To avoid cluttering, we do not report the relative output, making it accessible upon request.[24]

Thus far, by estimating separate regressions, we have assessed the impact of preferential schemes on eligible countries. For instance, the impact of the Cotonou regime has been investigated by considering only countries that are eligible for this scheme. The question we now try to address is whether the pattern that emerges using estimated measures of costs holds true if we use a non-estimated proxy of costs.

[23]To ensure that the Cotonou results are not driven by some extreme values, observations laying in the first and last percentile of the costs distribution have been omitted from the estimations. Results obtained without trimming the cost distribution are analogous, the Cotonou effect being only slightly higher.

[24]The output obtained when using Models 1 and 3 is analogous and available on request.

In other words, we seek to exclude that the main result obtained so far (i.e., the preferential margin influence on *IMPORTS* varies according to the costs level) is generated by idiosyncrasies of our estimated measures of costs. To this aim, we consider an alternative proxy for compliance costs by making the following working hypothesis: compliance costs tend to rise with the degree of processing, as proving the origin of more elaborated products should be more problematic than for unprocessed commodities (on this point see also Bureau et al. 2007a). We create a categorical variable, assuming value zero for raw commodities, one for slightly processed products, two for highly processed ones.[25] As a consequence, costs vary for different tariff lines, but – differently from our estimated measures – are homogeneous across different countries and schemes. On one hand, we acknowledge that this feature represents a limitation of the measure, which fails to capture fixed costs that are specific to each country and/or regime. On the other, the same characteristic allows us to estimate a single regression including all countries on which data are available. When using our non-estimated measure of costs, we consider the maximum margin that the EU grants to each country for each product line as the measure of the preference benefits. The assumption underlying the use of this indicator is that, *ceteris paribus* (therefore, for a given level of costs), countries tend to utilize the scheme they have access to, which grants the highest margin of preference. As not reported results show – similarly to what has been observed thus far considering the schemes separately – the margin influence decreases as the proxy of compliance costs increases. The overall margin impact appears significant for 37% of the observations. To save on space, we omit these estimates and the graph based on them.

As a final robustness check, to verify that our main findings do not depend on the hypotheses underlying one specific estimation method, we replicate our gravity estimations by adopting a Negative Binomial model, in which the Poisson model is nested. To be more precise, the Negative Binomial model relaxes the assumption of the Poisson model that the (conditional) variance is equal to the (conditional) mean. When the variance is larger than the mean the data are "over dispersed" and not Poisson distributed. The estimates, which tend to confirm the Poisson results, are reported in columns 2.1, 4.1, 6.1, 2.2, 4.2 and 6.2 of Table 10.6.[26]

[25]To give an example, we consider grapes fresh (HS6 080610) as a raw commodity, grapes dried (HS6 080620) as slightly processed, wine of fresh grapes (HS6 220410) as highly processed.

[26]When adopting a Negative Binomial model, the main finding of this chapter is confirmed also if we use an alternative measure of the degree of processing: a dichotomous variable coded 1 for processed products and zero otherwise, on the base of the FAO classification (employed also by Bureau et al. 2007a).

10.5 Conclusions

In this chapter a gravity model approach has been used to estimate the impact of the EU preferential schemes on the agricultural export flows of recipient countries, conditional on the costs of compliance associated to the schemes themselves.

The main findings of our analysis may be summarized as follows: there is evidence of a positive and increasing impact of the preferential margins as the costs of compliance decrease. The preferential margin appears to exert a statistically significant effect across all regimes, displaying the highest potential influence in the Cotonou case and the lowest in the GSP one. Furthermore, the influence of costs on the preferential margin impact is proportionally higher for the Cotonou and GSP-Drugs schemes, the latter representing the preferential regime with a smaller significance region, i.e., a smaller number of countries/lines for which the scheme appears to have been beneficial.

We acknowledge that these findings need to be qualified in some respects. First, the results obtained could depend on the estimated compliance cost measures we retrieve – in particular on the model specifications we employ – though numerous checks have been carried out and the same pattern is observed when we use a cost proxy based on the commodities' degree of processing. Second, due to data availability, we consider a cross-section of countries, instead of applying a panel analysis. Therefore, the present contribution represents a first step for further research. We believe that, with a larger database, one could develop a more sophisticated analysis. On the other hand, considering a single year makes our estimations less exposed to reverse causality problems: it is plausible that past (rather than contemporary) import volumes tend to affect current preferential margins.

Our findings confirm that recipient countries have not been able to reap the full potential benefits of the EU preference programs. Indeed, compliance costs appear to cancel out part of the preferential margin benefit. Therefore, there is scope to invoke actions and policy measures that will improve the ability of beneficiary countries to actually use these schemes. In other words, since granting higher preferential margins to developing countries does not appear sufficient to boost developing countries exports, the EU should also make an effort to reduce to a minimum the costs of proving eligibility for preferences. To make NRPTA more effective, the EU should help recipient countries boosting their ability to meet scheme requirements, reinforcing initiatives that enhance their human and institutional capacity to utilise the preferences. Direct assistance could be a way for fostering such a crucial capacity. To limit rent-seeking phenomena and funding diversion often associated with direct payments, such initiatives could be coordinated multilaterally. Indeed, in recent years, international institutions (for instance, the World Bank through its trade related programmes) have tended to refocus their trade assistance to increase export supply capacity via investment in infrastructure and skills (IEG 2006). Above and beyond, considering that the EU ultimate goal when granting preferential access to developing countries is to allow their exports – and, more generally, their integration into the world trading system – to become a powerful engine of growth, the challenge facing the EU appears to be twofold: not only assisting recipient countries to build their capacity to meet scheme requirements, but also supporting them to ease many other obstacles, such as low technological capacities and underdeveloped financial sectors, to produce and trade goods and services in the global economy.

Acknowledgments Financial support received by the "New Issues in Agricultural, Food and Bioenergy Trade (AGFOODTRADE)" (Small and Medium-scale Focused Research Project, Grant Agreement no. 212036) research project, funded by the European Commission, and by the Italian Ministry of Education, University and Research (Scientific Research Program of National Relevance 2007 on "European Union policies, economic and trade integration processes and WTO negotiations" – PUE&PIEC) is gratefully acknowledged. We are indebted to Giovanni Anania, Luca De Benedictis and Luca Salvatici for their precious observations and suggestions, which reshaped the original manuscript. Special thanks go also to Paola Cardamone, Anne Célia Disdier and Sophie Droguè for their useful comments. Any remaining errors are solely our responsibility.

References

Agostino MR, Demaria F, Trivieri F (2010) Non-reciprocal trade preferences and the role of compliance costs in the agricultural sector: exports to the EU. J Agr Econ 61:652–679.

Aiello F, Agostino MR, Cardamone P (2006) Reconsidering the impact of trade preferences in gravity models. Does aggregation matter? TradeAG Working Paper

Aiello F, Agostino MR, Cardamone P (2010) Evaluating the impact of non-reciprocal trade preferences using gravity models. Appl Econ 42:3745–3760.

Aiello F, Cardamone P (2010) Analysing the effectiveness of the EBA initiative by using a gravity model. Pue&Piec Work. Pap.n. 10/7

Aiello F, Demaria F (2009) Do trade preferential agreements enhance the exports of developing countries? Evidence from the EU GSP. PRIN PUE&PIEC 2007 Working Paper No 2009/18 (available via http://www.ecostat.unical.it/anania/PUE&PIEC%20Working%20Papers.htm)

Aitken ND (1973) The effect of the EEC and EFTA on European trade: a temporal cross-section analysis. Amer Econ Rev 63:881–892.

Alesina A, Spolaore E, Wacziarg R (2005) Trade, growth and the size of countries. In: Aghion P, Durlauf S (eds) Handbook of Economic Growth, Chapter 23. North Holland, Amsterdam

Anderson J, Neary P (1996) A new approach to evaluating trade policy. World Bank Econ Rev 63:107–125.

Anderson J, Neary P (2003) The mercantilist index of trade policy. International Econ Rev 44(2): 627–649.

Anderson JE (2011) The Gravity model. Annual Review of Economics, 3.

Anderson JE, Neary P (2005) Measuring trade policy restrictiveness: a non-technical introduction. In: Anderson JE, Neary P (eds) Measuring the restrictiveness of international trade policy. MIT Press, Cambridge, MA

Anderson JE, van Wincoop E (2003) Gravity with gravitas: A solution to the border puzzle. Amer. Econ. Rev. 63: 881–892.

Anderson JE, van Wincoop E (2004) Trade costs. J Econ Lit, 42:691–751.

Anderson JE, Yotov YV (2010) The changing incidence of geography. Am Econ Rev, 100(5), 2157–2186.

Anderson, JE (1979) A theoretical foundation for the gravity equation. Amer. Econ. Rev. 69: 106–116.

Angrist JC, Pischke J-S (2008) Mostly harmless econometrics: an empiricist's companion. Princeton University Press, Princeton

Anson J, Cadot O, Estevadeordal A, de Melo J, Suwa-Eisenmann A, Tumurchudur B (2005) Rules of origin in north–south preferential trading arrangements with an application to NAFTA. Rev Int Econ 13(3): 501–517.

Antimiani A, Conforti P, Salvatici L (2008) Measuring restrictivenness of bilateral trade policies: a comparison between developed and developing countries. Rev of World Econ144(2): 207–224.

L. De Benedictis and L. Salvatici (eds.), *The Trade Impact of European Union Preferential Policies*, DOI 10.1007/978-3-642-16564-1,

Arkolakis C (2008) Market penetration costs and the new consumers margin in international trade. NBER Working Paper No. 14214, Washington, DC.
Armington, P. (1969) A theory of demand for products distinguished by place of production. IMF Staff Papers 16(3):159–176.
Ashenfelter O, Harmon C, Oosterbeek, H (1999) A review of estimates of the schooling/earnings relationship, with tests for publication bias. Labour Economics 6:453–470
Bach M, Martin W (2001) Would the right tariff aggregator please stand up? J. of Policy Modeling 23(6): 621–635.
Bagwell K, Staiger RW (2002) The economics of the world trading system. MIT Press, London, England.
Baier SL, Bergstrand JH (2001) The growth of world trade: tariffs, transport costs and income similarity. J. Int. Econ. 53: 1–27.
Baier SL, Bergstrand JH (2004) Economic determinants of free trade agreements. J. Int. Econ. 64 (1): 29–63
Baier SL, Bergstrand JH (2007) Do free trade agreements actually increase members' international trade? J. Int. Econ. 71: 72–95.
Baier SL, Bergstrand JH (2009) Bonus vetus OLS: a simple method for approximating international trade-cost effects using the gravity equation. J. Int. Econ. 77: 77–85.
Baldwin R (2006) The Euro's trade effects. European Central Bank Working Paper n. 594
Baldwin R, Taglioni D (2006) Gravity for dummies and dummies for gravity equations. NBER Working Paper N° 12516.
Baldwin RE, Skudelny F, Taglioni D (2005) Trade effects of the euro evidence from sectoral data. European Central Bank, Working Paper Series No. 446.
Baldwin RE, Taglioni D (2010) Gravity chains: Estimating bilateral trade flows when parts and components trade is important. NBER Working Paper No. 16672
Baltagi B, Egger P, Pfaffermayr M (2003) A generalized design for bilateral trade flow models. Econ Letters 80:391–397.
Baltagi B, Egger P, Pfaffermayr M (2007) Estimating models of complex FDI: are there third country effects? J of Econometrics, 140: 260–281.
Baltagi B, Egger P, Pfaffermayr M (2009) Estimating Regional Trade Agreement effects on FDI in an interdependent world. J of Econometrics, 145:194–208.
Bergstrand JH (1985) The gravity equation in international trade: some microeconomic foundations and empirical evidence. Rev Econ Stat 67: 474–481.
Bergstrand, JH (1989) The generalized gravity equation, monopolistic competition, and the factor-proportions theory in international trade. Rev. Econ. Statist. 71: 143–153.
Bernard A, Jensen JJ, Redding S, Schott P (2007) Firms in international trade. J of Econ Persp, 21:105–130.
Blum BS, Goldfarb A (2006) Does the internet defy the law of gravity? J Int Econ 70(2):384–405.
Borchert I (2009) Trade diversion under selective preferential market access. World Bank Policy Research Working Paper 4710.
Bouët A, Decreux Y, Fontagné L, Jean S, Laborde D (2004) A consistent, ad-valorem equivalent measure of applied protection across the world: The MAcMap-HS6 Database, CEPII Working Paper No 2004–22
Boughner D, de Gorter H, Sheldon I (2000) The economics of tariff-rate quotas in the agricultural agreement in the WTO. Agric Resour Econ Rev 20:58–69
Boumelassa H, Laborde D, Mitaritonna C (2009) A consistent picture of the protection across the world in 2004: MAcMapHS6 version 2. AgFoodTrade Working Paper 2009–04 (http://www.agfoodtrade.eu/public-working-papers).
Brambor T, Clarck W, Golder M (2006) Understanding interaction models: improving empirical analyses. Political Anal 14:63–82.
Brenton P (2003) Integrating the least developed countries into the world trading system: the current impact of EU preferences under Everything But Arms. World Bank Policy Research Working Paper 3018.

Brenton P, Ikezuki T (2005) The impact of aricultural trade treferences, with tarticular tttention to the Least Developed Countries, in global agricultural trade and developing countries. Edited by Aksoy M and Beghin J. The World Bank, Washington, DC.

Brenton P, Manchin M (2003) Making EU trade agreements work: the role of rules of origin. World Econ 26(5):755–769.

Broda C, Weinstein D (2006) Globalization and the gains from variety. Quarterly J of Economics 121(2): 541–585.

Brooke A, Kendrick D, Meeraus A, Raman R (1998) GAMS, A User's guide. GAMS Development Corporation, Washington, DC

Brun J-F, Carrère C, Guillaumont P, de Melo J (2005) Has distance died? Evidence from a panel gravity model. World Bank Econ Rev 19:99–120.

Bun M, Klaassen F (2002) The importance of dynamics in panel gravity models of trade. Tinbergen Institute Discussion Paper, No. 02–108/2.

Bureau JC, Chakir R, Gallezot J (2007a) The utilisation of trade preferences for developing countries in the agri-food sector. J Agric Econ 58(1):175–198.

Bureau JC, Disdier AC, Ramos P (2007b) A comparison of the barriers faced by Latin American and ACP countries' exports of tropical products. ICTSD (International Center for Trade and Sustainable Development) http://ictsd.org/i/publications/3086/. Accessed 2007.

Bureau JC, Salvatici L (2004) WTO negotiations on market access in agriculture: a comparison of alternative tariff cut proposals for the EU and the US. Topics in Econ. Analysis & Policy 4(1) Article 8, 2004. (http://www.bepress.com/bejeap/topics/vol4/iss1/1).

Bureau JC, Salvatici L (2005) Agricultural trade restrictiveness in the European Union and the United States. Agricultural Economics 33:479–490.

Burger MJ, van Oort FG, Linders GM (2009) On the specification of the gravity model of trade: zeros, excess zeros and zero-inflated estimation. Spat Econ Anal 4(2):167–190.

Cameron AC, Gelbach J, Miller D (2010) Robust Inference with multi-way clustering. J of Business and Econ Stat, forthcoming 2010.

Cameron AC, Trivedi PK (2005) Microeconometrics. Methods and Applications. Cambridge University Press, Cambridge.

Candau F, Jean S (2009) What are EU trade preferences worth for sub-Saharan Africa and other developing countries? In: Hoekman B, Martin W and Primo Braga CA (eds) Trade preference erosion: measurement and policy response. Palgrave-McMillan and The World Bank, Washington DC.

Caporale GM, Rault C, Sova R, Sova A (2009) On the bilateral trade effects of free trade agreements between the EU-15 and the CEEC-4 countries. Rev of World Economy 145:189–206

Card D, Krueger AB (1995) Time-series minimum-wage studies: a meta-analysis. Am Econ Rev 85:238–43

Cardamone P (2007) A survey of the assessments of the effectiveness of Preferential Trade Agreements using gravity models. International Economics 60(4):421–473.

Cardamone P (2011) The effect on monthly fruit imports of preferential trade agreements granted by the European Union. Europ Rev Agr Econ, forthcoming.

Carr DL, Markusen JR, Maskus K (2001) Estimating the Knowledge-Capital model of the multinational enterprise. Am Econ Rev 91(3):693–708.

Carrère C (2006) Revisiting the effects of regional trading agreements on trade flows with proper specification of the gravity model. Europ Econ Rev 50:223–247.

Carrère C, de Melo J, Tumurchudur B (2008) Disentangling market access effects for ASEAN Members under an ASEAN-EU FTA. CEPR DP paper #5047

Carrère C, de Melo J, Wilson J (2009) The distance effect and the regionalization of the trade of low-income countries. CEPR Discussion paper No 7458.

Carrère C. and J. de Melo (2007), Are different Rules of Origin equally costly? Estimates from Nafta, in Cadot, O., Estevadeordal, A., Suva-Eisenmann, A. and T. Verdier (eds), The Origin of Goods: Rules of Origin in Regional Trade Agreements, Oxford University Press.

Chaney T (2008) Distorted gravity: the Intensive and extensive margins of International trade. Am Econ Rev 98:1701–1721.
Chen M X, Joshi S (2010) Third-country effects on the formation of free trade agreements. J of Int Econ 82:238–248.
Choi EK, Hartigan JC (2004) Handbook of International Trade. Volume Two. Economic and Legal Analyses of Trade Policies and Institutions, Blackwell Handbooks in Economics, Blackwell, Oxford, UK
Cioffi A, dell' Aquila C (2004) The effects of trade policies for fresh fruit and vegetables of the european union. Food Pol 29:169–185.
Cipollina M, Laborde D, Salvatici L (2010) Do preferential trade policies (actually) increase exports? A comparison between EU and US trade policies. Paper presented at ETSG 2010 in Lausanne, Switzerland, 9–11 September.
Cipollina M, Salvatici L (2007) EU and developing countries: an analysis of preferential margins on agricultural trade flows. TradeAg Project Working Paper 07/11 http://www.agfoodtrade.eu/public-working-papers. Accessed 2007.
Cipollina M, Salvatici L (2010a) The impact of European Union agricultural preferences. J of Econ Policy Reform 13:87–106.
Cipollina M, Salvatici L (2010b) Reciprocal trade agreements in gravity models: A Meta-Analysis. Rev of International Econ 18:63–80
Cipollina M, Salvatici L. (2008) Measuring protection: mission impossibile? J. of Econ Surveys 22 577–616.
Coe DT, Subramanian A, Tamirisa NT, Bhavnani R (2002) The missing globalization puzzle. IMF Working Papers 02/171 http://www.imf.org/external/pubs/cat/longres.cfm?sk=16104.0. Accessed 2002
COGEA (2009) Evaluation des measures de la PAC relative au sector du riz. November 2009, http://ec.europa.eu/agriculture/eval/reports/rice/fulltext_fr.pdf
Commission Regulation (EC) 214/2007, Official Journal of the European Union, L 62/6, 1.3.2007.
Commission Regulation (EEC) No 2454/93, Official Journal, L 253, 11.10.1993.
Costantini J, Melitz MJ (2008) The dynamics of firm-level adjustment to trade liberalization. In: Helpman E, Marin D, Verdier T (eds) The organization of firms in a global economy. Harvard University Press, Boston, MA
Council Regulation (EC) No 2501/2001, Official Journal of the European Communities, L 346/1, 31.12.2001.
Council Regulation (EC) No 732/2008, Official Journal of the European Union, L 211/1, 6.8.2002.
Council Regulation (EC) No 980/2005, Official Journal of the European Union, L 169/1, 30.6.2005.
Daude C, Stein E (2007) Longitude matters: time zones and the location of foreign direct investment. J Int Econ 71:96–112.
Davison AC, Hinkley DV (1997) Bootstrap methods and their application. Cambridge University Press, Cambridge and New York
De Benedictis L, De Santis R, Vicarelli C (2005) Hub-and-Spoke or else? Free Trade Agreements in the enlarged EU. European Journal of Comparative Econ 2:245–260.
De Benedictis L, Tajoli L (2010) The World Trade Network. World Economy, forthcoming.
De Benedictis L, Vicarelli C (2005) Trade potentials in gravity panel data models. Topics in Econ Anal & Policy 5(1):1–31
De Benedictis L, Vicarelli C (2009) Dummies for gravity and gravity for policies: mission impossible? Mimeo.
Deardorff, AV (1998) Determinants of bilateral trade: does gravity work in a Neoclassical world? In: Frankel JA (ed) The regionalization of the world economy. University of Chicago Press, Chicago
Demaria F (2009) Empirical analysis on the impact of the EU GSP scheme on the agricultural sector. Dissertation, University of Calabria

Demaria F, Droguè S, Matthews A (2008) Agro-food preferences in the EU's GSP scheme: an analysis of changes between 2004 and 2006. Devel Pol Rev 26:693–712.
Diewert WE (1976) Exact and superlative index numbers. J of Econometrics 4:114–145.
Disdier AC, Head K (2008) The puzzling persistence of the distance effect on bilateral trade. R E Stat 90(1):37–48.
Djankov S, La Porta R, Lopez-De-Silanes F, Shleifer A (2002) The regulation of entry. The Quart J of Econ 117(1):1–37.
Eaton J, Kortum S (2002) Technology, geography and trade. Econometrica 70(5):1741–1779.
EC (1992) Fourth ACP-EEC Convention, Protocols No 5, 6 and 7, Office for Official Publications of the European Communities, Luxembourg.
EC (1996) Green Paper on relations between the European Union and the ACP countries on the eve of the 21st century, Challenges and options for a new partnership, COM (96) 570, final.
EC (2005) Communication from the Commission to the Council, the European Parliament and the European Economic and Social Committee: The rules of origin in preferential trade arrangements – Orientations for the future, COM (2005) 100, final.
EC (2008) The European Community's rules of origin for the Generalised System of Preferences: a guide for users, http://ec.europa.eu/taxation_customs/customs/customs_duties/rules_origin/preferential/article_839_en.htm
EC (2010) Proposal for a Regulation (EU) of The European Parliament and of The Council amending Council Regulation (EC) No 732/2008 applying a scheme of generalised tariff, COM (2010) 142 final.
Egger P, Larch M (2008) Interdependent preferential trade agreement memberships: An empirical analysis. J of Int Econ 76(2):384–399.
Egger P, Leiter A, Pfaffermayr M (2010) Structural estimation of gravity models with market entry dynamics. Mimeo
Emlinger C, Chevasuss Lozza E, Jacquet F (2008) Tariffs and other trade costs: assessing obstacles to Mediterranean countries' access to EU-15 fruit and vegetable markets. Europ Rev Agr Econ 35:409–438.
Engel C (2002) Comment on Anderson and van Wincoop. In: Collins S, Rodrik D (eds) Brookings trade forum 2001. The Brookings Institution, Washington
Erkel-Rousse H, Mirza D, (2002) Import price elasticities: reconsidering the evidence. Canadian J of Economics 35:282–306.
Evenett S, Keller W (2002) On theories explaining the success of the gravity equation. J Pol Econ 281–316.
Feenstra RC (2003) Advanced international trade: theory and evidence. Princeton University Press, Princeton
Felbermayr GJ, Kohler W (2006) Exploring the intensive and extensive margins of world trade. Rev World Econ 142(4):642–674.
Feyrer J (2009) Distance, trade, and income – The 1967 to 1975 closing of the Suez canal as a natural experiment. NBER Working Papers 15557.
Fidmurc J, Fidmurc J (2003) Disintegration and trade. Rev Int Econ 11:811–829.
Fidrmuc J (2009) Gravity models in integrated panels. Empir Econ 37:435–446
Fisher RA (1932) Statistical methods for research workers. Oliver and Boyd, London
Francois J, Hoekman B, Manchin M (2006) Preference erosion and multilateral trade liberalization. The World Bank Econ Rev 20:197–216
Francois JF, Reinert K A (1998) Applied methods for trade policy analysis. Cambridge University Press, Cambridge.
Frankel J (1997) Regional trading blocs. Institute for International Economics, Washington, DC
Gallezot J (2003) Real access to the European Union's agricultural market. http://www.tcd.ie/iiis/policycoherence/index.php/iiis/eu_agricultural_trade_policy/agricultural_protection_measures. Accessed 2003.
Gallezot J (2005a) Database on European agricultural tariffs, DBTAR. TradeAg Project Working Paper 05/07 http://tradeag.vitamib.com/. Accessed 2005.

Gallezot J (2005b) Database of EU preferential trade, TRADEPREF. TradeAg Project Working Paper 05/08 http://tradeag.vitamib.com/. Accessed 2005.

Gallezot J and Bureau JC (2006) The trade effects of the EU's Everything but Arms Initiative. CEPII-INRA, Report prepared for the Commission of the European Union –DG Trade, (http://trade.ec.europa.eu/doclib/docs/2006/november/tradoc_131254.pdf)

Gallezot J, Bureau JC (2005) The utilisation of trade preferences: The case of agricultural and food products in the EU and the US. OECD, Paris.

Garcia-Alvarez Coque JM (2002) Agricultural trade and the Barcelona process: is full liberalization possible? Europ Rev Agr Econ 29:339–422.

Garcia-Alvarez-Coque J-M, Martinez-Gomez V, Villanueva M (2010) Seasonal protection of F&V imports in the EU: impacts of the entry price system. Agric Econ 41:205–218

Garcia-Alvarez-Coque JM, Martì-Selva ML (2006) A gravity approach to assess the effects of Association Agreements on Euromediterranean trade of fruit and vegetables. TRADEAG Working Paper No 2006–15.

Gasiorek M et al (2010) Mid-term evaluation of the EU's Generalised System of Preferences. Report for DG Trade, CARIS, University of Sussex. http://trade.ec.europa.eu/doclib/docs/2010/may/tradoc_146196.pdf

GATT (1979) Differential and more favourable treatment: Reciprocity and fuller participation of developing countries. L/4903, Decision of 28 November 1979.

Geie Agrosynergie (2008) Evaluation of the system of entry prices and export refunds in the fruit and vegetables sector. European Commission, Agricultural and Rural Development Evaluation.

Ghosh S, Yamarik S (2004) Are regional trading arrangements trade creating?: An application of extreme bounds analysis. J Int Econ 63:369–395.

Glass GV, McGaw B, Lee Smith M (1981) Meta-Analysis in social research. Sage, Beverly Hills, CA

Goetz L, Grethe H (2009) The EU entry price system for fresh fruits and vegetables – Paper tiger or powerful market barrier? Food Pol 34:81–93.

Gorman WM (1959) Separable utility and aggregation. Econometrica 27:469–481.

Gradeva K, Martinez-Zarzoso I (2009) Trade as aid: the role of the EBA-trade preferences regime in the development strategy. Ibero-America Institute for Econ. Research (IAI) Discussion Papers, No 197.

Greenaway D, Kneller R (2007) Industry differences in the effect of export market entry: Learning by exporting? Rev. World Econ 143(3):416–432

Greene, WH (1993) Econometric analysis, 2nd edn. Macmillan

Grethe H, Tangermann S (1999) The EU import regimes for fresh fruit and vegetables after implementation of the results of the Uruguay round. Diskussionsbeitrag 9901. Institute of Agricultural Economics, University of Gottingen, Germany.

Griliches Z, Hausman JA (1986) Errors in variables in panel data. J of Econometrics 31(1):93–118.

Guiso L, Sapienza P, Zingales L (2009) Cultural biases in economic exchange? The Quart J of Econ 124(3):1095–1131.

Guo M (2009) Hierarchical Bayesian Method for the Gravity Equations. in progress.

Hamermesh DS (2007) Replication in economics. Canadian J of Econ 40(3):715–733.

Harrigan J (2001) Specialization and the volume of trade: do the data obey the laws? NBER Working Papers, 8675.

Harrigan J (2010) Airplanes and comparative advantage. J Int Econ 82(2):181–194.

Head K, Mayer T (2000) Non-Europe: the magnitude and causes of market fragmentation in the EU. Weltwirtschaftliches Archiv 136 (2): 285– 314.

Head K, Mayer T (2004) Market potential and the location of Japanese investment in the European Union. R E Stat.

Head K, Mayer T, Ries J (2010) The erosion of colonial trade linkages after independence. J of Int Econ 81(1):1–14.

Heckman J (1978) Dummy endogenous variables in a simultaneous equation system. Econometrica 46:931–959.
Heckman J (1978) Dummy endogenous variables in a simultaneous equation system. Econometrica 47:153–161.
Heckman J (1979) Sample selection bias as a specification error. Econometrica 47(1):153–161.
Helpman E, Krugman P (1985) Market structure and foreign trade: increasing returns, imperfect competition and the international economy. MIT Press, Cambridge
Helpman E, Melitz M, Rubinstein Y (2008) Estimating trade flows: trading partners and trading volumes. Quart J Econ 123(2):441–487.
Henderson DJ, Millimet DL (2008) Is gravity linear? Journal of Applied Econometrics 23:137–172.
Higgins JPT, Thompson SG (2002) Quantifying heterogeneity in a meta-analysis. Statistics in Med 21:1539–58
Hudec RE (1987) Developing countries in the GATT legal system. Gower, Aldershot, Hampshire, U.K, Brookfield, Vt., USA.
Hummels D (1999) Toward a geography of trade costs. GTAP Working Paper 17, Global Trade Analysis Project, Purdue University.
Hummels D, Lugovskyy V (2006) Are matched partner trade statistics a usable measure of transport costs? Rev of Int Econ 14(1):69–86.
Hummels D, Skiba A (2004) A virtuous circle? Regional tariff liberalization and scale economies in transport. In: Estevadeordal R, Taylor V (eds) FTAA and beyond: prospects for integration in the America. Harvard University Press, Cambridge, MA
Hummels D, Skiba A (2004) Shipping the good apples out? An empirical confirmation of the Alchian–Allen conjecture. J Pol Econ 112(6):1384–1402 (December).
IEG (2006) Assessing world bank support for trade, 1987–2004. World Bank.
Imbens G, Wooldridge J (2009) Recent developments in the econometrics of program evaluation. J of Econ Lit 47(1): 5–86
Inama S (2003) Trade preferences and the world trade organization negotiations on market access. J World Trade 37(5):959–976.
Isard W, Peck MJ (1954) Location theory and international and interregional trade theory. Quart J Econ 68(1):97–114.
Jacks D, Meissner C, Novy D (2008) Trade costs. 1870–2000. Am Econ Rev 98(2):529–534.
Jackson M O (2008) Social and economic networks. Princeton University Press, Princeton
Jayasinghe S, Sarker R (2008) Effects of Regional Trade Agreements on trade in agrifood products: evidence from gravity modeling using disaggregated data. Rev. Agr. Econ. 30: 61–81.
Kerr WA, Gaisford JD (2008) Handbook on International Trade Policy. Edward Elgar Publishing.
King G (2003) The future of replication. Int Stud Persp 4:443–499.
King G, Tomz M, Witten J (2000) Making the most of statistical analyses: improving interpretation and presentation. Am J Political Sci 44 (2):347–361
Krugman P (1980) Scale economies, product differentiation, and the pattern of trade. Am Econ Rev 70:950–59.
Lai H, Trefler D (2002) The gains from trade with monopolistic competition: specification, estimation, and mis-specification. NBER Working Paper No. 9169.
Lai H, Trefler D (2004) On estimating the welfare gains from trade liberalization. Working paper, University of Toronto.
Lai H, Zhu S. C (2004) The determinants of bilateral trade. Canadian J. of Economics 37 (2):459–483.
Lawless M (2010) Deconstructing gravity: trade costs and extensive and intensive margins. Can J Econ 43(4):1149–1172.
Leamer EE, Levinsohn J (1995) International trade theory: the evidence. In: Grossman G, Rogoff K (eds) Handbook of International Economics, Volume 3. Elsevier, North-Holland
Leamer EE, Stern RM (1970) Quantitative international economics. Allyn and Bacon Inc, Boston.

Lederman D, Özden Ç (2004) U.S. trade preferences: all are not created equal. Central Bank of Chile Working Papers no 280.
Leen AK (2004) The Tinbergen Brothers. Nobelprize.org (downloaded the 17th of June 2010).
Limao N and Venables T (2001) Infrastructure, geographical disadvantage and transport costs. World Bank Economic Review 15:451–479.
Linders GJM, de Groot HLF (2006) Estimation of the gravity equation in the presence of zero flows, Tinbergen Institute Discussion Paper, TI 2006-072/3.
Lindgren KO (2010) Dyadic regression in the presence of heteroscedasticity – an assessment of alternative approaches. Social Network 32:279–289
Linnemann H (1966) An econometric study of international trade flows. North Holland, Amsterdam
Low P, Piermartini R, Richtering J (2005) Multilateral solution to the erosion of non-reciprocal preferences in Nama. WTO Staff Working Paper, ERSD-2005-05, http://www.wto.org/english/res_e/reser_e/wpaps_e.htm. Accessed 2005.
Maertens M, Swinnen JFM (2008) Standards as barriers and catalysts for trade growth and poverty reduction. J Int Agr Trade and Devel 4: 47–61.
Maertens M, Swinnen JFM (2009) Trade, standards and poverty: evidence from Senegal. World Devel 37:161–178.
Magee C (2003) Endogenous Preferential Trade Agreements: an empirical analysis. Economic Analysis & Policy Vol 2 Issue 1, article 15.
Magee C (2008) New measures of trade creation and trade diversion. J of Int Econ 75:340–362.
Manchin M (2006) Preference utilisation and tariff reduction in EU imports from ACP countries. The World Economy 29:1243–1266
Martin P, Mayer T, Thoenig M (2008a) Make trade not war? Rev Econ St 75(3):865–900.
Martin P, Mayer T, Thoenig M (2008b) Civil wars and international trade. J Eur Econ Ass 6:541–550
Martin W, Pham SC (2008) Estimating the gravity equation when zero trade flows are frequent. World Bank
Martínez-Zarzoso I, Nowak-Lehmann DF, Horsewood N (2009) Are regional trading agreements beneficial? Static and dynamic panel gravity models. N Am J Econ Finance 20(1):46–65
Matyas L, Sevestre P (2007) Econometrics of panel data. Kluwer Academic Publishers
Mayer T, Ottaviano GIP (2008) The happy few. Bruges
McCallum J (1995) National borders matter: Canada–US regional trade patterns. Am Econ Review 85 (3):615– 623.
Melitz MJ (2003) The impact of trade on intra-industry reallocations and aggregate industry productivity. Econometrica 1695–1725.
Melitz MJ (2003) The impact of trade on intra-industry reallocations and aggregate industry productivity. Econometrica 71(6):1695–1725
Millimet DL, Tchernis R (2009) On the specification of propensity scores, with applications to the analysis of trade policies. J Bus Econ Stat 27(3)397-415.
Minten B, Radrianarison L, Swinnen JFM (2006) Global retail chains and poor farmers: evidence from Madagascar. LICOS Discussion Paper No 164, Leuven.
Narayanan B, Walmsey TL (2008) The GTAP 7 database. Center for Global Trade Analysis, Purdue University.
Nielsen CP (2003) Regional and preferential trade agreements: a literature review and identification of future steps. Fodevareokonomisk Institut, Copenhagen, Report n. 155.
Nilsson L (2002) Trading relations: is the roadmap from Lomé to Cotonou correct? Appl Economics 34:439–452
Nilsson L (2009) Small trade flows and preference utilization. Mimeo, European Commission, DG Trade
Nilsson L, Matsson N (2009) Truths and myths about the openness of EU trade policy and the use of EU trade preferences. Working Paper http://trade.ec.eu.europa.eu/doclib/docs/2009/july/tradoc_143993.pdf. Accessed 2009

Norton EC, Wang H, Ai C (2004) Computing interaction effects and standard errors in logit and probit models. Stata J 4(2):154–167.

Novy D (2010) Gravity redux. Measuring international trade costs with panel data. University of Warwick, mimeo

OECD (2005) Preferential trading arrangements in agricultural and food markets. The case of the European Union and the United States. Paris, ISBN 92-64-00932-9.

Oguledo VI, MacPhee CR (1994) Gravity models: a reformulation and an application to discriminatory trade arrangements. Appl Econ 26:107–120

Olper A, Raimondi V (2008) Agricultural market integration in the OECD: a gravity-border effect approach. Food Policy 33:165–175.

Ongluglo BP (1999) Developing countries and unilateral trade preferences in the new. International trading system. In Rodriguez M, Mendoza P Low, Kotschwar B (eds) Trade rules in the making: challenges in regional and multilateral negotiations. The Brookings Institution Press/ Organisation of American States, Washington, DC.

Özden C, Reinhardt E (2005) The perversity of preferences: GSP and developing country trade policies, 1976–2000. J Devel Econ 78:1–21.

Panagariya A (2002) EU preferential trade arrangements and developing countries. The World Economy 25(10):1415–1432.

Péridy N (2005) The trade effects of the Euro-Mediterranean partnership: what are the lessons for ASEAN countries? J of Asian Economics 16:125–139

Persson M, Wilhelmsson F (2007) Assessing the effects of EU trade preferences for developing countries. In: Bourdet Y, Gullstrand J, Olofsdotter K (eds) The European Union and developing countries. Trade, aid and growth in an integrating world. Edward Elgar Publishing

Persson T (2001) Currency Union and trade: how large is the treatment effect. Economic Policy 33:433–462.

Piermartini R, The R (2005) Demystifying modelling methods for trade policy. World Trade Organization, Discussion Paper 10, http://www.wto.org/english/res_e/reser_e/discussion_pa-pers_e.htm. Accessed 2005

Pishbahar E, Huchet-Bourdon M. (2008) European Union's preferential trade agreements in agricultural sector: a gravity approach. J. of International Agricultural Trade and Development 5(1):93–114.

Pöyhönen P (1963) A tentative model for the volume of trade between countries. Weltwirt Arch 90:93–99.

Proenca I, Fontoura MP, Martìnez-Galàn E (2008) Trade in the enlarged European Union: a new approach on trade potential. Portuguese Econ J 7:205–224

Puhani PA (2000) The Heckman Correction for Sample Selection and Its Critique. J of Econ Survey 14(1):53–69.

Pusterla F (2007) Regional integration agreements: impact, geography and efficiency. IDB-SOE Working Paper, January 2007.

Raimondi V, Olper A (2010) Trade elasticity, gravity and the gains from trade: evidences from the food industry. PUE@PIEC Work. Pap. 10/5. downloadable at http://www.ecostat.unical.it/anania/PUE&PIEC.htm

Raimondi V, Scoppola M, Olper A, (2010) Preferences erosion and the developing countries exports to the EU: a dynamic panel gravity approach. PUE@PIEC Working Paper 2010/21.

Ravallion M (2008) Evaluating anti-poverty programs. In Handbook of Development Economics, vol. 4, Schultz TP, Strauss J (ed), 3787–846. Amsterdam: North-Holland.

Ravenstein EG (1885) The laws of migration. J Royal Stat Soc 52:241–310.

Romalis J (2007) NAFTA's and CUSFTA's impact on international trade. Rev Econ Statist 89:416–435.

Rose AK (2004) Does the WTO make trade more stable? NBER Working Paper N. 10207.

Rose AK (2006) Size really doesn't matter: in search of a national scale effect. Journal of the Japanese and International Economies 20:482–507.

Rose AK, Stanley TD (2005) Meta-analysis of the effect of common currencies on international trade. J of Econ Surveys 19:347–365

Roy AD (1951) Some thoughts on the distribution of earnings. Oxford Economic Papers.

Ruiz JM, Villarrubia JM (2007) The wise use of dummies in gravity models: export potentials in the Euromed region. Documentos de Trabajo N. 0720, Banco de Espana Eurosistema.

Santos-Silva JMC, Tenreyro S (2006) The log of gravity. Rev Econ Statist 88:641–658.

Savage IR, Deutsch KW (1960) A statistical model of the gross analysis of transaction flows. Econometrica 28:551–572.

Siliverstovs B, Schumacher D (2009) Estimating gravity equations: to log or not to log? Empirical Economics 36:645–669

Skully D (2001) Liberalizing tariff-rate quotas. In: Burfisher ME (ed) Agricultural policy reform in the WTO – The road ahead. Economic Research Service U.S. Department of Agriculture, Agricultural Economic Report No. 802, Washington

Stanley TD (2005) Beyond publication bias. J of Econ Surveys 19:309–346

Stanley TD, Jarrell SB (2005) Meta-regression analysis: a quantitative method of literature surveys. J of Econ Surveys 19:299–308.

Subramanian A, Wei SJ (2007) The WTO promotes trade, strongly but unevenly. J of Int Econ 72(1):151–75.

Sutton AJ, Abrams KR, Jones DR, Sheldon TA, Song F (2000) Methods for meta-analysis in medical research. John Wiley, Chichester

SwinbankA, Ritson C (1995) The impact of the GATT agreement on EU fruit and vegetable policy. Food Pol 20:339–357.

Szenberg M (1992) Eminent economists. Their life philosophies. Cambridge University Press, Cambridge

Tinbergen J (1951) Econometrics. Allen and Unwin, London

Tinbergen J (1962), Shaping the World Economy, The Twentieth Century Fund, New York.

UNCTAD (2003) Trade preferences for LDC: an early assessment of benefits and possible improvements. UNCTAD/ITCD/TSB/2003/8, United Nations, Geneva.

van der Mensbrugghe D (2009) The Doha development Agenda and preference erosion: modelling the impacts. In: Hoekman B, Martin W, Braga PC (eds) Trade preference erosion. measurement and policy response. Macmillan and World Bank, Washington, DC

WDI. World Development Indicators (Washington, DC: World Bank, 2008) CD-ROM.

Wei SJ (1996) Intra-national versus international trade: how stubborn are nations in global integration? National Bureau of Economic Research Working Paper 5531.

Westerlund J, Wilhelmsson F (2006) Estimating the gravity model without gravity using panel data. Unpublished. School of Economics and Management, Lund University.

Winters LA (1984) Separability and the specification of foreign trade functions. J. of International Economics 17:239–263.

Wooldridge JM (2002) Econometric analysis of cross-section and panel data. MIT Press, Cambridge MA

Wooldridge JM (2006) Introductory econometrics: a modern approach, 3rd edn. Thomson South-Western, Cincinnati, OH

WTO (2001) WT/MIN(01)/15 of 14 November 2001.

Zipf GK (1946) The P1P2/D hypothesis: on the inter-city movement of persons. Am Sociol Rev 11:677–686.

Index

GPSR Compliance

The European Union's (EU) General Product Safety Regulation (GPSR) is a set of rules that requires consumer products to be safe and our obligations to ensure this.

If you have any concerns about our products, you can contact us on ProductSafety@springernature.com

In case Publisher is established outside the EU, the EU authorized representative is:

Springer Nature Customer Service Center GmbH
Europaplatz 3
69115 Heidelberg, Germany

Batch number: 10614744

Printed by Printforce, the Netherlands